A Short History of Celebrity

A Short History of Celebrity

Fred Inglis

<small>PRINCETON UNIVERSITY PRESS</small>   *Princeton & Oxford*

Copyright © 2010 by Princeton University Press

Published by Princeton University Press, 41 William Street,
Princeton, New Jersey 08540

In the United Kingdom: Princeton University Press, 6 Oxford Street,
Woodstock, Oxfordshire OX20 1TW

Library of Congress Cataloging-in-Publication Data

Inglis, Fred.
A short history of celebrity / Fred Inglis.
p.   cm.
Includes bibliographical references and index.
ISBN 978-0-691-13562-5 (hardcover : alk. paper)
1. Celebrities—History. 2. Celebrities—Biography. 3. Fame—
Social aspects—History. 4. Fame—Psychological aspects—
History. 5. History, Modern. 6. Popular culture—History.
7. Civilization, Modern. I. Title.

D210.I525 2010
305.5'2—dc22   2009050143

British Library Cataloging-in-Publication Data is available

This book has been composed in Adobe Garamond and
ITC Golden Cockeral

Printed on acid-free paper. ∞

press.princeton.edu

Printed in the United States of America

1 3 5 7 9 10 8 6 4 2

For Jessie and Abby

Guardians of the Middle Station

Contents

Acknowledgements   ix

PART I   Fame and Feeling

1. The Performance of Celebrity   3
2. A Very Short History of the Feelings   19

PART II   The Rise of Celebrity:
A Three-Part Invention

3. The London–Brighton Road, 1760–1820   37
4. Paris: Haute Couture and the Painting of Modern Life   74
5. New York and Chicago: Robber Barons and the
    Gossip Column, 1880–1910   108

PART III   The Past in the Present

6. The Geography of Recognition: Celebrity on
    Its Holidays   135
7. The Great Dictators   158
8. The Stars Look Down: The Democratisation
    of Celebrity   187
9. From Each According to His Ability: Sport, Rock,
    Fashion, and the Self   217
10. Stories We Tell Ourselves about Ourselves   247

    Envoi: Cherishing Citizens   270

    Notes   289
    List of Illustrations   303
    Index   305

Acknowledgements

This book was first conceived while I was Visiting Fellow at the Institute for the Humanities at the University of Connecticut, and I am exceedingly grateful to its director, Dick Brown, and to my co-fellow, Ross Miller (Arthur's nephew), for their encouragement and suggestive criticisms; in particular I would also like to thank the institute's admirable administrator, JoAnn Waid, for all her kindness and energetic thoughtfulness during my stay.

In the event, I later put this book aside to work on my biography of R. G. Collingwood, *History Man*, and it was during that period that I came so happily under the attentive care of my present editor at Princeton University Press, Ian Malcolm, and he was readily persuaded to take my proposal to his colleagues and return with a contract.

I then wrote the thing headlong, for some of the time while occupying a Visiting Fellowship in the handsome surroundings of the Humanities Research Centre at the Australian National University in Canberra to whose director, Debjani Ganguly, I owe repeated thanks for her intellectual hospitality. I also aired some of these thoughts at Massey University, New Zealand, at the invitation of my old and cherished friend, Joe Grixti, as well as at the University of Warwick, thanks to two other such patrons and honoured friends, Joe Winston and Jonothan Neelands, as a result of whose good offices I am now an honorary professor at their university.

Mostly, however, the writing of this book was done at home in my study in Somerset, and its large, indistinct, and protean subject matter came and went according to the rhythms of domestic life and the great happiness of scholarly retirement. A useful hand was early loaned by Richard Howells, and the manuscript was much exhilarated as well as improved by the readers' reports written by Dr. Howells and by Professor Tara Brabazon at a later stage. As usual, a difficult and handwritten manuscript was regularly dispatched to Carol Marks and punctually returned in perfect electronic form. Finally, the presence of my late and much mourned friend and guide, Clifford Geertz, is discernible in every chapter.

Essentially, however, the book was written in solitude which, given its civic subject matter, is a bit rum. I suppose that nonetheless it represents an effort by an ageing citizen-scholar, unregenerate Englishman and old Labourist, devoted husband, father, grandfather, to name for what it is what is horrible in our society. But it is also, and much more so, an argument with which to resist uttering any slack-jawed curse over the tendencies of the times to be going to the dogs, and a search in our public narratives as these are dramatised by celebrity and told by history, for all there is to celebrate indeed, of the best we can do on behalf of our anxious happiness, and of all manner of things that are well.

PART I   Fame and Feeling

Chapter 1

The Performance of Celebrity

This is a history book. Insofar as it offers a theory of itself, it is a theory of historical sedimentation, transformation, re-creation. It is the theory that we live, wittingly and involuntarily, the assorted versions of our selves and our society which history has deposited within us. Nothing much to say about that except that history is not a vast undifferentiated force coming at us with a capital H, but an irresistible series of tiny, invisible infiltrations which sidle along our bloodstream and oscillate in our thoughts and feelings.

Insofar as we become conscious of these invasions, we do so by way of shaping them into narratives grand or small, but even the grandest are made up and made out of the bits and pieces of the many disjointed experiences and unintelligible events of the past, rearranged and re-created for a different present.

The usefulness of fame for the purposes of this simple historical lesson is that the concept serves to pick out those lives and ways of life which shaped themselves into the significant constellations of the past and provided quite a lot of people with stars to steer by. When we add to that the general scholarly agreement that modernity may usefully be taken as picking up speed from round about the middle of the eighteenth century, then a history of the fairly new concept of celebrity may tell us plenty about what is to be cherished and built upon as well as what is to be despised and ought to be destroyed in the subsequent invention of modern society.

My most pointed moral is that the business of renown and celebrity has been in the making for two and a half centuries. It was not thought up by the hellhounds of publicity a decade ago. Consequently, if we load its discussion and evaluation down with the mass of time, we might be able to lend some gravity to the shallow and violent lightness of being attributed to fame in our day. What follows is full of such historical *examples*, of individual life stories which neither constitute a sample nor provide epitomes.

They are instances of something, cases in point. Examples instruct; they do not prove.

II

Celebrity is everywhere acknowledged but never understood. It is on everybody's lips a few times every week; it is the staple of innumerable magazines on either side of the Atlantic, whether in the glossy and worshipful guise of *Hello!* and *Glamour* or the downright fairytale telling and mendacity of the *National Enquirer* and *Sunday Sport*; it fills a strip cartoon in (where else?) *Private Eye* and provides *all* the dailies, whether tabloid or broadsheet, with the contents of news, op-ed, gossip, and, not infrequently, contributed columns.

Celebrity is also one of the adhesives which, at a time when the realms of public politics, civil society, and private domestic life are increasingly fractured and enclosed in separate enclaves, serves to pull those separate entities together and to do its bit towards maintaining social cohesion and common values. Nonetheless, in societies like ours priding themselves on having reduced the aura of deference; on having opened their élites to popular talent; on their mingling of high old art and new low popular culture with a fine egalitarian hand, it is something of a surprise to find quite so many people in thrall to the power of that same celebrity, and to those who, involuntarily or otherwise, carry it along with their lives. One way to catch hold of this change will be to notice how celebrity has largely replaced the archaic concept of renown.

Renown, we shall say, was once assigned to men of high accomplishment in a handful of prominent and clearly defined roles. A sixteenth-century jurist, cleric, senior mercenary, or scholar was renowned for bringing honour to the office he occupied. He might be acclaimed in the street, but the recognition was of his accomplishment—his learning (in the case of John Donne, for instance), his victories (as Othello is acclaimed in the play), his implacable power (in the case of Cardinal Wolsey). Renown brought honour to the office not the individual, and public recognition was not so much of the man himself as of the significance of his actions for the society.

This historical difference is readily studied by way of the fame of one of the very few women of historical renown in the period before celebrity became a feature of the individualisation of fame. We have a detailed record of the Royal Progresses of Elizabeth I, and these bring out their ceremonial meaning as *pledging* monarch to people, and vice versa. What is publicly affirmed by her attire and adornments, and by her words, on the one hand, and by the people's witness of themselves and their self-display (masques, banners, cheering, children's presenting of posies to the queen), on the other hand, is nothing less than the mutual duties of each to the other.

This picturesque prologue serves to mark off honour and renown from glamour and celebrity. The rise of urban democracy, the two-hundred-year expansion of its media of communication, together with the radical individualisation of the modern sensibility made fame a much more transitory reward and changed public acclaim from an expression of devotion into one of celebrity.

III

The distinction can only be made historically. As I suggested, Royal Progresses provide a simple instance of the way in which fame and power express and confirm themselves by way of spectacle. The adjective "spectacular" as applying to something eye-filling, imposing, dramatic, and ambitious makes its *Oxford English Dictionary* appearance only in 1901 and has since been vaguely enlarged to take in *any* event or accomplishment of impressive consequence or display ("she's a spectacular pianist"), visible or not.

In 1967, as the extraordinary year of unprecedented spectacle which succeeded it was about to open, a Parisian leftist published a striking and prophetic little book of *pensées* which, a few months later, became the primer for analysts of the "May events." In *Society of the Spectacle* Guy Debord took it upon himself to announce the advent of a quite new dimension to the idea of the political spectacle and the power it dramatised.

[T]he principle of commodity fetishism [taken from Marx's Capital], the domination of society by intangible as well as tangible

things … reaches its absolute fulfillment in the spectacle where the
tangible world is replaced by a selection of images which exist above
it, and which simultaneously impose themselves as the tangible *par
excellence*.

The world at once present and absent which the spectacle makes
visible is the world of the commodity dominating all that is lived.[1]

Debord proposes a spectacle of quite different significance to the Eliza-
bethan Progresses describing which will, I hope, provide a little more purchase on the image of celebrity first adumbrated in 1770s London and
brought to its extraordinary compulsion by the infinite reproducibility of
all contemporary imagery. The display of Queen Elizabeth I was certainly
spectacular, whether or not the adjective existed then, but the meaning the
spectacle dramatized was not celebrity but renown. Elizabeth is renowned
as being the monarch; her fame is conferred by her people on behalf of
God and England; the enacted theory of her rule partakes equally of her
pious receptiveness and her subjects' supplication and approval.

She set out on January 14, 1559, the day before her coronation, seated
in an open carriage, followed and preceded by a thousand horsemen, her
whole attire stiff with glittering jewels and flashing gold leaf, the innate
radiance of which was still believed to possess mysterious magic. "As she
moved, a vast didactic pageant unfolded, stage by stage, settling her into
the moral landscape of the resilient capital."[2] In Fenchurch Street, a child
was appointed to present her with gifts of tongues to praise and hearts to
serve her; at Cornhill, another child on a throne was supported by four
citizens representing the cardinal virtues; they in turn were provided with
their moment of fame in a little cameo during which they trod underfoot
four other citizens attired as the contrary vices. On to Cheapside, where
Elizabeth passed down a thoroughfare lined with great poster paintings of
the English monarchs culminating in herself, paused (in Little Conduit)
at two large stage mountains, one bare and barren (bad government), one
green and flowering ("a flourishing commonweal"), met Father Time, who
gave her a copy of the *Book of Truth*, listened to a Latin oration in minatory
praise of herself by a schoolboy of St. Paul's, to another schoolboy oration
at Christ's Hospital, and wound up at Temple Bar to read tablets carried

by the giants Gog and Magog summarising all the honour and admonition offered to her.

It makes a sumptuous story and marks a very wide space between the political imagination of the Elizabethans and our own. Theirs was allegorical, specific, and plain as day. The queen stood for clear moral absolutes, a whole medley of them: "Chastity, Wisdom, Peace, Beauty, and Religion" is Geertz's list. But the point of the progress was for her royalty to be instructed by her people in its duty and significance towards them, hence the presence of so many children. She in her turn knew her place and took the lessons to heart, promising on Cheapside "that for the safetie and quietness of you all, I will not spare, if nede be, to spend my blood."[3]

Exotic, indeed, and a long way from the Notting Hill carnival. Yet not so *very* far. Elizabeth's Progress was a confection of charisma, where that slippery concept connotes the public location of authority and its benefits, of fame and its supernatural aura. Charisma, first made much of by Max Weber,[4] is at once the personal radiance and gravity of a publicly recognized figure and the symbolic halo of value and meaning lent to that figure by those rituals which declare and create centrality and importance.

In Elizabeth's case, the worshipful rituals at once claimed and ratified her. They connected her reciprocally to her people. So, too, with presidents and prime ministers, monarchs and dictators, and in a quite intelligibly scaled diminuendo, with the carefully shaded circles of significance which surround them: ministers and secretaries of state; solemn figures of lasting achievement, businessmen, clerics, admirals, marshalls, artists, scientists; leading figures of more or less democratic communication without which we would all be lost in the world, television commentators, announcers, journalists, opinionators; and out beyond these circles which surround the very centre, the obviously whirling and transitory porters of fame created by the cultural industries and the huge happiness and misery brought by the industrialisation of leisure: the stars of film, sport, rock, kitchen, soap, and a dozen other pastimes.

This is not to pretend that our world view, like that of the Elizabethans, conceives society as a great chain of being stretching from thrones, principalities, and powers down through the wretched of the earth and culminating in a similar chain in the animal world. It is to say that the centres of value and meaning in the societies of the wealthy nations have indeed their own decided order, contested and opposed no doubt but intelligible and upheld quite securely. It is also to say that the not-very-old phenomenon of celebrity, borrowing assiduously from past spectacles and rituals (there being nowhere else to find them) generates by its dramas the structure and the strength with which to hold things in their proper place.

IV

This book offers an explanation of this no more than 250-year-old phenomenon. It finds the reasons for the persistence, the vigour, and the apparently limitless energy of the new spectacle and its peculiar allegory in its history. Mid-eighteenth-century London is our starting point, half a century after the capital replaced the court as the centre of social dynamics. Spontaneously, the city bred its version of a new social figure, famous for his and her urban accomplishments: Dr. Johnson and his self-appointed circle of public opinion–makers in literary journalism; Wilkes and his raffish radicals; Lady Mary Wortley Montagu and the lead she took as a solitary woman tourist (getting into the Sofia mosque disguised as a man), as philanthropic proselytiser for the new science of immunisation (herself disfigured by smallpox), as friend of poets (Alexander Pope) and audaciously free-loving free-liver; the amazing Joshua Reynolds, all were treated as first, authentic celebrities. Above all, the late eighteenth and early nineteenth centuries provide the earliest opportunity to study the way in which the *theatre*, distorting and magnifying mirror of its society, assumes the significance it never loses as providing the leading ladies and men of the cast of celebrities. Sarah Siddons, David Garrick, and Kean anticipate Bernhardt, Ellen Terry, and Irving and point forward to Hollywood.

In the new urban culture of London and the passionate competitiveness of its new and old rich, the theatre takes a special place as the occasion both to be seen moving in the best society and to see that society mirrored, magnified, parodied, and satirised onstage. Sheridan's great play *The School for Scandal* is a brilliant seizing of the significance of *gossip* in this unprecedented sort of society, for gossip is only the means of preserving one's own respectability and that of one's own little class by counting other people out of it. Actors then act out in public, both onstage and off it, the delicious contents of this scandal. Their reward, paid in kind for well over two centuries, for losing their respectability is to be celebrated for scandalousness. As you would expect, actors learned to live up to this reputation as long as they were paid enough. Jane Austen provides a mordant insight into the process in her treatment of the scandalous play *Lovers' Vows* staged in *Mansfield Park* while the master of the house, Sir Thomas Bertram, is away from home. In doing so, she captures the sexual thrill still at the heart of theatre celebrity.

These throngs of biography, vastly magnified by the fat figure of the Prince Regent, gradually effected the institutionalisation of the underlying forces which composed celebrity: first, the new consumerism of eighteenth-century London; second, the invention of the fashion industry with department stores to match in mid-nineteenth-century Paris; third, the coming of the mass circulation newspaper, its gossip columns, and its thrilled, racy transformation of city life in New York and Chicago into the glitter of publicity.

These three new social formations provide a simple dynamic for the advent of the industrialisation of celebrity. London's consumer society invented with astonishing speed the forms and content of the new urban leisure. Not just the theatre, but the pleasure gardens, the coffee houses, the novels and journalism, the sudden expansion of those making the Tour, and of the holiday industry to take in Bath and Brighton, Weymouth and Scarborough, define certain conventions of sociable life which still hold. The leisure timetable of the London *haute bourgeoisie* of 1820 is immediately familiar to us today. It was given direction and excitement by being punctuated by glimpses of the famous. Gainsborough's painting of fashionable young women dressed to the nines eyeing each other's fashions in St. James's Park is a gleeful instance of this. The scandalous life of the Prince Regent in the Brighton Pavilion marks the passage of the royal heir from sanctity to celebrity.

Stage two of the process takes us to Paris after the return of the Bourbons. London's invention of spectacular leisure is there vastly extended, and the city's lead in making the celebrity-conscious consumer society overhauled. When Baron Haussmann pulled down great swathes of old Paris to make his *grands boulevards*, he may have intended to ease the passage of the riot police on their way to put down insurgent *citoyens*, but he certainly arranged things for the benefit of the fashionable crowd out in its finery to see and be seen. He also made things easy, as Walter Benjamin was the first to notice, for the new invention of plateglass to be installed all the way down the Rue de Rivoli and up the Boulevard Malesherbes in order to show off the goods of *haute couture* and the new department stores.

After 1851 Paris swiftly becomes *the* city of the urban spectacle, and thereafter the astonishing new painters who picture this development—Manet, Renoir, Toulouse-Lautrec—provide us with a sumptuous album of the dress, the poses and posiness, the delights and agonies of living city life in public.

Paris is the first place to put sheer *appearance*—good looks, smart clothes, swank and show—at the centre of celebrity. New York, in its turn, customises gossip and glamourises money. Money mattered in London and Paris, for sure, but the New York and Chicago of the gilded age, in the absence of a settled ruling class and in the presence of a polyglot throng of immigrants offering to fill the bill, lent the prodigious sums of new money cascading into their banks an unprecedented magnetism. The people who possessed it were magnetised along with the money, and Pulitzer's mass-circulation presses assigned them whole columns of gossip in which goggle-eyed admiration mingled with trifling and malice (veins of mixed feelings richly exploited over the next century, as gossip columnists themselves won celebrity).

London, Paris, New York: the leisure timetable, window-shopping and *haute couture*, money and the gossip column—the mechanisms of celebrity take on their modern outline from these forces. They are then given mass and energy by two dramatic phenomena created by world war, its consequent technology, and its fabulous reorganisation of society.

The First World War ended with governments confidently directing and unconsciously directed by their new instruments of propaganda; over the same years the momentous invention of Hollywood brought to birth the sacred infant of the century, the star. Celebrity, it is a commonplace to say, is the product of culture and technology. The new media of film and radio worked each in their different way to restore immediacy and intimacy to human narrative at just the moment when mass modernity made everything in city life seem so anonymous and fragmentary. In the cinema, for instance, the audience could see the stars in colossal close-up, could watch their gigantic lips meet and touch, but could only do so sitting in the dark, more or less solitary, and eerily without any physical propinquity to these intimacies. No wonder then that the stars became imbued with such magical emanations, especially at a time when people in their masses were struggling to find a politics and ethics capable of expressing this strange modern world. Cinema stars, like the political leaders who made themselves into similar stars, offered the reassurance of individual recognisability at a time when that was proving increasingly hard to find. Hence, whether you were a politician in 1919 or merely a millionaire investor in movies, you could have no doubt that these dazzling new media would do everything for your power or your pocket.

The tale of the twenties and thirties is first of all, therefore, a story of how the great dictators and indeed the everyday victors of electoral politics—Mussolini, Hitler, and Stalin, along with Woodrow Wilson and Lloyd George—made themselves into stars on the world stage of politics and corralled the public spectacles of celebratory propaganda—the rally, the armaments parade, the Olympic Games, the Cup Final, the ticker-tape drive through Manhattan, the state openings, the royal weddings, the Mayday march—which then became essential adjuncts of power. All such occasions lent themselves, with the help of newsreels and hugely amplified martial music and megaphone rhetoric, to the public dramatisation of power. The mass political spectacle, no less sumptuously orchestrated at the 1937 coronation of King George VI than at Nuremberg—marching men, drums, banners, horses, and the mute power of the crowd—is *the* feature of political life between the wars. It affirms for each society some of the most important of the social values and traditions and makes the small public figures at the centre of such vast attention uniquely recognisable and still sacredly remote.

This is the powerful contradiction at the heart of our phenomenon. It combines knowability with distance. Political leader and cinema star are intensely familiar (one of the family) by way of the cinema screen, and (at first) by way of their voices on the living room radio, but physically and in terms of how we all need to feel the directness of experience, they have the remoteness of the supernatural. This is the compound which makes for the sacredness of celebrity and may suggest the reason why people both worship *and* vilify the famous. The invention of stardom and the instantaneous mass publicity it released by way of the new media from 1919 onwards twined together in a strong rope of meaning some of the strongest and strangest passions of modern society. The irresistible shine of money was added to the new emphasis given by the advertising industry to physical desirability and youthfulness. The industrialisation of leisure offered new locations in which to display its conspicuous consumption—holiday attire, seaside games, expansive freedom, informal intimacy all as watched by the envious and their hired eavesdroppers, the gossip columnists and photographers.

All these ingredients come together in the compulsion of the new value, *glamour*. Our nineteenth-century history prepares the ground, and the twin forces of propaganda and stardom join in completing the manufacture of celebrity as it will be constituted from the 1920s to the present. The early forms of celebrity life were lived in the public gaze but in the pretence of privacy. Conspicuous leisure enjoyment became the public action of the damned and beautiful people. Mind you, the leisure of the very wealthy which boiled over onto the beaches of the Riviera at this date was staffed by a very mixed bag: the politically unemployed (the Windsors), the big names in literature and art (the Fitzgeralds, the Lawrences, the Hemingways, Picasso, Segovia), the international sporting set (the Murphys, the Donald Camerons, the Richthofens), the latest thing in *haute couture* (Coco Chanel), and of course the film stars (too many to choose from just now). So it is that a brief history of the Cote d'Azur in the 1930s discovers the shape and meaning of the weird new value it will find on the beaches, in the bedroom, at the baccarat tables, the logic of its composition and the way in which such an odd assortment of candidates concentrated the attention of the publicity industry and, in its turn, held such fascination for its vast audiences.

V

The essential foundations of the Halls of Fame are completed by the second bout of world warfare, which brought renown to the soldiery and black-and-white news photography to a world desperate to know what was happening to sons and husbands, wives and daughters, in mortal danger and torn apart by flight, combat, starvation, high explosives, and High Command. *Picture Post, Life, Paris Match*, ten dozen imitators and the newsreel lent unprecedented size, reproducibility, and immediacy to the representative features of leaders and ordinary people and set the pace and tone for this new industry which would turn the vividness and intimacy of ordinary humanity into the remoteness of glamour. As it did so, one unacknowledged consequence of its industrial muscle was that it defined a new and universal content for what counts as supreme success in life in the postwar world. If, however, that supreme success is what celebrity defines for society, it is no surprise if the uncelebrated multitudes want to blow a raspberry at it.

It is important, however, to emphasise that this book will not be a long and lofty malediction spoken over the celebrity cult. Certainly there are bleak judgements to be made about people's being *quite* so entranced with very small numbers of unevenly gifted and frequently unattractive individuals. Just as surely, the stars have looked down at the adoring faces looking up and brought home to them the blessing of unrealisable fantasy, the respite of escape from harsh lives, the glimpse of possibility of a better future, of a decent home, of a just world. Hence, the biographies of a handful of stars on either side of the Atlantic, each of whom assumed a special place in international affections, may be said to have taught by example an imitable way of being in the world. People model themselves in part on the lives of those they admire; it has long been a routine jeremiad from older people to say that private morality has been corrupted by Hollywood. Very well, let us ask ourselves what has been the contribution to public ethics of the lives and careers of some of the stars. This is the moment to oppose the jeremiahs by celebrating the celebrity of a generation of film stars who held out the promise of happiness to millions, and who indeed provided a respite from harsh lives as well as a rousing image of a better society, a decent home, a just world. Cary Grant, for instance, was held all his life in such a *personal* affection, almost as if it could dissolve the star's remoteness and he become ordinarily likeable. He combined dazzling charm (and dazzle is inextricable from glamour) with blithe ruthlessness—one thinks of *His Girl Friday* or *Indiscreet*—but always brought the well-dressed raffishness of this mixture safely home to tenderness and the marriage bed, and all the time he remains somehow untouchable by moral contamination. James Stewart's exemplary career as a bomber-pilot (1,800 hours of combat flying) throws into relief his unique gift to register moral hesitation, self-uncertainty, the silent loss of a gift for kindness and then its doubtful recovery. Marilyn Monroe, of course, figures for *her* heart-melting genius for the projection of schoolgirlish sexuality and a settled, mature sadness whether on-screen or off it. Gratitude for such brief lives as these cuts down any intellectual hauteur or mere snobbery.

Stardom once offered *such* solace; its consolation and rapturous reassurance remain embedded in our faith in fame, even though so much has happened to us and to them since its cinematic peak in the 1950s. One way of grasping the history of celebrity since then is to see how admiration has become twisted by spite, gossip by vindictiveness, and how the careless envy with which teenagers once adored the Beatles turned into the purposeful malignance with which Princess Diana was pursued to her death.

VI

The film stars are, in a way, easy to talk about. There is a copious literature, and their faces are still so familiar from remaining on television and in Blockbuster Video stores. But what may be thought of as the most serene decades of the history of celebrity—roughly 1945 to 1975—are also the period when television comes to command all media. The victory over fascism not only brought to fame wartime heroes and heroines who became moral examples of the day, but the poets of this metamorphosis, journalists and radio reporters, themselves became starring storytellers of war, new and necessary presences just to one side of otherwise vast and unintelligible events. Celebrity is a natural award to such men as Walter Cronkite and Ed Murrow, Richard Dimbleby and William Hardcastle, and the invention of the mature, benign, intelligent broadcaster ordering celebrity by telling us the news of the world, and in doing so helping us ride out its dizzy whirl, is one best part of our history.

The hinge of our epoch turns with the coming of mass television; the story of celebrity turns with it. Lit by the bright noon of the Pax Americana, the era of mass politics is gradually dissipated and replaced by a different kind of intimacy between the unknown lives of mass audiences watching in solitude and the individual but personally unknowable celebrities doing *their* living only in the windless spaces on the other side of the television screen.

Television is by now so inextricably part of all our domestic lives that it resists analysis. But the truth of what I say is surely borne out by the enthusiasm with which people rush to glimpse the physical actuality of celebrities they think they know well from their screen lives. The stars from the soaps will always pull a crowd, but their stardom depends on still keeping their distance. "A woman is not a duchess a hundred yards from a carriage" goes the old saying, and the conservation of celebrity (it is very precious; it is quickly lost) depends on the peculiar conventions of performance.

The first and most obvious way to follow this making of celebrity by television is to tell the tale of politicians as they perform the dance of power between 1960 and the present day. John F. Kennedy was the first president imaginatively to grasp the momentousness of television, and his remains the most gripping moral fable of celebrity politics. His thousand-day creation of a television president and his combination of exhilarating and energetic charm, flagrant sexual allure, fixity of will, and the delighted possession of absolute political power is a fearful object lesson. Later politicians have to be judged by his lights. So Ronald Reagan, first *professional* actor in the White House, teaches much about the importance of craggy charm, unpretentious likeability, and easygoing disengagement from the urgency of world history, as attributes commending themselves to a citizenry gradually turning away from politics. Bill Clinton shows us much in his strange compound of dazzling intelligence and cretinous behaviour (and the issues each of these factors raises in general for the celebrity) but also reveals more about the place of *scandal* as well as popularity in our ruminations. These star figures may be set off by comparative asides on the parallel careers of, say, Charles de Gaulle, Willy Brandt, Nelson Mandela (all of whom in different ways may be said to be *renowned* for their moral strength). Margaret Thatcher adorns a different moral. In each case, the moral point is to grasp how a powerful man or woman dramatises and enacts, *both for himself or herself and for us*, values essential to the self-image and self-esteem of his, her, and our society.

VII

Outside the big political story, as you would expect, are smaller narratives. But if we pursue the gradual transformation of sporting heroes from local figures familiar to those they passed in the street of their hometowns to world-famous, personally unknowable multimillionaires with no closer ties binding them to their sporting attachments than a signature on a contract, there is a common theme. Take the contrastive stories in footballing Britain of Stanley Matthews and David Beckham: Stanley Matthews, first footballer to be knighted, belonged to the local people of Stoke, the small-ish capital of the five pottery towns, and kept a small hotel in Blackpool when he retired from first-class football at fifty-one. Beckham, the partial subject of a box-office movie (*Bend It like Beckham*, 2002), husband of an equally famous pop singer, owner of a huge country house-home, and an undoubtedly wonderful athlete, is a very different kind of man, embodies very different virtues, from Matthews. So, too, in the parallel contrast between Bobby Jones, courteous southern gentleman and amateur golfer, and Tiger Woods, first black champion golfer, fabulously rich, rigidly quiet and self-contained with it. These few instances may be used to elaborate what celebrity *does to* people, whether grandly world-historical people or limitedly gifted ones, and how—as it was put a moment ago—personal character adapts itself to the demands of celebrity and, insofar as it is successful, alters the demands to suit itself. (A useful paradox is provided by George Best, whose career as a drunk has been as celebrated as his career as a footballer.)

Throughout this third, more or less contemporary, part of the book, particular stories bring out that strange combination of cruelty, sentimentality, touching affection, and downright superstition with which the famous are treated, and in terms of which they have to respond. We know how the photographers hurtled after Princess Diana on motorbikes, and how the massed displays of flowers down the Mall reproached them and pitied her. If one follows one or two celebrity victims through the demented pages of the fanzines and takes time to consider them as a meaty part of the general theme, one notes not only their proliferation over the past few years but also the hardening of their viciousness, their increased disregard for mere truth, and their fierce circulation rivalry, itself no doubt a strong component in the business of celebrity manufacture.

Against such a grisly excursus, we may nonetheless pit examples of celebrity biography in which the hero remains in sufficient possession of him- or herself, lives a worthy life, and grows gracefully old in the public gaze. A few dignified politicians manage this; a durable story such as that provided by Paul McCartney, who has sustained so calm an advance to present respect and affection; or Paul Newman, who refused public celebrity and committed a private fortune from his salad dressing company to relieving the wretchedness of mortally ill children and to supporting the overdraft of the radical journal *The Nation*.

Meanwhile, of course, new social roles and characters are added to the register of those eligible for celebrity treatment—the chat show hostess, the chef, and the gardener have all been recently recruited—and many of those who fill them are conspicuously unequipped by either intelligence or formation to carry things off with any success. Indeed, the whole notion of what constitutes success in consumer and celebrity society becomes a crux in the book, as do, inevitably, the prodigious rewards and expenditures of both cash and character in the whole amazing cavalcade. So it is that understanding celebrity turns more or less obtrusively into an inquiry into the best and worst values of contemporary Western society. These public lives embody key meanings of the day: success and wealth first, perhaps; then niceness, generosity, honesty, integrity, spontaneity, sympathy (on the good side); and arrogance, insolence, cruelty, narcissism, irresponsibility, greed (on the bad).

Any such bit of moralizing will find these debits and credits on *both* sides of the barriers: for it is a commonplace of celebrity that its figures are transformed into what they are by the compulsions and fantasies of those who throng to see them. The domestic passions and civil affections of the historical present are compressed into and dramatised for us by the public lives of private and ordinary people suddenly awarded fame. Our celebrities are made to carry in public the values and contradictions of private muddle.

The category itself is disorientingly large. Think of the saintly figures of our time—men and women of the stature of Aung San Suu Kyi, Dorothy Hodgkin, Andrei Sakharov; in what way are they comparable to a bunch of chefs or the desperate boringness of the people hanging out in the unrealities of reality television? It is expected of public intellectuals and moral commentators that they sufficiently match their status to their convictions and their moral practice; how can such a balancing act be placed in the same sentence as the self-mutilations of Jim Morrison, Jimi Hendrix, Freddie Mercury? If Oprah Winfrey is, as I believe, an admirably steady, morally capacious, chat show counselor, what sort of creature is Jerry Springer? If it is a cliché to say that modern identity is made by the form of consumer society, the question is then, what are we worth to ourselves if we pay such attention to celebrities?

And then one asks, what may celebrities do for us in return? To tackle these blunt and disobliging matters, we need an even shorter history than this book embodies. It is a history of how we learn to feel, and feel differently from our ancestors, as well as how we contrive to match our moral beliefs to those veering passions.

Chapter 2

A Very Short History of the Feelings

The history of celebrity therefore demands a kind of history which is largely missing on the shelves. It is a history of what the greatest commentators of our origins in the 1760s or so would have called the moral sentiments. David Hume, greatest of them all, wrote *A Dissertation on the Passions*, and Adam Smith, his close friend, admirer, and executor, now best known for his authorship of the first indisputable classic of economics, *Wealth of Nations*, wrote *The Theory of the Moral Sentiments*, which ran into six editions before Smith died in 1790.

These men—and many others in the great surge of conflicting ideas we now generalise as the Enlightenment: Kant, Herder, Condocet, Hegel, de Tocqueville, Wordsworth—were pulled to the idea of explaining the massive social change they saw about them in terms less those of old textbook narratives of the Age of Reason and the efforts of reasonable men to control the passions, and more of the way reason and passion were mutually formative and inextricable. The key for us, 250 years later, is to learn the lesson they can be said to have inaugurated, that passion is as historical as everything else, and that what we now call the feelings and, in exalted moments, our emotions, are quite differently formed from those which blazed out in the streets of England and Scotland during the second half of the eighteenth century. That same formation of our feelings, what is more, occupies a quite different space in our social identities, themselves highly differentiated by class and education. The business of learning how to feel and what to do about it is now a business of itself, staffed by psychotherapists, agony aunts, relationship counsellors, social workers, priests, and schoolteachers. The present point of being and seeing celebrities is a very long way from those who went peeking and gossiping in their best finery to St. James's Park and Vauxhall Gardens in 1770.

Yet those are the origins of our strange topic. Spotting and gaping at Sarah Siddons and Joshua Reynolds and, a little later, at the satisfyingly

disgraceful Prince of Wales is the opening of our tale, gleeful and shameful as it is. To fix that narrative line against some kind of moral horizon,
to prevent its becoming a mere sequence of snapshots—1770s London
theatre, 1848 Parisian revolution and haute couture, Gilded Age New York
and Newport, the founding of Hollywood, and the self-invention of Mussolini and Hitler—we need our own rough-and-ready theory—a *historical*
theory—of the moral sentiments. Thereafter, the lived life recounted in the
book itself is intended to give the necessary historical thickness, nourish-
ment, and energy to the sketch which follows.

A brief warning first. There is no presumption here of an old Marxist
kind that, in the slogan, social being determines consciousness, or that
the economic base dictates the cultural superstructure, including human
passion. Nor is this an essay in classical or Durkheimian sociology, to the
effect that both passion and action are ordered expressions of prior and
all-powerful social structures and interests.[1] On the contrary, the sketch
of the feelings which follows, and the play of mind upon those feelings,
might once have been characterised as old-fashioned idealism, that is, the
notion that it is not the material forces of the world which shape history and economics, rather the *ideas* which human beings direct upon the
world, which make history up for the final reckoning. What follows is only
"idealist" in the sense that the dramas of everyday life configure, define,
and perpetuate "a constellation of enshrined ideas." The phrase belongs
to Clifford Geertz,[2] and, elaborating the approach to historical enquiry
labelled by Kenneth Burke "dramatism," Geertz is at pains to emphasise
how human conduct, impelled both to obey and to disobey its history,
presents, expresses, and *argues over* the principles and passions of life in
the very drama of ordinary life. That drama is at one and the same time
a historical segment of the life of the community and an enacted theory
about how that life should go.

One dismal and prevalent way of picturing society practised at present
in the human sciences is to see absolutely everything in terms of the power
relations at work. But, as Geertz tells us, "to reduce [the public drama of
the theatre state] to such tired commonplaces, the worn coin of European
ideological debate, is to allow most of what is most interesting about it to
escape our view. Whatever intelligence it may have to offer us about the
nature of politics, it can hardly be that big fish eat little fish or that the rags

of virtue mask the engines of privilege."[3] If the theory of symbolic action as professed here teaches us indeed to see human conduct as "a constellation of enshrined ideas," we will need to read it aloud as an apostrophe in rhetoric, *not* a natural history of dependence. The poetics of a polity, which is to say the story a society tells itself about its politics, makes up a match between its official and its unofficial knowledge and values. Thus, one comes to see what kind of thing it is, in all its restless and assured complexity, by seeing quite literally how it *acts*. Seeing like this frees one from the culpably simpleminded view that power is a synonym for politics, and that the political is (simply) the transcendent domain of social action.

II

My potted theory of the moral sentiments (a swooping historical ride across two and a half centuries) will therefore intervene at only four points of the period, displaying at each point a cartoon of the social drama as it so passionately enacted its theories of what it was. Since we must, to avoid an infinite regress, start somewhere, the 1760s will do, as the decade when Smith published *Moral Sentiments* (1759); when the peace treaty which concluded the Seven Years War was signed (in 1763) and the Grand Tour became a central part of every well-off young Englishman's aesthetic, geographic, acquisitive, and sexual education; when David Garrick enlarged Drury Lane Theatre (in 1762) to make it the most important and accessible theatre in Europe; when George III came to the throne (in 1760) and James Boswell came (in 1762) to seek his fortune, by way of a commission in the Guards, in London, and to write the first celebrity classic.

Fortune seeking, as we shall see, was all the rage by the time that same Boswell decided against the army, and London was the place to find and lose it again. For over the three generations since the restoration of the monarchy and the peaceable, venal settlement of Toryism under Walpole's long rule, London had become the progressive centre of the European and North American imagination, as well as the actual, practical centre of economic activity. The court and the city changed places, as John Brewer puts it,[4] and as even that admirable textbook *1066 and All That* acknowledges, "all the gents drank coffee all the time, and winked at all the girls."

The point of the commotion invoked in this chapter is for the moment not so much that old historical standby, the rise of new middle classes, as the consequence for those on the make and the rise in the feelings they confected about themselves and others, and how such feelings issued in action.

In his *Dissertation on the Passions*, David Hume distinguishes between pride and humility. Pride is constituted by "a certain satisfaction in ourselves, on account of some accomplishment or possession which we enjoy," and Hume emphasises that this happy condition only has actuality insofar as it is ratified by the attitude of others. It will only fortify us

> if to the agreeable impression which arises in the mind, when the view either of our virtue, beauty, riches or power makes us satisfied with ourselves, there answers in others a corresponding agreeable impression.... Nothing flatters our vanity more than the talent of pleasing by our wit, good humour or any other accomplishment; and nothing gives us a more sensible mortification than a disappointment in any attempt of "that kind."[5]

Hume's vision of human conduct is of tense, obvious, but unspoken exchanges of deference and condescension. To be "condescending" at this date was to show oneself at once superior *and* accessible to one's inferiors; the shift in meaning which has since turned "condescending" into a derogatory term catches exactly one aspect of the history of the sentiments we are considering. A celebrity of 2010 cannot be caught out in an act of condescension and be left unpunished.

We have necessarily to turn to some rather catchall explanations in order to say something useful but approximate about feeling formation at our distance from the strong-smelling ground in which celebrity sprouted and old renown died off. The coefficient of social friction was located between the grand landowning families and the tumultuous entrepreneurs of manufacture whose absolute desire was to emulate, elaborate, and supersede those who condescended to them. Social bonds of class, region, occupation, and family were all much tighter then, for sure, but the flashy, jumbled world of London, whose fashions were omnipotent, left plenty of room for newcomer money to play in. In his sweeping scan of the social drama, Roy Porter finds the source of social energy as generated precisely by the contradictory frictions of snobbery (a force impossible to overestimate in class society), of the mutual requirement that class rulers be popular and well acclaimed, as well as simultaneously sneered at and mistrusted, both from below; at the same time they must be confident and ruthless in the maintenance of their power and the enlargement of their riches. [6] The play of respectful deference, sardonic resentment, terrific self-assurance in public and permanent self-doubt in private is what produces in the classic plays of the theatre of the day their continuing epiphany. For along with our contemporary pleasure at Sheridan's and Goldsmith's disdain for the fop and the oaf, for the pretence of high cultivation and the satisfaction of low malice, no one can doubt the readiness with which we can recognise these unedifying ingredients in the formation of our own, different, twenty-first-century feelings. Stooping to conquer is still a frequent and useful strategy of advance, and every celebrity has been a pupil in the school for scandal.

Porter unsympathetically marks out the matrix of the passions, when he observes that "magnates were on the horns of a self-created dilemma. Acquisitiveness urged them to maximise agrarian profit, pride to bask in undisturbed private grandeur, yet both would undermine their hegemony." Hence the Wentworths in South Yorkshire ripping the coal out from under the beautiful prospect in front of Wentworth Woodhouse *and* commissioning Gainsborough or Wilson to paint pastoral landscapes for the rooms inside. "The richer they got, the more they cultivated tastes—Palladian [architecture], French fashions, Italian music, artistic connoisseurship—which risked distancing them from their natural right hand men, homespun squires and freeholders." (It was of course one main point of these tastes to put at such a distance their nearest subordinates.)

"Patricians grew more snooty about the vulgar world.... And yet popularity was the kiss of life. Lacking private armies, in the end they had to court popularity and rule by bluster and swank. Authority could be upheld only by consent, through a tricky reciprocity of will and interests, give and take." Therefore those who ran for parliamentary office had to pay for the drunken meetings and postelection parties; the high style of landowning hospitality, aesthetic exhibitionism, lavish condescension, was built on very long credit (it still is), and the subordinate creditors got their own back in both senses by muffled overcharging.

Porter concludes brutally that "the fraternising game, however nauseating, however phoney, had to be played." We might now say, a bit more forgivingly, that the dance of social status is endless; *it is what there is*, and eighteenth-century England, if it was to escape the social detonation due across the Channel, had to devise a theatre in which savage rivalry and pitiless competition were softened by concessions and courtesy and common kindness.

The sentiments learned and the passions expressed in these exchanges were quick and subtle. A man's will and his interests were likely to be at odds ("I must assert my proud superiority; no, better if I condescend with due humility"); a woman could not "bluster and swank," rather she learned, in the appropriate social stations, to balance ardour with feasibility, pride against serenity, modesty against resentment.

In the busy jostle of the competition, feeling was, as David Hume unforgettably tells us, primary and imperious. "Reason is, and ought always to be, the slave of the passions" was his most famous dictum, by which he meant that one will select a reasonable course of action by way of accommodating the feeling which starts one off.

This serves as the originary algebra in our cartoon history of the passions. The function of reason is so far as possible to equip the passions with pleasurable action, where pleasure connotes a far less self-referring or privately sensuous condition than it does by the time we arrive at the year 2000. At its simplest, Hume's and Adam Smith's theory of the "moral sentiments" directs passion towards appropriate and reasonable conduct. That passion may be trivial and transient, or grand and philanthropic; it may be for a pretty girl or a monstrous meal, it may be to encourage peacefulness and magnanimity in the ruling classes. All ways, the aim of reason is to discover courses of action which will, in Hume's formula, respond to the initiating passion by bringing it to a "pleasant" fulfilment, and this pleasingness will be of a reasonably "civil" or recognisable kind. Hume is entirely scornful of the extremity and delusions of what he calls "enthusiasms, ... such as appears from numberless instances; of the Anabaptists in Germany, the commissars in France, the levellers and other fanatics in

England and the covenanters in Scotland ... [all inspired] with a contempt for the common rules of reason, morality and prudence."[7]

The first of our four stages of the passions is therefore Hume's. Alasdair MacIntyre explains of Hume's theory and its actualisation in the daily life of London in the 1770s that "the [motivating] passion is not and does not provide the reasoning with its initial premise."[8] It just *is*. Reasoning is then a matter of determining action which will, as a matter of practicality, "serve" and satisfy the passion. By the same token, when those members—let us say, half—of the eighteenth-century social structure who could afford the privileges of emotional discrimination in "the fraternising game"[9] responded to the actions of others, their attention was directed towards identifying the passion which produced the action. Social education and the institutional etiquette which dramatised it defined what counted as the permissible passions and gave rise to the vocabulary of critical interpretation and moral judgement which issued as Lady Teazle's gossip in *The School for Scandal*, on one hand, and Hume's essays, on the other.

A vehement and counterposed riptide was, however, beginning to tear across these long undulations of European feeling by the end of the century. (It is always worth remembering that the two great geniuses who rode the wave most boldly, Wordsworth and Beethoven, were both born in 1770.) The Romantic movement in the arts and the revolutionary one in politics spoke alike in the accents of egalitarianism and the shared humanity to be found in common feeling. The very fact of common feeling and the joy of celebrating its expression became the grounds and justification of artistic creation which have lasted until the present. Jean-Jacques Rousseau, perhaps the most compelling philosopher of the new sentimentality, wrote of Hume's sociably reciprocal "man of society" that "he is always out of himself," "he cannot live but in the opinion of others, and it is from their judgement alone that he derives the sentiment of his own existence."[10] Scorning such dependence on the gaze of other people (without which, no doubt, there could be neither persons nor society at all), Rousseau led the way to the thrilling viewpoint that feelings are given by nature; that an individual is most in possession of his or her self when feeling deeply; that what one feels is best discovered in solitude; and that being true to one's feelings is the surest guide to moral conduct.

The new doctrine did not simply supplant the old. Jane Austen, for instance, saw it coming and wrote *Sense and Sensibility* to warn against its dangers, just as, balanced and judicious in everything, she wrote *Pride and Prejudice* a year or two later to mark the limits not to be overstepped by grandee arrogance, and to insert into the hatefulness of the fraternising game the cool excellence of Elizabeth Bennet's self-respect and dignity. The new doctrine intertwined with the old. It gave rise to the quite new valuation of spontaneity as opposed to the stifling rules of correctness and decorum. It was commended, among many, by Madame de Staël, doyenne of the Parisian salons, when she cried out, "One should never put oneself by choice in a situation where morality and feeling are in conflict; for the spontaneous is so beautiful that it is appalling to be condemned to be for ever dominating one's own actions, and to live with oneself as one's own victim."[11]

The hearts of a new generation gave back an echo to that. Even the horrible atrocities of the revolution borrowed a righteous glow from the idea that revolution is intrinsically iconoclastic. Only by a smashing up of the old icons—above all, as Malevich was to say in Russia in 1921,[12] those beautiful images whose destruction you will most regret—will new feelings and good societies be brought to birth. Meantime, on less apocalyptic, more English occasions, poets made their poems, in Wordsworth's wonderful phrases, "in the real language of men" and "out of the spontaneous overflow of passionate feeling," while nonetheless "being recollected in tranquillity."[13] Thus, the English heroes of Romantic poetry: Keats listening to his nightingale in a Hampstead garden; Shelley turning on his monarch after the cavalry charged the demonstrators at Peterloo—"An old, mad, blind, despised and dying King"; Byron jauntily pursuing himself and Don Juan through a series of insincerely sincere love affairs and dying, an authentic hero, in defence of Greek sovereignty.

These works were both type and token of the new criterion of true feeling, learned by opening oneself to the chance of personal spontaneity, and catching it on the wing, above all in the passionate love affair. For as we shall see (as we know already), the space of social action is very curtailed. If, as for Hume and Henry Fielding, passion is your motive power, or if, as for the Romantics, spontaneity is the beautiful sign of your freedom and individuality, it is still damnably hard to know what to *do* in order to retain your self-possession. For the good Humean gentleman or gentlewoman must needs hang on to the virtues of moderation in the middling station of life and is in honour bound to slight the fraternising game, while on the whole the Romantic woman can only be spontaneous in the tiny area of passionate love either before or outside marriage.

Her rival and her suitor, the Romantic man, has, however, two arenas for action. The first is also, of course, that of the love affair; the second, however, has since proved, for a sufficient multitude of (mostly) men, a vivid, mobile, and exhilarating action for the fulfilment or the expression of the passions. It is the action of money. A passion for money is, for the Humean, preconceptual and intelligible. Practical reasoning lends it purpose and direction and issues in action. For the Romantic, making money is supremely liberating and spontaneous in expression (so, too, as Marx was to show, is passionate hatred of the capitalist). Money is present from the start of this local history as crucial to a sentimental education. A love of it, nonetheless, must always be mitigated or disguised, even in post-Christian society, and as a consequence learning how to feel about it is never straightforward.

It was therefore the love affair which triumphed as the key lesson in and example of the advent of Romantic feeling, with a due feeling for nature and art, so framing and pervading the love affair as at times to seem the same thing. Hence the force of, say, Verdi's *La Traviata*, as blazing typefication of our second station. For *Traviata* not only dramatises the beauty of the spontaneous, it has also much been used as itself an education in and a prompt to the passions. [14]

Breaking momentarily with the exchange of deference and condescension certainly typical of bourgeois Paris in 1840, the wonderfully rapturous music corroborates the myth of the love story, since corroborated in art and real life countless times. Alfredo, son of a cosmopolitan landowner, falls for Violetta, the bewitching and beleaguered courtesan. Her voice and his, from offstage, intertwine in a soaring affirmation of true love as transcending social convention. In the natural beauty of the forest of Fontainebleau, the pair live in the delirious certainty of mutual devotion. Feeling of this intensity is its own rational justification.

Alfredo's father arrives while Alfredo is away, pleading with Violetta to renounce his son and save his daughter from the disgrace of the connection. In a wonderful moral and emotional touch, Verdi understands how such a woman as Violetta, desperate to win the social approval of such a man, knowing also that in Paris of the 1840s a courtesan will never regain the respectability she craves, complies.

In a painful scene in a packed gaming room, Violetta, back under the protection of her cynical old lover (a baron, inevitably), is publicly humiliated as Alfredo flings his winnings in her face. In the poignant last act, Violetta, dying of consumption, longs for Alfredo's arms and the limitless restorations of love. In the nick of time, Alfredo, accompanied by his now remorseful father, rushes in, and in a transport of reunion the lovers swear that their love is deathless. Verdi then kills off his much betrayed heroine, and the social order, of both passionate love and marital propriety, is paid on both sides. The opera is an intoxicating declaration of allegiance to the new treaty of the passions, and a low-key subversion of it. The forces of deference and condescension have the luck to find death on their side.

The relevance for our purposes of such a tale, and of the music which sustains it, is to vindicate the contradiction that selfless devotion and passionate love are all-imperious, prerational, and close to the meaning of life. Lovers become famous for their feeling, and celebrity itself borrowed the glow of ardour with which to adorn itself in public, never more so than when music was being played. Thus the virtuoso—singer, conductor, soloist[15]—joined the actor as the publicly celebratory *sign* of the splendour of passion.

All this spectacularity notwithstanding, passion's reason became thereafter much ramified and complicated by a very different account of its working. The grand simplicities of *Traviata* and *Rigoletto*, of *Pagliacci* and *Cavalleria Rusticana*, the private-passion-enacted-in-public by such artistic celebrities as Georges Sand, Chopin, Liszt, Madam Butterfly, and Anna Karenina, lent their transfiguring force to the everyday formation of feeling on either side of the Atlantic. But the real transfiguration of feeling and the rewriting of the emotional curriculum took place—for the record at least—in novels: the novels of George Eliot, Henry James, Marcel Proust, Thomas Mann, Virginia Woolf. Indeed, Tolstoy set things in motion in *Anna Karenina* by showing, as F. R. Leavis put it, that, setting themselves up "to live *in* the pride of their passion, Anna and Vronsky found that they couldn't live *on* it." [16]

The grave, careful, and reflective prose of the great novelists bears witness to a reconceptualising of feeling and emotion over the period from about 1870 to 1920, a process, moreover, given a horrible jolt between 1914 and 1918 when it became so difficult to know what to feel at all apart from horror, and when most feeling was in any case so painful. This strange process, fundamental to our historical movement, relocated emotion in what MacIntyre, my guide in this elaboration of his suggestion, calls "a patterned regularity of dispositional and occurrent feeling, judgement and action."[17] By this, I take it, he means that the careful processes of reflection upon and revision of feeling chronicled by Henry James and his fellow novelists broke off the direct line Hume saw from passion to action and replaced it with an intermelding and integration of feeling with judgement, of both with reflection and deliberation upon both, until action itself is dissolved into a studious uncertainty about the place of rationality in the understanding of feeling and the object of emotion becomes emotion itself, while action is infinitely postponed.

For an intelligent gentleman in 1900, Henry James shows us the diffidence as well as the tenacity with which his hero moves between an evaluation of his feelings, a correction of the evaluation, an aligning with these of his tentative judgement about each, and a pause while indistinct entities swirl together and commend to him a possible course of action, perhaps never to be taken.[18] By the time we come to Virginia Woolf, twenty years later, we find her giving life, in *Mrs. Dalloway*, to a woman (women in any case being, as she sardonically noted, forbidden to act meaningfully) whose emotions have disintegrated into moments of pure consciousness, divorced from the sociable world, unavailable as guides to what she should actually do, and not even considered for that purpose. The point of the novelist's reflection is to watch how feelings gleam and flash and dislimn into subsequent feelings.

In part, one supposes such a quandary besets us all, ninety years later. It is very hard in the modern world to discover forms of rational and significant action. One reason for the popularity of ludicrous television action games and the grotesque car crashes and high explosions of thriller movies is that thereby eager (mostly male) spectators can briefly escape into a world in which physical strength and personal decisiveness about killing other people win the day. Back in 1920, as E. M. Forster remarked of

T. S. Eliot's *The Love Song of J Alfred Prufrock*, it was just a relief, the war just over, to find a poem concerning an ineffectual American intellectual worried about his bald spot.

Emotional rumination and diffident theories of action as commended by the Bloomsbury group and the not very rich, fairly cultivated English middle classes in the 1920s have therefore something good to be said for them. That allowed, one cannot doubt that they helped us towards our fourth, contemporary stage of the history of feelings. What they did then was to plot the manifold matrix of emotion, evaluation, reflection, and (doubtful) intention which is the moral foundation of the present day. The world of personal therapy, of the admirably careful protection of small children, of domestic self-analysis and family democracy,[19] was founded then.

As far as the confection of celebrity was concerned, this radical tendency may be said to have done three things. It made the criterion of worthwhileness the private reason; intimacy became the space of judgement. Thus the private life of the film stars turned into the stuff of fame; their acting only signified as a point of access to the truth of their feelings. The abdication of Edward VIII in Britain was a testing ground of the process, and his intimate life failed the test, while that of his kindly, pallid, and helplessly stammering brother and his wife came up to scratch.

The second thing the Bloomsbury settlement brought slowly about, at least across Europe and North America, was the entire rejection of the Great Dictator as a tolerable type of political leader. Hitler, Stalin, and Mussolini, celebrities like no other, had mean, vicious, or paltry intimate lives, and in the end even the Russians came to welcome Mikhail and Raisa Gorbachev.

The third contribution made by the delicate emotional reckonings of such as Henry James and Virginia Woolf was to settle the idea of the *individual* at the centre of modern ethics, and that individual is defined as such in virtue of the self-possession of his or her feelings. These feelings express the moral preferences of the person,[20] and there is no arguing about how those preferences are arrived at. Each individual is defined as such by being in possession of preferences arising from his or her feelings and held as a matter of right as well as accorded the respect due to rights.

Long before the twentieth century turned, this version of a new character role, the individual, clarified and moved centre stage. The colossal swirlings of what we now generalise as "globalisation," the obvious delights brought to enough people by consumer capitalism for it to count as victorious over a longish season, softened social ties, eroded cultural identity for better and worse, obliterated neighbourhoods, and cancelled old tokens of social class.

We come therefore to a historical moment at which community and membership are constituted by individuals vigorously defending their individuality, largely in terms of their feelings. This has led to a political world of citizens each standing on individual dignity for recognition of the preferences and wants of each. Nor is there any agreed mode of argument for determining which wants, arising from which feelings, should take precedence over which others. The business of the democratic polity is to devise ways of ordering the wants so that the most popular may be satisfied. The common good is now separated utterly from its earlier meaning as just that and becomes instead the good ranked first in the order of preferences by electorates, governments, or pollsters. Politics can retain no vision of a polity in these conditions but must confine itself to the dictum of utilitarianism and discover agreement on the greatest good of the greatest number, as discoverable by way of elections, social survey, focus groups, and national media.

The individual himself or herself is meanwhile increasingly in a hole. In this book, he or she scrutinises and revises the available states of feeling and not infrequently is at a loss to know what to feel. This gives birth to a familiar figure in our time which is the educated, intelligent person withdrawn from all social contact and commitment, frozen in a fearful condition of nonfeeling, locked into inaction. When the same condition repeats itself in a sensibility with fewer intellectual resources and in a person without even a job to provide a daily patterning of time, then the frozen sensibility may well break out into violent rages or uncontrolled hilarity precisely to force feeling of some kind into its veins.

Mostly, no doubt, the individual keeps up the defence of individuality by feeling something. But it is a feature of the modern sensibility and its regulated circulation of feeling, reflection, revision, evaluation, that this orderly sequence, while to itself seeming perfectly rational, need lead to no consequent action. Carefully considered inaction is the daily condition of modernity, accompanied by those feelings we find appropriate to our dispositions, all this largely confirmed by the sheer difficulty of discovering significant forms of action in the corporate and institutional routines of bureaucratised life.

This is not a curse spoken over modernity. Freedom and happiness are more liberally distributed by and across these processes than they were for Hume's comrades. But the stock of meaning for reflection and resolution to draw upon has shrunk even as the demand of individuality for more opportunity has enlarged. So the fulfilments offered, on the one hand, by parenthood and, on the other, by career, over here by leisure life, over there by the acquisition of things, seem to many people stretched and worn thin. They are uncertain what to desire for their children's good and their inheritance; they are unlikely to enjoy the commemoration of long employment in a single career and a circumscribable place; impressed by learning of individuality and its habits of consumption, they are quick to say to themselves "I want" and to treat such a statement not as needing justification but as a fact about the world and a condition to be met as of right. The value which has lost most weight in this history is love, at best replaced by kindness, mostly smiled at regretfully, as a lost illusion.

In these particulate times, celebrity serves as a kind of magnifying screen onto which these doubts, aspirations, and predicaments are projected. The screen, of course, is television, and television is so magical a theatre that it sits intimately in the family's main room. Often it remains unswitched off, unignorable, omnipresent, repeated in several rooms of the house and then, when people are gathered round in attention to its garish fairground effects and costume, its revelation of intimacy, of the bodies and spirits of those it pictures, it serves to mimic significance and action merely by being there. The audience then comes to suppose that the dream of successful action is best, even only, realised on television. To be on TV is the pure form of the successful, fully realised individual.

Those who make it are enviable. It has been an imaginative as well as a revoltingly seedy development by programme planners to invent so-called reality TV. It is cheap—inexperienced newcomers get sudden money and then the sack. It is flagrant and intimate—its characters practise the analysis of their feelings, so familiar to the audience, not exactly in public but in colossally visible intimacy. Far from being feelingless, it shows feelings worked up to a high temperature by the hothouse lights and the millions of glass windows through which the victim-victors are watched and derided. These petty quarrels and reconciliations are recognised and repeated in miniature by audiences not so much rapt as distracted.

To be on television is to be enviable. But envy is a tense, psychotic passion. It revolves through desire to fulfilment to disappointment to dislike. The great satisfaction is to see those who are enviable humiliated. This is a primary rhythm of celebrity, easy to see in the accelerated psychosis played out in *Big Brother* and suchlike.

In the further galaxies of stardom, the psychosis has its way, no doubt, as psychoses will. But the earlier frames of feeling are still embedded in the new ones, and the quadruple frames of feeling as enumerated here are still detectable in the manufacture of today's celebrities.

The British royal family, the American presidents and their First Ladies, can still play the fraternising game of will and interests, of condescension met by deference. But they are also figures in the psychosis of envy and disappointment, playing it up or down as best they can. The continuing power of the love story, "Still promising to solve and satisfy, / To set unchangeably in order," as Philip Larkin has it, is still in force, if shorter lived.[21] The companion idea of art and nature as together a cathedral of true and good feeling thrives busily in opera houses, art galleries, literary prizes, and, for the thousands of people, ourselves among them, walking the hills of the Lake District and picnicking in the national park beside the Pacific.

The celebrities who project these ideas owed the feelings they express onto the screen of the national imagination to artists, writers, actors, who enjoy a longer life in the public gaze than the wretches who take the cheque and the abuse of reality TV. The further from good art they are, the more liable to the destructive whirl of the psychosis, as expressed on behalf of the people by the unspeakable yellow press. Then gossip, scandal, mere mendacity, and brutal, phoney condemnation fill the entrails of the audience with brief satisfaction.

These are the sewerish manifestations of celebrity; they were there in the nineteenth century, they are here now. But as the feeling formation of history made its turn by way of the novelists towards our deliberative matrix of feeling, reflection, revision, and judgement, then "the talking cure" (as the Freudians came to call therapy) coloured the representation of celebrity and, as I suggested, perhaps tempered for some the sheer inhumanity of political celebrity as circulated by despots.

However that may be, deliberative feeling gradually took priority over rational action, and the celebrity, offering to act as a magnified projection of ourselves and our dominant, most cherished meanings and feelings, is set, by film, television, press, the whole spectacle of modern life, to dramatise the best and worst of our passionate puzzlement. Insofar as we are at a loss without the help of traditional customs and culture, neighbourhood, local long-standing jobs—all that is gestured at by "community," that wistful value—then the tale of our celebrities is here presented as the primary tale of our times, long prepared in the making of modernity, now come not to a conclusion but to our kind of apotheosis.

PART II The Rise of Celebrity: A Three-Part Invention

Chapter 3

The London–Brighton Road, 1760–1820

By 1760 London was the first city of the known world. By this I mean not just the most important one but also the first city to construct itself *as* a city in a form which would prove recognisable to modernity. It missed the chance, which Paris gave itself when the 1848 revolution was over, to rebuild itself as a city of squares and parks and boulevards after the great fire and according to Wren's plans. But it rebuilt a good deal of the wealthier areas in any case, and its delineation of itself in terms of fairly clear localities, each with its distinguishing status and market—meat, fish, fruit and vegetables, dockland, money, garments, transport, print, prisons—as well as its sheer condensation, the tightly packed, crammed nature of its construction, all made for its unprecedented success.[1]

The politics of the seventeenth century had displaced monarch and court from the centre of society; the city replaced it, and the city turned itself into one vast and roaring marketplace into which rivers of money poured from new imperial ventures, successful new wars, new technology, and its industrial expression. The reduction of the monarch to constitutional head of state, and the self-congratulatory but not vacuous welcome given by the new country of Britain to its incomparable liberty, made possible the terrific expansion of economic activity and social imaginativeness which followed the break. There is a century-old argument about where to place the historical beginning of capitalism, but no one can doubt the rate of its acceleration in London in the second half of the eighteenth century. The city, jammed, filthy, dangerous, small, domestic, unsplendid as it mostly was, was the ideal place for this to happen.

I say "dangerous," and it was. At such a time, footpads, cutpurses, rapists, whores, madmen, and drunks made up a plentiful proportion of the thronged streets, and respectable London could hardly avoid pursuing its business among all of them. But although riots broke out often enough to be considered normal—riots about bread prices,[2] about the establishment of turnpikes, against popery (the Gordon riots of 1780 when the soldiery killed 290 people and 25 looters were executed[3]), in derision of the rich and unpopular, even in exuberant support of popular heroes such as John Wilkes the radical, and Charles James Fox the libertarian member of Parliament, who could rally a mob in the street in minutes—the social order itself remained stable, only touched rhetorically by the revolution across the Channel.

The danger of the city was inseparable from its vitality, and one essential ground of its functioning. The old landowners were the masters of the regime all through, and Robert Walpole, for twenty-one years prime minister (until 1742), was their shrewd Tory protector, custodian, and, when he needed to be, disciplinarian. Their power and visibility was vastly increased over the century by the colossal rise in land values and the rapid climb in rent-rolls, as well as the legislation which created mortgages, and the licence this gave them to build and keep great mansions with a large staff in both the capital and the country. They ran their local shires like caliphs, carrying off or suborning all local offices, gerrymandering elections, and, in Parliament, assigning themselves all the profits from the countryside, whether the royalties from coal, the receipts from roads and canals, all the way down to legislating a monopoly of the game populating their huge acreages.[4]

Yet, as we saw, they had to play the game. Many were benevolently paternal towards their tenants, and all acknowledged the reality of the "free-born Englishman," in law and in the political feeling they shared with the common people. Their importance for our purpose, however, is twofold: they set taste and taught right feeling by the sheer conspicuousness of their example. Whatever new developments—theatres, concert halls, pleasure gardens, publications—emerged in the culture of the city, they could not thrive without the endorsement and the money of the mighty. Second, the great landowners were themselves *notable*. To be recognised as worthy of note, one would have to carry oneself like the aristocrat, mimic his dress, manners, lavishness of expense and then, after emulation, extend and seek to supersede his mode of being celebrated. It was not, I would say, until the 1960s that the ruling class in both Britain and the United States (in the United States, after 1865, "The 400") stopped being the glass of fashion and the mould of form. Not that the aristocracy (and the very rich) lacked critics through all the period under discussion—even old Tory Samuel Johnson asked, "If every man who wears a lace coat was extirpated, who would miss them?"—but they kept up on their eminence and lost emulability only very gradually.

Nonetheless, by the time Joshua Reynolds was knighted in 1768, his had become a grander and more awe-inspiring name than that of many a titled bravo with huge debts and no talent. Reynolds, whose brief illustrative biography is to come, was a leading version of a new kind of the London entrepreneur class mobility had made possible by means, indeed, of the new kind of capital and its very own new capital. New fortunes were made outside the city; their beneficiaries brought the money to town. The Whitbreads started out as minor Bedfordshire squires, and three generations later their brewery brought in £8,000 a year. The Cooksons and the Liddells discovered the Durham coalfields.[5] George Culley, another northerner, started out driving a coal-cart and ended master of Fowberry Tower. "England could boast more prosperous folk than perhaps any nation other than the Dutch Republic."[6] And they took their money to London, to build there, to vacation, to gape and bow at their betters, to gamble, to buy industrial plant for their businesses and dresses for their wives, to patronise coffeehouses, brothels ("bagnios"), theatres, pleasure gardens: to look at, to be seen, to spend.

J. H. Plumb, Neil McKendrick, and John Brewer were the first historians to say roundly that what was invented in eighteenth-century Newcastle, Norwich, York, Bath, Leeds, and, above all, London was the first consumer society.[7] It is always a slightly disparaging term, as indicating (correctly) that its members are impelled by a passion for going to market not to subsist, to buy and sell necessities, but to buy for the joy of it, to consume more than their dinner (and more dinner than they needed), to take home new clothes, of course, new furniture, carriages, carpets, wines (this is the moment at which wine begins to acquire its own intellectual discipline), full-grown trees, books, prints, paintings, and their gorgeous frames.

In point of fact, "consumption" is not a very accurate metaphor and earns no right to its derogatory inflexion. A painting or a building are still there after being looked at, trifling erosion apart; novels may be reread and plays revisited, and even fashions have their use-values. But insofar as a

consumer society is one in which demand insatiably outstrips supply, and
money is made for the spending of it, then England was such a society long
before the eighteenth century was over, and London was warehouse, marketplace, shop window (a new consumer invention), fashion showroom,
factory and its outlets, mint, bank, and crowded bankruptcy court.

Knowing now as we do what are the conditions of celebrity production,
it is not hard to see each buoyant and greedy innovation of the capital as
another turbine driving forward the juggernaut of fame. The rock-bottom
stability of the society was assured by the Whig-and-Tory settlement and
the unshakable position of the ruling class it invented.[8] But these men,
and the wives and families they ruled with a calm class arrogance, not
only needed a lively but uncontrollable money market with plenty of loose
change available, the rhetorical expression of their grandeur which dramatised their power and preeminence also demanded a new class fraction
of, so to say, grandee-advertisers. They needed architects, writers, painters,
landscape gardeners, interior decorators, and where once, at court and in
its satellite mansions, such artisans would have been entirely subordinate
to the rule of the master, in the much more open market created by the
new cities and their capital (by the time Walpole resigned in 1742 the population of London had passed half a million, one-tenth of the nation, just
like the present) things were much freer, opportunities more numerous,
buyers far more plentiful, bloodyminded independence less expensive.

In such a world, renown was still hard and solitarily won; fame, however,
was more quickly acquired because conferred not slowly by one patron but
competitively by several. Fame became a commodity, to be invested like
capital in a life's work, and to yield dividends of itself as the work won
esteem. Celebrity, its consort, stood to fame as marketing to production.
(This is only metaphor, not the real thing; I would be the last person to
suppose that a political economy of art says all there is to say about the
relations of art production under capitalism.)

In other words the ambitious artist, whose success depended on sufficient patrons finding what he (and, gradually at least in fiction writing,
she) created to their taste, made a name into a style of life. To do this, the
artist must become *known*: known for character qualities, artistic personality, moral, political, aesthetic originality—mixed with familiarity (not too
much of either). In the city, this meant that not only must the work exhibit

such qualities, but the life also. Deference must be acted out with a fine self-reliance; social insubordination played off against sheer accomplishment; the manner, and if possible the talents, of genius must be the well-handled weapon of the artist against the detestable lordliness of the Lords.

II

So celebrity comes into being as a portioning out of the posture and position of power. What the graded differentiations of the propertied and wealthy possessed, from the great dukes through the baronets, new and old, to ironmasters on the make and solid squires with a handsome income, they possessed only as they were able to display it, either as wealth itself or wealth made evident as taste. Since they depended on the artisans who produced the symbols of wealth and taste, dynasty and its certainty, they had to concede some of their own standing to these employees. It was a zero-sum game. What artists, writers, architects, composers, actors, all gained was at the expense (in all senses) of the mighty. Celebrity was the shine rubbed off the great and polished onto their hired (but unreliable) publicists. Hence the closeness of celebrity and art.

We can follow this relation most easily and excitingly through a potted history of the eighteenth-century theatre. This will provide two of the most telling persistences in our theme. The first is that it is by way of the theatre that the definition of celebrity takes its indiscriminate composition of private and public life, where private turns out to be synonymous with sexual. The second is that contradictory presence of rapturous acclamation and vicious will-to-wound on the part of the audience and the media of opinion which bestow and withhold the award of celebrity. The intimate life of actors is greedily pursued, starting in 1760 (let us say); this is because it is the actors' art to present the intimate life of fictional others while suppressing their own. They assume the greatness of kings and queens while being themselves nobody. It isn't hard to see why, having been made distraught to the point of tears or helpless merriment, having been abandoned to joyful applause, a spectator will turn on the cast and spitefully demand recompense for such a loss of self-possession. "Who is *she* to make me cry like that? No better than she should be, I'll be bound."

Those feelings were bound up in a long-standing tradition of fear and loathing of theatres and their players. After all, during the Commonwealth after the English Civil War, the Puritans did all they could to keep theatres shut. Their attitude had a long provenance, running from the fierce censorship exercised upon Shakespeare and his fellow playwrights by way of Puritanism, and still going strong in a delirious 1757 pamphlet called *The Players' Scourge*, asserting that "Play-actors are the most profligate wretches, and the vilest vermin, that hell ever vomited out ... they are the filth and garbage of the earth, the scum and stain of human nature ... the debauchers of men's minds and morals.[9] John Brewer goes on to say that, throughout this period of unfailing theatrical success, packed auditoriums, a pantheon of great actors, scholarly editions of the playwrights, "for many Protestants, especially clerics, it was a cardinal principle that playgoing and going to mass were both forms of idolatry."

Yet theatre life fairly stormed across these decades. David Garrick, actor extraordinary of course, but also impresario, producer, theatre-owner, financial speculator in theatre, and ultimately knight of the theatre, made himself its first celebrity and also, a much harder task, taught the London audiences, bit by bit, to suppress their chatter, their zoo noises and bursts of ribald song, their bombardments of fruit onto the stage, indeed the whole cultural supposition that the theatre was just another fairground, and to presage that so very civilised silence and sitting-in-the-dark which became, by the end of the next century, the appropriate reverentiality in which to receive great literature or music.

He swept the audience off the stage itself; he enlarged Drury Lane Theatre to take three thousand people; he battled to replace the hugely popular programmes of song and recitation, of pageant and light operatic fragments, with a serious repertory, seriously performed. Shakespeare was the key and this the moment—the moment of more or less conscious nation-building and consolidation of the overlapping identities of Britain, Britannia, England, Albion[10]—during which Shakespeare was canonised as the greatest *English* writer, and pride of the nation's literature.

So Garrick had his work cut out to adapt the tumult of the sociable theatre to his version of a decorous submission to strictly aesthetic experience. And of course, as well he might, he loved the noise and the acclaim he won and deserved, even as he battled to raise the social standing of actor and theatre, and sought successfully to become a man of letters about town, close friend of Dr. Johnson and his writers' circle, genial, courteous, gentlemanly. Johnson, who knew Garrick as well as anyone besides being the most percipient man in town, spotted the twistpoint of the whole business of the new fame when he wrote that Garrick "by an uncommon assemblage of private virtue, adorned the highest eminence in a public profession."

Garrick was one main artificer of the role and character of this new figure in metropolitan life (and not just in the capital, either—dozens of country towns had their own theatres, Norwich's and Nottingham's each seating a thousand; all these theatres drew repertory touring companies, each boasting at least one star name). He made it his life's task to turn acting into a noble art and to this end conscripted Shakespeare, the nation's own genius, as partner and his curriculum.

He succeeded, of course, splendidly, and bequeathed to us the nationally acclaimed figure of actor-producer-knight, mingling in his manners inevitable scandalousness and lordly remoteness, offstage untouchable, onstage the people's personality. When Garrick came onstage in certain of his very popular roles, the audiences claimed him for their own in excessive displays of enthusiasm and affection. At times, the same audiences would interrupt the dialogue from the boxes (a convention still exploited by the Crazy Gang at the London Victoria as late as the 1950s), and meanwhile anybody down in the pit believed himself free to shout interjections during the action. On a number of occasions on which the pit thought poorly of the play, they cheerfully caused it to be closed down, indicating their critical disapproval by smashing the gilt mirrors of the auditorium and pulling up the benches.

Garrick did more than anyone else to make the position of the actor not just respectable but conspicuous, not merely an officer in the entertainment infantry but a professor of the nation's taste and signal custodian of its art. By every contemporary account, he was a wonderful performer; by the evidence of such a trio as Dr. Johnson, Edmund Burke, and the great philosophe and theatre-lover Diderot, Garrick was a man of handsome manners, devoted seriousness, unshakable rectitude, perfect taste, even grace of spirit. Established at his fine villa at Hampton, he built a shrine to Shakespeare and was painted beside it by the society portraitist Johann

Zoffany; he collected a remarkable library with, as one would expect, a singular collection of play texts; he set this off with paintings by Perugino, Rembrandt, Van Dyck, Watteau;[11] he entertained at home the great aristocrats and his writer friends. But he knew his place. The definition of great actor and impresario which he contrived so single-mindedly remained necessarily in thrall to his public. Once having offended his audience by his choice of play and performance, he came onstage to remonstrate with the uncontrollably noisy spectators, only to have his contrition demanded by chants of "kneel." Garrick obeyed.

Garrick was capacious enough—no man more so—to carry off the contradictions in the role he had himself contrived. His irreproachable private life as well as his public munificence on behalf of the theatre meant that he was able to play out his signal version of the theatre celebrity who unites business with art, wealth with popularity, gregariousness with an immaculate self-conception.

Theatrical mythology, however, was what it was, and remains. All around Drury Lane were the bagnios, brothels, licentious taverns, and the deep squalor of the street. To be famed for a life of achievement in such a setting was necessarily to carry something of its malodorousness and raffish flair in spite of all Garrick could do to throw it off. Sarah Siddons, Garrick's equivalent among the actresses, had the same trouble, for all her friendship with Queen Charlotte, her stage embodiment as Britannia, her ostentatious mothering of her children: "One . . . gentleman . . . found Mrs. Siddons at her sick child's cot, rocking it with her foot and holding another at her breast, her new role in hand which she was learning."[12] This is immediately familiar to us as standard celebrity fare. But even stately Sarah Siddons, devout Tory, pious mother, queen of the tragic muse, was gossiped about as mistress of the painter Thomas Lawrence and—my dear!—of a well-known fencing master.

She and Garrick shaped the character of the actor as high-minded and cultivated aesthete, the public's own defender of the arts, guarantor of the nation's patriotic self as compacted in its theatre. All around them, however, their adoring, hypercritical, hypocritical, duplicitous, and often indifferent public smacked their lips over the trivial sexual misdemeanours, studiedly outrageous fashions on and offstage, high jinks and low drunkenness of such of the male actors as Colley Cibber (derided to his grati-

Mrs. Siddons, 1785, by Thomas Gainsborough (1727–1788). Oil on canvas, 126 × 99.5 cm. Bought, 1862 (NG683). National Gallery, London. Photo Credit: © National Gallery, London / Art Resource, NY

fication by Pope[13]), Garrick himself, his painful respectability notwithstanding, Charles Macklin, greatest of Shylocks, and Siddons's brother, the
second great actor-manager-theatre-owner, John Kemble. The actresses,
still objects of sanctimonious horror simply for doing the job, took heavier
obloquy, and several had the wit to turn this attention to advantage. They
were, in any case, treated as pretty well indistinguishable from Kitty Fisher,
Emma Hart (later Lady Hamilton), and the courtesans, and so the women
set and were set by the double standards which still shape such lives. Kitty
Clive, Peg Woffington (notorious for her "principal boy" roles and a showing off of her excellent legs), Cibber's sister Susannah, Anne Oldfield and
her illegitimate children, Sophia Baddeley, painted by Zoffany, much
courted (and won) by noble lords and ignoble indigent actors alike, were
all feted and reviled, lips pursed over just desserts (illness, death, poverty,
loss of good looks) moments after the selfsame women were objects of
envy and acclaim.

This paying-on-both-sides is probably the predominant structure giving
the concept of celebrity its multiple moral force. The word carries both
denigration and acknowledgement; its mere presence invites instinctive
salaciousness and fastidious withdrawal. It at once attributes charisma and
strips it off. It magnetises an audience, but only briefly. Celebrity glows
only while it passes by. These ambiguities were laid down during the last
four decades of the eighteenth century. They were the effects of a new kind
of performing society in which *appearance*, itself a concept with multiple
meaning, began to count as much as standing, longevity, tradition. These
things being so, it is to be expected that the institution of the theatre, the
very locale of specialised appearance, should engender the contradictory
passions so concentrated by the pretence of truth enacted within its great
cathedrals.

III

The theatre provides the simplest control for our historical venture. The
lineaments of eighteenth-century celebrity are reassuringly familiar in the
twenty-first century, whatever the differences in the direction of present-

day sentiment. Theatre is easy to add to film and television by way of grasping that celebrity, if not under that name, has been with us for 250 years.

The theatre, however, did not bring off the trick by itself. The fine simplicity of its workings requires at least softening in its outlines by a brief attention given to other manifestations of the new consumerism. The industrialisation of leisure, which is to say the shaping and organisation of the personal disburdening of work and its resulting freedoms (none more pleasurable than "free time" itself), demanded the invention of new daily routines and the spaces within which to live them out. A wealthy gentleman's leisure had been previously adjusted to the wide open spaces of his country home, to arranging to make killing wildlife interestingly spacious and difficult (hunting, stalking, shooting). Those pastimes sanctioned themselves as immemorial and English at just about this time, and old and new rich alike defined themselves by affording them.

The crammed, raucous life of the city, however, demanded new forms of leisure which were, in turn, much demanded by those new arrivals in the fields of leisure, well-off womenfolk. There had always been the limitless pleasure of music as a womanly pastime, of course, and during the period in hand, the concert, like everything else, moved from court to city. Handel's is the formative name in the narrative, and his music is forever attached to the idea of fresh-air performance, where king and country could enjoy what Handel wrote to be heard across the waters of the Thames or before the fireworks burst above the public gardens. Indeed, Handel has good claim as a main ancestor of musical celebrity; he threaded his way across the courts of Hamburg, Naples, Hanover and came to London in the service of the Hanoverian monarch. But unlike Bach, who remained a jobbing musician in the pay of the town council, Handel won not just fame and wealth but such recognition by his adopted city that the city celebrated his centenary in 1784 with one of the spectacular musical occasions, with mass choirs, professional and amateur players, large audiences, fireworks of course, which proved such a happy innovation of the day.

Such occasions formed the centrepiece of a rich and populous musical culture in London once Handel's music, especially the oratorios, had been transformed into patriotic repertory. This same transformation has also lasted comfortably into the present and formed the stock-in-trade of dozens of choral societies nationwide. As Brewer tells us, it became possible, then as now, to attend a big concert every night,[14] and this publicity (a useful example of concept predating word) drew the best composer-performers from the European courts to the British capital. J. C. Bach, Mozart, Haydn, each came to dazzle the concert-going city and, in J. C. Bach's and Haydn's cases, to remain, astonished by fees and salaries quite dwarfing anything Prince Esterhazy could pay.

The concerts were only one system of production in a city mass-producing leisure pastimes. For one thing, concerts, like plays, needed their characteristic venue, and the colossal classical swank of the Pantheon on Oxford Street, with its huge vaults and arcades, was a very different affair from the much rebuilt, twice burned to the ground Drury Lane Theatre. In the provincial towns, both county towns and spas, so-called assembly rooms and pump rooms were built on similar lines, modestly reduced, to those of the Pantheon and the Hanover Square Rooms, and these, generally giving onto parks or at least a large, open, tree-lined square, prefigured a new and very particular kind of assembly. (Somerset House and the Courtauld Gallery still provide a vivid reexperience of the visual aesthetics.)

Such an assembly arrived to converse, to read the newspapers, to take coffee (or at Bath, Cheltenham, Droitwich and Harrogate, to drink the dire and doubtfully medicinal waters), to "promenade," that is, to see and be seen in good company, to show off one's fashionable attire and one's eligible daughters, to vindicate one's taste at the concerts, to confer condescension and to receive deference, to offer respectfulness and conceal malice.

These were much more restrained and genteel places than the theatres, and the entrepreneurs of the leisure industry were quick to shape a novel stage environment around these elaborate comedies of manners. There had been "pleasure gardens" at Vauxhall since before the beginning of the century, but for many decades thereafter they were the workplace of the artisans of the pleasure industry, harlots, hard drinkers on the spree, cruising homosexuals, destitutes. The new men set themselves to change all that. An elaborate concert hall, decorated with (to modern taste) impossibly overdone swags, pillars beribboned in plaster, copious floral effects

very ornate and carefully devised in contrast to the Ottoman picnic gardens

on a looped and folded ceiling plastered to look like tenting, was built in the 1750s at Vauxhall by its keen new proprietor, Jonathan Tyers, as he turned respectable. New gardens, with all the desired consumer effects— prospects, ornamental water and waterfalls, coulisses, closures, sudden clearings and vistas, classical bridges, and little mausoleums—were constructed at Ranelagh in Chelsea, which centred on its splendidly ornate Rotunda, at the Ring in Hyde Park, in St. James's Park, Spa Fields, Marylebone Gardens, and in imitation countrywide from Brighton to Scarborough, Glasgow to Clifton, high above the seething docks on Bristol harbour. [15]

The pleasure gardens shook off as much low life as they could (by no means all of it). Most of the poor were debarred by the price of admission, a shilling at Vauxhall, half a crown at Ranelagh, and once inside the promenaders could enjoy the pleasures of the landowner as he sampled his prospects, paths, and specially imported trees from China or the Lebanon. The promenading family at Ranelagh could thereby fall into a rapture of fashionable emulation, parading, greeting, displaying, masquerading, not just like their betters but often alongside them, before turning to the bewitching medley of amusements inside the main buildings: concerts, *thés dansants* (which also lasted until the 1950s), print and picture galleries, tumblers, pageants, coffee stalls and muffin men, booksellers, pantomimes, gymkhanas, prize fights. "No one was to wear a sword, and all were to minuet in strict rotation, ignoring aristocratic precedence." [16]

The pleasure gardens were solvents of social distinction even while the point of one's visibility was to declare one's distinction. In a wonderful painting by Thomas Gainsborough already mentioned, the artist paints groups of ladies of the very *haut ton* promenading in St. James's Park some time in the summer of 1783. [17] It has been speculated that the women in the central group are the king's daughters, but however this may be, all the figures are, avidly but discreetly, assessing the others, for fashion, for deportment, for correctness of condescension and deference, for good looks (and their decline), for fame and privilege and sheer wealth. (The glorious duet sung and danced by Fred Astaire and Judy Garland in the movie musical *Easter Parade* is affectionate parody of the same social ritual taking place on Fifth Avenue nearly two hundred years later.) The beady little eyes

The Mall in St. James's Park, c. 1783, by Thomas Gainsborough (1727–1788).
Oil on canvas. © The Frick Collection, New York

of Gainsborough's women, missing nothing but never to be caught out
looking, serve as an early commemoration of the performance of celebrity.

IV

The rules of cultivated conventions, urban and urbane, were fixed across
these same years, and the discursive markers—polite as opposed to rough,
elegant not boorish, genteel rather than coarse, proper not indelicate—put
down. The language of self-reflection, of that naming and sorting of the
inner subject which is to be rendered so complex by the novelists a century
or so later, starts here. The historical archaeologists Norbert Elias and Mi-

chel Foucault agree, by their very different methods, that it is about now that becoming civilised turns out to mean the subjugation of the body to rules of civilised or surveillant order, whichever you choose, of manners, of propriety of motion, of work (and therefore leisure), of time.[18]

Foucault has his system of mighty historic changes, archaeological stratifications which mark off great splits in the historical formation of persons and peoples. These correspond little with the amiable gradualism of this book, proposing its moves from eighteenth-century reciprocities, to Romantic passion, to the early modern intensity of reflectiveness, to the contemporary practices of feeling-postponement and the carceral solitude of life-puzzlement. Yet Foucault matches two of these divisions of ours. He discovers one radical split in the forms of thought and feeling opening up around the turn of the eighteenth century, when Enlightenment doctrines of scientific classification and taxonomies (as taught by Linnaeus) are superseded by Hegel and Marx, sure that history was the prime mover of things and explicator of their causes and effects. Foucault's second rupture, coinciding with the advent of modernity, takes place either side of 1900, when Freud and Nietzsche inaugurate an age Foucault populates with such phantoms as "the scattering of the profound stream of time," "the absolute dispersion of man," "the return of the masks."

These slogans, Foucault being who he is, bear more weight than one might at first suppose. But his most daring assertion is that these shapes are not just forms of thought or of life itself, but frameworks devised as structures of power as coerced by the workings of a "discourse," the language conventions which power itself bolts onto the manacles and cages it prefers.

We do not have to swallow Foucault whole to accept that what his disciples call "discourse formation," and we might call codes of linguistic conduct, direct us, in 1760 and after, to attend to the new class of writers who flocked to London, whose works constituted the conversation of culture, a victory for one set of the stories people believed about themselves over another. The definitions of art and art's directive influence upon the good life, the (coercive, certainly) enumeration of etiquette and decorum, the early promotion of equality, and the naturalisation of the individual all transpire from the innumerable writers' clubs, the efflorescence of fiction in the magazines, particularly those written for women,[19] the amazing heaps of periodical literature, from Addison's *Spectator* to Johnson's *Rambler*.

The authority of these writers turned into something very like extra-political power, and it was inevitable that the masters of discourse were not at all invisible, as Foucault would say, but famed, recognised in public, celebrated.

The drama of our historical theory has therefore its living characters. The men of the Kit-Kat Club, first meeting after 1700 in the Cat and Fiddle in Gray's Inn Lane, had certain high-minded purposes on behalf of the arts and the drumming up of patronage, and they had some big names from the literary world as well as the aristocracy. But they also preserved the rakehell, coarse, all-male heavy-drinking-and-eating ways of the restoration court. They had nonetheless their direct descendants, especially under the leadership of George III's son in the latter part of the century. The soberly named Literary Club, however, of which the first advocate was Joshua Reynolds, was a very much more portentous, serious-minded, and public affair. Conscientiously sober, dressed in the new black of the gentle-man scholar, they embodied perfect politeness in its new sense.

Reynolds and eight other members began the club at the high peak of London's clubbishness in 1764. The names of the members it accrued over the thirty years of its incarnation vindicate its claims to both serious-ness and influence. Reynolds himself, Edmund Burke, Oliver Goldsmith, James Boswell (on his merits as well as Johnson's ticket), Garrick, Sheri-dan, Gibbon, Adam Smith, even Charles James Fox, demagogue and radi-cal MP, were the cream on an intellectually very rich jug of talent.

Talent was the point. These were or became men of high achievement, who were quite purposefully in search of fame and public recognition, the first formula of celebrity. The first nine members Johnson himself in a ringing roll call (modestly omitting himself) marked out as describing the circle of the arts, the sciences, and their disciplines: "we have Reynolds for Painting, Goldsmith for Poetry, Nugent for Physics, Chamiere for Trade, Politics and all Money concerns; Mr Burke for Oratory, Mr Beauclerk for Polite Literature, Langton for Ecclesiastical History ... Sir John Hawkins for Judicature and Ancient Musick."[20]

They met to talk and separated to write the results of their delibera-tions, which then turned out to be some of the main and most forceful determinants of taste ever written, utterly formative then, authoritative now. Reynolds's *Discourses on Art*, Johnson's edition of Shakespeare and his *Lives of the Poets*, Smith's *Theory of the Moral Sentiments*, Hawkins's musicological history, Nugent's medical textbooks, Malone's translations from the Greek and Latin masters, Gibbon's astounding *Decline and Fall of the Roman Empire*, all could be said to have been fired by the intensely learned and collaborative debate at "the Club."

These men were canonising a new curriculum of the arts and sciences on behalf of the new kind of cosmopolitan readership. They had patrons no doubt, when they could get them, but they looked on them with some ruefulness. As Johnson said bitingly to his, Lord Chesterfield, "such treatment I did not expect, for I never had a Patron before." He went on: "Is not a Patron, My Lord, one who looks with unconcern on a Man struggling for life in the Water, and when he has reached ground, encumbers him with help?"[21] Patrons were a hindrance or a help, but members of the Literary Club, whether Whigs, Radicals, Tories, or nothing much in the political line, were wholly their own men, and their true independence, their mitigations of the exchange of deference and condescension, were a centre ground of their solidly built fame, just as these qualities, guaranteed by the integrity of the work, gave their appearance (even Johnson's) a glamorous patina, and their presence the presaging aura of celebrity.

It is safe, however, to say that at this juncture, celebrity was inseparable from the public acknowledgement of achievement. These men attached the glitter of celebrity to the solidity of what they had accomplished by merely appearing in public; they were recognised for who they were as a result of what they had done. A genius, however, like Reynolds, could turn these simple recognitions into the manufacture of himself-as-a-famous-painter. It took prodigious hard work but that was nothing to him. He loved it, and he loved what it brought.

V

The history of both theatre and letters demonstrates, in its noisy, confusing, and jaunty style, how the new city culture mingled art and entertainment, intellectual endeavour and the morning coffee, lasciviousness and poetry, just as we do now, and it was the eighteenth century which taught us to delight in and to deride it all as well. Mighty though the men of letters were, quick on their heels the women, and morally ambiguous the stars of the stage, one could not say that any one figure among the writers was a great inaugurator of the peculiar life of each corner of the culture. In the case of painting, however, we can. Joshua Reynolds pretty well single-handedly invented the role of painter as public celebrity, threw off by sheer industry the heavy encumbrance of the patron, devised an unprecedented harlequinade of social life, compounding sexual licence, gluttony and drunkenness, gaming and court appearances before the king, all along with a ruthless business acumen for later artists to copy and embellish. Since he also possessed the necessary talents to accompany the show, he provides a sumptuous object-lesson for our theme. Hogarth was, by contrast, an artisan who picked up status by a judicious marriage. To contemporary taste, his bawdy, caustic realism, heir to Brueghel and Jan Steen, may make for a keener response in the sensibility, but beside Reynolds, Hogarth cut a very small dash.[22]

The idea of fame lasting into posterity had been an artistic ambition since Augustan Rome and Horatian poetry, and Reynolds certainly aimed for it. But he also sought contemporary recognition in the most literal sense. He longed and he planned to be known by name in the best circles and in the street; to be larger than ordinary life because a great artist; to flout the rules of gentlemanliness because bigger than a gentleman; to go to bed not only with courtesans but with great ladies as well, and to do so because of the fame his painting had brought him and would brush off on them.

Fame was his aim from boyhood, as his headmaster father observed, and Reynolds chose his first master shrewdly.[23] Thomas Hudson taught him to paint portraits and in 1744 introduced him into one of the best of the new clubs springing up to discuss and buy paintings. After statutory study for three years in Italy, Reynolds planned his return very carefully, for "by being in too great a hurry I shall ruin all and arrive at London without reputation and nobody that has ever heard of me."[24]

He timed things right, not least in ensuring his own high visibility by investing heavily in large dinner parties (a new and attractive craze) and canvassing for election to innumerable clubs (failing at White's). The much publicised pleasure he took in painting straight courtesans as well as the more uninhibited ladies of fashion (Kitty Fisher of the nursery rhyme, Emily Warren, Nelly O'Brien) was the more gratifying to him for its being so generally assumed that sitting for him was not the only favour they granted. Johnson's dear friend Mrs. Thrale tried to make a match between Reynolds, in his late fifties and a bit shaky, and the young, bright, much admired new novelist Fanny Burney.

Reynolds did everything, including paint, on a big celebrity scale. In 1760, his name already made but a long way still to go, he bought a large house in Leicester Square and opened it with a show of his old masters and his own paintings, setting these off with a grand and (according to the *Gentleman's Gazette*) debauched ball. He assumed a robustly undeferential manner to men of rank, one of them describing him, after soliciting a portrait, as "so vulgar and familiar a forward fellow."[25] Maybe the manner came naturally, maybe it was a product of Reynolds's belief that the artist was a better man than any of them; but he handed down entire the celebrity model of man or woman given by genius and achievement: freedom, stature, self-reliance, absolute indifference either to the subservience or the derogation of others, bad manners if called for, bursts of hospitable generosity if not.

What was never in doubt were his giftedness and his dedication. He worked prodigiously hard, painting over two thousand portraits during his career (taking a hundred commissions a year at his peak) and able by its end to charge 150 guineas standardly and a thousand guineas a picture if he felt like it. The amazingly wide social range of his sitters—actors, certainly (Garrick and Sarah Siddons), courtesans as already listed, writers (Goldsmith, Sterne, Johnson—more than once—Sheridan), politicians (Charles James Fox, Burke), generals (Gentleman Johnny Burgoyne), admirals, all the most prominent hostesses and their children, and of course the king and the crowds of the titled heads of the great families. He also did much to commemorate the transient status of celebrity by painting assorted figures of brief publicity, such as the soldier hero of the American war, Robert Orme, the Polynesian prince Omai brought to London by Captain Cook as a kind of anthropological trophy in 1774, and the Cherokee chieftain Scyachet Ukah, visiting London in 1762 on a diplomatic visit much impeded by the death of the interpreter and the inability of anyone else in London to speak Cherokee.

Reynolds was well aware, nobody more so, both of the social standing of his subjects and of his own power to confer status on the sitters in virtue of his agreeing to paint them. He did much therefore, as it may be put, to lend the aura of celebrity to those already selected for renown by their talent as writer or soldier or sailor. To have been painted by Reynolds added a recognisable gleam in the social circles of *haut ton*, whether or not anybody had ever seen the portrait.

His huge fame did something else, much more radical by way of consolidating the social status of the newly mobile class of producers in the arts. Reynolds made sure that the writers and actors he painted appeared in his canvasses as figures just as worthy of celebration and public recognition as the *grands seigneurs* and their wives who owned and ran England and Scotland. As we saw, the novel city of London and its terrific creativity gave these scribblers and the whoreson players their chance; Reynolds was their generous and uncondescending advertiser. He redefined their public relations and, in doing the same for the office of courtesan, did much to underline and magnify what will prove to be the unbreakable connection between public life and private busyness, between cultural display and sexual activity, between high-mindedness and scandal.

What was no doubt unknown to eighteenth-century London society, although there is a glimpse of it in the portrait of Prince Omai, is the idea of fame as residing merely in the fact of being and of being recognised and talked about in public. That is to say, what Reynolds celebrated was power, status, or talent, and what he did for Sheridan or Garrick or Mrs. Siddons was ensure that their fame shone so brightly in his paintings as a consequence of their achievements in *art*. The good life as lived by the passably devout, conscientiously cultivated, sufficiently prosperous, and youngish parents of the day was urged upon their children as given moral timbre and spiritual gracefulness by familiarity with and accomplishment in the arts. This inheritance is still solidly visible in all definitions of a decent education from that day to this. In particular, responsibility for the inheritance has been handed over to women, and it was from about 1760 or so that women came to be not only conspicuous consumers of the arts as well as hostess and patroness to artists, but also its practitioners. The great tradition of British women writers and women actors starts in London from that date. Given the propensity of men to battle to keep their women under, it is no surprise that the trade of writer or actor when practised by women is routinely linked to sexual scandal.

One cannot say that Reynolds's successful, even brilliant manipulation of the ingredients of fame, for himself and for fellow artists (including the artistes of sex), *caused* the coming of celebrity. But his efforts certainly throw into relief most of what we now understand as the effects and conditions of celebrity: public recognisability, the interplay of envy, admiration, generous acclaim, malicious denigration, prurient attentiveness, swift indifference. Fame was and remains either the reward of social achievement in the public field or the tribute necessarily paid to power, wealth, and privilege. (In either case, such rewards may be arbitrary and uneven.) Celebrity, by contrast, is either won or conferred by the mere fact of a person's being popularly acknowledged, familiarly recognised, attended to, selected as a topic for gossip, speculation, emulation, envy, groundless affection, or dislike. In either case, fame or celebrity bestows an aura on its proprietor, magnetises a crowd, swivels heads, and clears a path through the multitude for its carrier to pass. When Reynolds entered a social occasion, one of his servants recalled, "the people all turned round and stared so, upon hearing Sir Joshua's name announced, and they even made a lane for him to pass through, whereas when a duke or an earl was announced, few of the people took any notice."[26]

This is celebrity in action, but Reynolds (on our definition) combined it with fame: he is still a *renowned* painter, a figure in the pantheon of art; so are Garrick and Sarah Siddons and Dr. Johnson; but not so Kitty Fisher and Emily Warren. These little distinctions are at the heart of this book, and eighteenth-century London their first flourishing. Those beginnings, however, were rooted, obviously, in a much more restricted society, one which offered its chances of mobility and fortune making, for sure, but whose social frames were fixed by crown, church, aristocracy, property, and a capital city which, for all its multitudinous and incarnadine seas of people, could be walked across in two hours.

There are, no doubt, historical rhythms at work in the frequency and intensity with which both fame and celebrity distend and collapse. Reynolds died in 1792, knighted, president of the Royal Academy (which he had laboured to found with his eye on just that office for himself), painter to the king, and object of admiring dedications in a dozen tomes of literature, and of general veneration. Fame took him up and shook off the scandal he both courted and enjoyed. But celebrity as a social force was surging towards a brief crest, to do which it had devised a pleasure garden amounting to a city, and a star figure combining vast social status and reckless self-indulgence, combined if not with artistic achievement, then marked good taste and energetic patronage.

                                      VI

King George III's son, George, was born in 1762, two years after his father came to the throne aged only twenty-two. George senior was the first of the Hanovers to have been born in England, a man of pious and righteous conservatism and a decided political will which brought him into serious conflict with his ministers over American independence and (he being a devout Lutheran) over the emancipation of the Catholics. But the poor fellow has been recovered from historical almost-oblivion by Alan Bennett's remarkable play and then movie of 1994, *The Madness of King George*, which deals out such delicate-handed justice to the king's domestic propriety and personal rectitude while so painfully and comically dramatising his outrage at the treatment given him by his doctors and warders during the gibbering madness brought on by porphyria of the kidneys.

It was not only outrageous to him that he was straitjacketed, mustard-plastered, tied down to his bed, leeches stuck to his head,[27] his urine and excreta studied by servants and doctors; he was utterly humiliated by all this being common knowledge to the nation, everywhere reported in the press, openly discussed in Parliament, the small change of political chatter in the coffeehouses. George had always entertained much grander ideas of his own capacities and the power with which he wanted to express them than either the inexplicit constitution or his tough, trustworthy ministers—North, Pitt the Younger, even Fox—would permit. George never had the money he wanted, particularly to spend on building palaces commensurate with his dignity and his artistic tastes; his subjects crowded onto his very doorstep at Buckingham House; if he wanted to attend the theatre, why then he had to join his subjects in Drury Lane.

Yet the length of his reign, mad or not, the very publicity of his intimate ills, together with his stolid self-righteousness and marital decorum, slowly set a new royal style. When the Jacobins loosed the Terror on Paris in the four years after 1789, even the Radicals recognised the value of a sedate head of state retaining that head in both symbolic and corporeal ways. Once recovered from the first onset of the madness in 1788, King George was allowed a much more handsome exchequer to do as he wished to Windsor Castle and discovered, to everyone's satisfaction, that amiable prurience about his water across the nation had transmuted itself into a sort of affectionate tolerance, rising even to patriotic zeal at official occasions like the Jubilee of 1810.

The king's adventurous combination of publicised insanity, subdued showiness, and unself-conscious stolidity set a pattern for the monarch which proved amazingly durable. The madness made him vulnerable and sympathetic, and his peppery self-righteousness made him respectable. Such a figure, removed but familiar, acquired the aura of celebrity without having to work for it. The state required a dignified and dutiful sovereign; the people, in their turn, looked for a great personage who was at one and the same time neighbour, national possession (they could not make him kneel to them, as they did Garrick, but they could insist he showed himself to them), and type and token of the good life. Such a life should be compounded of a little art, a little money, a little munificence, British beef, and a proper patriotism.

The king filled each dimension of the role and the people applauded. For his eldest son, the Prince of Wales, the consequence was heavily overdetermined. He was, after all, eldest of eight surviving children (his big brother Frederick died young) and six stillborn. Given the leisure culture of ruling-class boys at the time, the sexual and aesthetic lessons of the Grand Tour, the necessary militarism of an age in which the country went so frequently to war with Spain and France, let alone the threat of civil war in 1745, all this mixed with wealthy idleness in the clubs of London and the grand houses on the estates, George Prince Regent was a predictable and not-so-very-awful product of such an education.

Sure, he loved the part of dandy, certainly he got very fat. Without any formal apprenticeship for the post, when he became Prince Regent for the first, fairly brief spell, the ministers naturally kept him well away from anything executive, about which, being petulantly accustomed to his own way on trivial matters among his sycophants, he was duly petulant. That is the unedifying way of heirs presumptive when the parent-monarch reigns for more than fifty years. Although when the prince became king he was widely derided, long since mocked in the Gillray cartoons, earnestly condemned for his treatment of his wretched and abandoned wife, Caroline of Brunswick, he (and his brothers) had done their intermittent best to establish the established throne as a fixed feature of British politics quite unlike the contemptible French, with their murderously dangerous Committee of Public Safety and their corporal-emperor. Prince George was, after all, grand master of the Masons at a time when freemasonry was a site of lower-middle-class and mercantile-egalitarian comradeship, for twenty-three years Freeman of a dozen cities, acknowledgeable in the street.[28]

The prince was satisfyingly vain, promiscuous, slothful, dissolute, drunken, and greedy. He was also cultivated, a generous patron, an appreciative connoisseur of art and townscape, and, when he became king, persuasive paymaster and codesigner of a projected new London, marble clad, high, wide, boulevarded, and handsome.

As prince, his contribution to the formation of celebrity was central and, for a major dimension of the concept, highly specific. Prince George invented Brighton, near enough to the capital not to be out of touch, far enough away to do whatever you liked in. (The fact that Brighton retains this ambiguity long after the train first cut the journey to ninety minutes is a testimony to the weightiness of cultural history.)

Brighton was invented as medical advice lit upon the healthful properties of salt water and sea air, just at the moment when walking out for a little exercise coincided with promenading for social display, and when the pleasures of holidaying in clean air away from the city created not only pleasure gardens but pleasure-and-leisure towns and spas, stiffened with a dose of medicament.[29]

Brighton would speedily provide all this, and the prince launched it by buying a farmhouse there which faced the river Steine in order to be near his mistress, Mrs. Fitzherbert, whom he had illegally married in 1784. So from the start Brighton (and all seaside resorts) was linked to lubricity, and royal heirs to sexual scandal. Prince George, however, did his scandal in theatrical

Brighton Pavilion. Shutterstock © Markus Gann

style, and the Marine Pavilion, as it first was called, was its stage. He and Henry Holland, the classiest architect in town, built a reflection of the farmhouse beside the original, added pagoda roofs, and connected them with a double-apsed rotunda, fronted by a stately colonnade. William Porden, the next architect, designed in 1804 Indian-Islamic stables, for "these were the years of the most insouciant playing with the forms of other peoples."[30] Finally, the great John Nash threw studiously fanciful adornments around the miniature court—Indian pinnacles, Gothic friezes, ogee arches. When the whole effect was completed by interior decor of oriental black and red and gold, gilt and lacquer and serpents in voluptuous chinoiserie, so fashionable at the time, one can see (splendidly restored, what is more, see it now) how royal celebrity framed itself with a pleasure-drome, the symbolism of which consciously celebrated the imagined sexuality of "the East" and the indolence and indulgence which were supposed to accompany it.

As you would expect, when the prince became King George IV in 1820, he never returned to Brighton. Like it did for Prince Hal before him, the crown compelled sobriety, and he turned his attentions to Windsor and to transforming his mere house into Buckingham Palace, which he did.

The years in Brighton had, however, consolidated two halves of royal celebrity—the domestic and the dissipated—and they serve to fasten with the authority of the crown the earliest components of the whole colossal business, as well as to remind us just how plentiful are the precedents of commotion in royal households, and the curious passions these quicken and fulfil in the national citizenry. The people deferred and the crown condescended; the people mocked and the crown placated; thus and thus were ruling and popular passions equalised. Given the attempt this book is making to find some point of balance and of rational judgement alongside the whole crazy charivari, it will be as well in a moment or two to conclude this chapter by an appeal to the steady judges of the "civil affections" which could keep us right about the eighteenth century, and the present too, come to that.

VII

Before we do so, however, our history demands of its very form that we sketch one more brief life in the genesis of celebrity. Thereafter we may turn with relief to the calm and minatory reflections of our favourite moralists, by way of retrieving from the hectic past the reassurance that craziness has always played the biggest part on the social stage, and that a steady kind of moderation was as defensible then as needful now.

The life in question is that of George Gordon, Lord Byron, and however perfectly he fits the outlines of early and self-created celebrity, it must be insisted that the other half of his studiedly and wilfully divided character was that of the Humean and Augustan gentleman. He was plentifully endowed with the arrogance of caste, and with the sudden generosity of purse or spirit (and whether or not he possessed at the time enough of either to give it away) which used frequently to go with it. In the one version of himself, he lived, as Rousseau and the sentimental novelists taught, at the full stretch of his passions, whether sexual and amorous, or political and radical. In the other, he was fine-mannered, dignified, courtly, and defender of the faith in reason.

Byron knew well enough that what other people make of us, makes us. As he wrote in a letter to John Murray, his eager, nervous, and exploitative publisher:

I know the precise worth of popular applause, for few scribblers have had more of it; and if I chose to swerve into their paths, I could retain it, or resume it, or increase it.... They made me without my search, a species of popular idol; they, without reason or judgement beyond the caprice of their good pleasure, threw down the image from its pedestal; it was not broken with the fall, and they would, it seems, again replace it—but they shall not.[31]

I suppose that in this last remark he was more or less right, for he spent most of the next five years, before he died of ureic fever in Greece, well away from England. But he could not claim in truth that his undoubted standing as "popular idol" was, if not sought, then gaily enjoyed and dramatically played out. He would never have kneeled to the popular, like Garrick, but nor did he ever keep it at a businesslike arm's length, like Reynolds. In a well-known *mot*, he said of himself to his fellow-poet and close friend Tom Moore that "I awoke one morning and found myself famous." But in saying so, he presages the false naivety of several hundred celebrities to come.

For the occasion of his sudden fame was the publication of his voluble, picaresque, narrative poem, *Childe Harold* (a "childe" was an archaic term for a knight-in-waiting). But there was never a more mocking essay in mock-heroic. Byron took up the genre of Pope but turned it into *True Confessions*. It was plain as day that the poem described the innumerable sexual escapades of its author. He was a lord of the realm, a well-known libertine, amazingly handsome, darkling curly-haired, dazzling and dashing *and* daring with an allusion, a courtly compliment, an insolent excuse. Add to all that dysplasia, a withered calf muscle which shortened his leg and twisted his foot inwards, and his Romantic uniform—his masterful nature *and* his winsome appeal—could not be bettered.

It is worth recalling, after our brief handshake with that stout party and genteel voluptuary, the Prince of Wales, just how publicly self-indulgent, faithless, arrogant, and rancorous the then ruling class was. Its single, cast-iron commitment was to the maintenance and showing off of its own wealth and power, and to that end its menfolk, pretty well supported by the women of due seniority, ruthlessly married off the girls to whomever would cover the debts or bring in the profits. In the meantime, the same system of connivance fostered wholesale adultery and adorned it with the savoury gratification of gossip and scandal. The novels of Jane Austen, written between 1812 and 1818, are at some remove from this large portion of the stage; Byron lived at its centre.

So he could never have doubted that, if his talent proved up to it (he never doubted *that*, either), fame in all its ambivalence would come down on his head in torrents. He had brewed up a flavoursome and intoxicating mixture, and done so in such a pacey, racy, easily memorable verse; its subject matter was, nearly enough, the stuff of melodramatic and romantic novels but lent his singular charm and taste for the gothick, for sure, and ablaze with the novelty of confessional poetry, artful prurience, hinted sex, and gentlemanly travel and heroics.

He took his lead in stylistics from the Corinthian *beaux* clubmen of the day, of whom Beau Brummel is the eponym, forever strolling the wide streets of St. James's with a silver-topped cane, after being shaken by his valet into drenched white buckskin breeches and held tightly in swallow-tail coats of swooning cut.[32] In point of fact, Byron was often scruffier than that, but he *too* had his specially made Albanian court attire and took Philhellene military helmets with him when he went to rescue Greece from Turkey. For everyday seduction, he carried off the uniform of Kean's Hamlet: raffish, loose black shirt, kerchief, breeches.

These manners, his good looks, his tearing high spirits, as well as the usual high jinks of titled young gentlemen at Trinity College, Cambridge—bull mastiffs fighting in his room, dancing bears in Trinity Great Court, *that* sort of thing—gave his literary success its Byronic timbre. In February 1812, at age twenty-four, he made a not unimpressive maiden speech of a radical tinge in the House of Lords; *Childe Harold* sold out the first print run in days; he made friendly acquaintance with the Prince of Wales; and then he captivated and was captivated by Lady Caroline Lamb, wife of the future Lord Melbourne, three years his senior, irrepressible, boyishly sexy, intelligent, literate, and utterly reckless.

Portrait of George Gordon (1788–1824), 6th Baron Byron of Rochdale in Albanian Dress, 1813, by Thomas Phillips (1770–1845). Oil on canvas. National Portrait Gallery, London / The Bridgeman Art Library

They flirted, they kissed in public, she fell for him, she loved him, it seems likely, for the rest of his life. They even staged a mock wedding.[33] She hid from him out of town; he found her. Byron took up simultaneously with the matronly and magnificent Lady Oxford, proposed to the heiress Annabella Milbanke (and was slowly accepted), and, pursued by the fame of his bestseller, cut a swathe across the West End.

He trampled blithely, even irritably, on many hearts, none more than poor Lady Caroline's. In his most extreme gesture of playful, bitter violation of social prohibition, he made his half-sister, Augusta, pregnant (as he was to do at least eight or nine other women, in London, Venice, Ravenna, and no doubt Cephallonia). This latter outrage he then placed, barely concealed, in the incestuous tale of *The Bride of Abydos*, which naturally sold out in a trice, while he tried, before a large, delightfully scandalised audience, to brush off the adhesive Lady Caroline.

The life became synonymous with the work. He placed no gap between passion and poetry. He wrote very fast and spontaneously, just as he lived. Scornfully refusing Wordsworth's "emotion recollected in tranquillity," his amazing plenitude of writing caught up all the most technicolour, odorous, and dizzy of Romantic themes and narratives—doomed dungeons (*The Prisoner of Chillon*), Arab horsemen in the desert (*The Giaour*), pirates (*The Corsair*), sublime and dangerous mountainscapes (*Manfred*), and above all, his own sexual biography, fictionalised and given to the legendary prince of all demon lovers. His special genius (it was the moment at which his trust in art changed into true self-knowledge) was to turn Don Juan, as Mozart did, into a comic (but absolutely serious) figure, fleet, venturesome, funny, a subverter of morality, dynamite to respectability, tireless defender of greater freedoms by far, whether of oppressed women or of oppressed peoples.

All these brilliant contradictions were played out under the noses of high society, until whispering turned into a roar. The tales of licence alongside the proofs of passion, courage, graceless brutality, and hardhearted irresponsibility were all told well beyond the circles of the *haut ton*. The tales had to be lived up to, and not just for the sales (although his whole life constituted a struggle between penury and extravagance, especially when his wife, Lady Annabella, withdrew and took her fortune with her). The tales of extremity in life had to be kept up as being the very source of his life.

In this Byron embodies the deep damnation of the celebrity, and he does it first and most completely. He was the first such figure publicly to live and act exactly on the split between sense and sensibility. Class formation, the gentlemanly aspect of his character, and ordinary instincts of conformism taught him the good sense of Hume's and Smith's judicious advice. He was, after all, born to a Scottish mother and was an alumnus of Aberdeen Grammar School after Mad Jack, his father, decamped, and before inheriting the title by way of a cousin killed in battle, thereafter moving up the school league table to Harrow.

So the canons of the Scottish Enlightenment left their traces in his intelligence and his taste. But far stronger in him was his ardent and narcissistic endorsement of the new doctrines of feeling and freedom. The French Revolution erupted the year after he was born, and its banners fluttered his heart, not with doctrinaire adherence to any principle of equality—he was always too delighted by his accidental accession to the aristocracy for that—but rather with a quick, reckless sympathy for victims of injustice, of summary and brutal punishment (he was against both slavery and capital punishment when such a stance was far from *bien-pensant*), of picturesque tyranny. He died, after all, leading a military-diplomatic sortie in and on behalf of Greece against the tyrant Turks.

But a zest for political justice and an early admiration for pre-absolutist Napoleon did little for fair conduct in the politics of the personal. He rode and reaped the whirlwind of romantic love and sexual sensation; indeed, he made little distinction between the two. He took up with new sweethearts, bedfellows and mistresses with what was even by the standards of a high-sybaritic and hypocritical society amazing, even deplorable, celerity and ease. Not that the captives he took were at all unwilling. He remains a byword for his kind of good looks, his charm; his gay, cheerful, teasing, tender, offhand personality flashes out from the poems as unmistakably as it must have done on the way to bed. Indeed, he incarnated both the melting and the haughty qualities of his great original as created by Mozart and handed them down to be inherited by fighter pilots and Mills and Boon.

Perhaps we can say, as far as this potted history is concerned, that it is during Byron's brief lifetime—he died at thirty-six in 1824—that charm and its distorted and magnified echo, glamour, become public values, and what is more, values looked for as attributes of celebrity. Charm would have been useless to Reynolds, tough and dignified and detached as he was. *His* prime value was success, certainly to be required, for a while at least, of celebrity. But charm, along with youthfulness, good looks, great gifts (preferably in the arts), and impulsive, dashing action—these were the qualities Byron brought to the newest dramatisation of fame.

And scandal. We have seen the necessity of scandal to the theatre, seen it put unforgettably on show by Sheridan, noted its bedroom preoccupations. Byron, however, turned scandal into an essential dynamo within the engines of publicity, only temporarily eliminated a century later by the methods of totalitarianism. Scandal turns on the torque of malicious laughter. (You cannot laugh at a dictator and survive.) For actions to give rise to the thrill of scandal, they must openly flout closed conventions or norms. The more closed the society in question, the more scandalous actions threaten it absolutely. When, for example, the Amish take a collective decision to shun one of their members, the collective emotion is less scandalised than horrified;[34] it is not a thrill but a violation. When high society led the way, and the self-consciously named *Tatler* followed, the scandal of Byron's rough trading, his public cruelties to Caroline Lamb and many others, the eagerly reported tales of his conquests of married Venetian housekeepers or the three pretty daughters of his landlady in Athens, all these misdemeanours delighted both author and audience. But they touched the audience also with envy, spite, gleeful incredulity, lascivious musings. This malodorous mixture thereafter steamed up from the system of celebrity, its very means of production. All celebrities would gradually be subjected to the test of scandal, and those who passed it become a kind of tedious disappointment.

Byron did not of course, pass the scandal test, he set the terms of its examination. In this he is augury of one aspect of the conceptual structure of celebrity. It is, obviously enough, a reciprocal idea; its manufacture is two-sided. The celebrity acts, necessarily in public; the public reacts by taking the action and, after transforming it for its own purposes, projects it, as a filthy or a glowing image, back upon its source. The wretched celebrity not only asked for it but must incorporate the image as amiably as possible, turning it for better or worse into corporeal reality.

There was for Byron, and for so many of his successors in this new social form, the consolation of good old time. If he could not pass the scandal test, he could *sur*pass it. Scandalised peering through his curtains was gradually replaced, first by ennui, no doubt, by repetition and the short duration of a thrill, but also by—well—a new maturity in the character concerned, let alone the loss of key attributes: Byron was going bald, was ill more frequently as he paid the price for pretending eternal youth, put on fat and dieted it ferociously away, went riding hell for leather in torrential rain, kept up hellfire drinking to match, and paid the price in doctors' bills.

Nonetheless, age was as usual settling something down in him. In 1819 (and revolted by official brutality in the carnage at St. Peter's Fields near Manchester) he quit England for Italy and Greece, leaving behind and, it seems, not missing his newspaper notoriety. Of course there was still a vast amount of poetry to come, in the case of *Don Juan* the best as well as the best-selling which he wrote, a poetic style which was indeed the man, audaciously mingling dandy's slang, classical Hellenic echoes, Popish satire, and plangent feeling, especially as Haidee fades sadly away, all this written down as no other English poet ever has or could.

Don Juan takes the measure of what Byron was becoming, and it may be said to mark the passage of his name from celebrity to renown. *He* knew exactly how good it was. As he wrote to his friend Douglas Kinnaird in 1819 (no missing the bluff charm, either):

Confess, confess, you dog and be candid—that it is the sublime of *that there* sort of writing—it may be bawdy, but is it not good English? It may be profligate but is it not *life*, is it not the *thing*? Could any man have written it who has not lived in the world?—and fooled in a post-chaise?—in a hackney coach?—in a gondola?—against a wall?—on a table?—and under it? [he's fairly going through his diary] ... I had such projects for the Don, but cant is so much stronger than cxxx [Byron's elision] nowadays, that the benefit of experience in a man who has well weighed the worth of both syllables, must be lost to despairing posterity.[35]

He is, however, as a roué does as he ages, just telling over his memories. For by now he was more or less stably attached and in honour bound (the honour of a gentleman) to Teresa, wife of one Count Guiccioli; by autumn

1821 he was a neighbour of the Shelleys on the Lungarno, still pursued by the desperate Caroline Lamb; and he gradually resolved to do what he could on behalf of Greek liberty, and throwing off the damnable Turks. He commissioned the brig *Hercules*, put together what was more a diplomatic than a war chest, and, without his Teresa, sailed to Cephallonia, and after comic-operatic but entirely sincere exchanges with bits of the Turkish fleet and despair at the factiousness of the Greeks, was drained of blood to death by his primitive doctors, soon after writing his timely and mournful lines in commemoration of his thirty-sixth birthday:

> Seek out—less often sought than found—
> A soldier's grave, for thee the best;
> Then look around, and choose thy ground,
> And take thy rest.

> Well! Nothing is here for tears, nothing to wail
> Or knock the breast ...

That was clear. Byron's death framed the image of celebrity as work of art. To the life of the rake, the drinker, the hard rider, the wit, the milord, was added the freeborn Englishman standing up, and falling, beneath the liberty tree. *How* he felt (always passionately) and *that* he felt (never needing to check) found rare aesthetic expression in a life larger than life, lived and written down as a mock-heroic poem.

It has remained as a huge example of one version of celebrity embossed by renown. In the past century, Ernest Hemingway, Norman Mailer, and perhaps Martha Gellhorn had a shot at the same thing. Byron, however, gave inimitable poetic dimensions to birth and copulation and death and became thereby that rarest of creatures, a celebrity worth celebrating.

VIII

The pictures I have painted of English life after 1760, particularly as they concentrate on London, then first city of the known world, have an exotic flavour. Those throngs and crowds, a fixed social order jumbled up together, royalty, officers, fops, harlots, beggars, cobblers, footpads, merchants, chandlers, scriveners, dressmakers, geniuses. The folk memories which are given such life by Sheridan and Dr. Johnson and Fanny Burney are still sufficiently familiar for us to feel envious admiration (all that colour, that style, those dresses!) and gratified revulsion (the smells, the illness, the grotesque hypocrisy of the manners!). It is time to listen once again to one or two voices which presage our present and confirm the steadiness, grace, and sanity of eighteenth-century London and, in two cases, Edinburgh.

The Scottish Enlightenment made its home in the Georgian beauties of Edinburgh's New Town. Out of a formidable group of progressive and like-minded men, David Hume and Adam Smith stand out as striking geniuses in any case, and as early shapers of the modern mind. Adam Smith has recently suffered the fate of annexation by the fanatics of neoconservatism, who have named an institute after him and claim him as ancestor and apologist for unimpeded free trade, the diminution almost to zero of the role of the state, the headlong division of labour, and the ruthless stripping of assets, all this guided by Smith's benignly "invisible hand" of the market system to ensure a certain road to prosperity.

In historical fact, Smith and Hume, his closest friend, beside him, do not lend themselves to such an ideological abduction. Smith's own *Theory of the Moral Sentiments*, already encountered, speaks an ethical language familiar to our own everyday morality but does so by aligning enlightenment premises alongside economic thought in what is now a wholly unaccustomed way.[36] Far from that unappetising invention of economic algebra, the rationally self-interested *Homo Economicus*, Smith reproaches everyday mercantile policy for being so disfigured by "falsehood," "jealousy," animosity, and "golden dreams"[37] and censures "self-love" for misrepresenting everything. His rejection of the state, so applauded by supporters of the colonel of the neoconservative dragoons, Friedrich von Hayek, is grounded on its unjust laws, "written in the blood of the poor," its mindless nationalism, a "mean principle of national prejudice," let alone the general disposition in society "almost to worship the rich and the powerful."[38] A better function for the state, Smith affirms, would be to educate the people that they might "feel themselves, each individually, more respectable" and that, led by education, "low people" might learn for themselves the freedoms of labour movement, the happiness of domestic virtue, and—for Smith and Hume alike—the paramount sentiment, "the nice security of friendship."

Finally, "It is the duty of sovereignty to protect every member of society against the injustice or oppression of every other member."[39]

These are bromides to which any devout reader of yesterday's *New Republic* or today's *Guardian* could sign up. Their force here is to show how ironically the intellectual leader of the day would view "the fraternising game," the exchanges of deference and condescension, how much larger than in the present day loomed Hume's reciprocal values, pride (nearer perhaps to dignified self-respect) and humility (closer to both humiliation and shame). The point for us is that these two fierce little sources of concentrated meaning played a counterpointed music to which society danced. Such music in the great houses and in the conversation of the coffeehouses had its resplendent chords, its pomp and circumstance. Everyone knows that from folkloric history. The same musical forms, however—you can hear them in musical actuality in Handel, Mozart, C.P.E. Bach—were perfectly capable of detachment from the social dance, of jokes at its expense, of a robust independence from convention. In music as in life, invention makes what it can of convention; the greater the inventor, the more complete this new freedom. The dance of society between 1760 and 1820 made for heroic emancipation as well as mass hypocrisy.

The best position from which both to watch and to participate in society was, Hume wrote, from "the middling rank of men, who are the best and finest basis of public liberty."[40] Speaking from their ranks, Hume reassures us as to the sanest parts of eighteenth-century life and convinces us not only that we have inherited much that we owe directly to him, but that he and we—at our best—would have come to roughly similar conclusions about the vices and pleasures of watching and being celebrities. For

> the great are too much immersed in pleasure and the poor too much occupied in providing for necessities to hearken to the calm voice of reason. The middle station as, it is most happy in many respects, so particularly in this, that a man placed in it can, with the greatest leisure, consider his own happiness, and reap a new enjoyment from comparing his situation with that of persons above and below him.[41]

Hume was calmly aware, and never more so, as Adam Smith reports in his famous memoir, than when on his deathbed, of "the feverish uncertainty and irresolution in human conduct" and of these disturbances as "altogether unavoidable."[42] His very recognition of these commends his "middling" (but exceptional) kinds of virtue to us, his very tone of voice, steely, humane, courteous, and cordial, softens the riotous noise of his city and ours, brings home with kindly certainty what to make, now and then, of fame and its hot spur, and of the fineness and nobility summoned up by characters worthily celebrated for what they show us of the best in human beings. Commending the virtue of friendship as "lying principally among equals" and therefore having the most room to grow in the middle station, he goes on: "There are more natural parts and a stronger genius requisite to make a good lawyer or physician [those two principal exports of his native Edinburgh] than to make a great monarch . . . courage and resolution are chiefly required in a commander; justice and humanity in a statesman; but [Hume's voice deepens and, surely, he smiles] genius and capacity in a scholar."[43]

Chapter 4

Paris: Haute Couture and the Painting of Modern Life

The two star figures of our first historical epoch stand at either end looking at each other with mutual incomprehension and distaste. David Hume, prince of moderation, had long since died of course, in 1776. But he made as good an end as any late-come, gentlemanly scholar could wish. His devoted friend reports him, calm and welcoming, hoping only for the end to hasten because its cause was bowel cancer and the symptoms, in the days before domestic sanitation improved things so much, such as naturally to be offensive to his own fastidious taste and that of his visitors.

When Byron died, half a century later, the news made the headlines and served to top off the delicious daring of his so very well-known and scandalous life story. There he was, dressed doubtless in his Albanian officer's uniform, captaining an improvised naval expedition intending to light the flame of Hellenic resistance and throw off the antique tyranny of Byzantine infidels. In youth, he had lived with utter audacity and nonchalance the role of poet and seducer; now in his late thirties, still a byword in the bedroom, he fought and died for the great new abstraction of postrevolutionary Europe, liberty. A peer of the realm (another juicy attribute for the spirit of celebrity to require), he gave his life also to the parallel names of equality and fraternity.

In doing so, whether as poet, seducer, or displaced patriot, he lived, and was recognised as so living even by those who were horrified by his conduct, as *true to himself* and in accord, that is, with his own deep nature. Thus was the quite new account of what and how to feel opened up by the tidal waves of Romanticism. Hume and Smith and their like-minded associates in the New Town and in London had agreed that life must be lived in congruence with the moral sentiments and the civil affections, as these regulated domestic benevolence and confirmed the rhythms of ordinary life. "Benevolence and sympathy are seen as natural," as Charles Taylor puts it, "as were the traditional limits on sensual fulfilment set by, say, Rousseau or Herder."[1] "But," as Taylor goes on warningly, "the way is open for a redefinition." Sensuality is itself a, if not the, natural force. Its fulfilments are themselves capable of leading to spiritual discovery; the road to Lady Chatterley's and Oliver Mellors' flower-bedecked picnic suddenly beckons ahead.

Between 1760 and 1820 ethics and aesthetics became intermingled, and they remain so to this day. Beauty and sublimity[2] became ascribable not just to objects, but to one's experience of them. A torrent of new treatises, in German, French, English, by Goethe, Schiller, Madame de Staël, Alphonse de Lamartine, Hogarth, Wordsworth, Blake, poured from the publishers, teaching the new doctrines of the feelings, their conjunction of aesthetics and ethics, their radical displacement of the stolid cardinal virtues, temperance, justice, fortitude, by such fiercer-burning and colourful passions and qualities as desire, spontaneity, abandon, ardour, eagerness— all these supremely the experiences of youth. One way of envisioning this historical surge is, for our purposes, as the sudden sweeping away of the authority of the elders by the blissful self-authorisation of the young. Its relevance, for our bit of history, is that celebrity is invented as a large screen upon which is projected a huge and distorted magnification of some of a society's most contested values.

So the cartoon version of Byron's life, like that of the not-so-very-wretched Prince of Wales, has packed into it by its author and his lip-smacking audience all the latest fashions in feeling. Nor is fashion in feeling a light thing: it is cut out of the cloth of our best and worst experiences, and you pay for it, all right, on the never-never.

Byron and the European Romantics of the history of publicity— Beethoven, Turner, Ruskin, Dickens, Shelley, Rossini, and, soon to arrive, Verdi, Liszt, Chopin, Baudelaire—announced a new bill of rights to feelings, in which art figured largely as both vehicle and tutor of those feelings. The artist, by this token, leads the way to the wonderful land where the new man and the new woman will come to realise in a perfect equality of being all that they might become, if only the everyday world were not too much with and for them.

These giddy phrases were not of course those on the lips of every artist, but enough of them were: Wordsworth's in his "Preface" to *Lyrical Ballads* in 1798, Schiller's in his famous *Letters on Aesthetic Education* at about the same time, Coleridge's in his vision of the sublime possibilities of the imagination in his *Biographia Litteraria* of 1817, supremely Shelley's in his manifesto for poets where he described them as "unacknowledged legislators of the world."

The artist took a lot on himself (and, Jane Austen, Fanny Burney, and Madame de Staël notwithstanding, it was until the 1860s or so mostly "him" in public debate and citation) and was given a reverent enough hearing. High art taught the goodness of nature, and nature was discerned in the attuning of the inner ear to the outer sublimity. As Charles Taylor summarises a fearsomely complex revolution in thought and feeling, nature and its human expression in natural being became a nontheistic but pious new source of grace. [3]

This shining conception of life naturally collided with and damaged traditional accounts of religious grace and cut across the other riptides of new feeling, in particular the great wave of freedom-seeking released by the revolution in France, corroborated by the artists, and at first violently repressed in England in the Gordon riots, the birth and death of Captain Swing, [4] the bloodshed in St. Peter's Fields, the hostility to the illegal trade unions and Chartism.

Mingled with the banners of freedom and her inseparable allies, equality and fraternity, were the tricolour flags of *La Patrie*, old England's Union Jack, America's Old Glory. For the new waves of political freedom brought a new nationalism, [5] not unattractively grounded in national language, myths of historic victories and prizes, and fables of national character taken from literature and folklore—Robin Hood and Prince Hal in England, Deerslayer and Davy Crockett in the United States, Liberty herself in France, Pericles in Greece, William Tell for everybody.

Such contrary currents swept ashore a peculiar kind of political and emotional monster, which was to lead the way, in the three most ardent and energetic nations of new nationalism, Britain, France, and the shapeless masses of the United States, to the Victorian settlement, and to bear as its progeny the Victorian versions of celebrity. In Britain the monster won its political garlands with the passing of the great Reform Acts during and after 1832. These brought the suffrage to a much enlarged electorate and, more than that, made access to the vote the unslakable thirst of all those without it. Britain in its obdurate way—or rather, England, for the show was run for an English ruling class trying to keep its membership manageable and its profits large—conceded the suffrage only inch by inch, to the male working class only by 1906, to the women only by the general election of 1929.

The Reform Acts no doubt prised open a little way the grip of the land-owning class upon power. In cultural terms the passions which impelled this shapeless revolution (for that is what it was)[6] turned the poem, the painting, the symphony into visions of judgement, and politics itself into a symbolic theatre. Hereafter the march, the demonstration, the staged rehearsal of slogans, the flag, the masses, but above all the *leaders*, embody the public narrative of politics. A demonstration or a march is a flop if not enough people turn up—its significance is measured by its numbers—but it can only be given point and identity by the figures who speak for it and, in being recognisable for what they are, win recognition for their moment and movement.

No wonder some of the artists caught up by and riding the waves of mass movement became dizzy. As we shall see in the cases of a great painter, Gustave Courbet, and a great poet, Charles Baudelaire, keeping your balance when so much feeling presses on you takes rare genius. That the same genius may turn out to be horrible is one of life's bigger disappointments.

For insofar as the artist was isolated and acclaimed by the new history being made on the streets of the city, in its meeting rooms and offices, its markets and parks, the artist was torn two ways: by the aesthetic doctrine of artistic singularity, and by speaking (or picturing or composing) in "the real language of men" and women. He and she had set themselves to live outside the conventions of everyday life, to invent new, more beautiful and fulfilling ways of being and making, to be therefore in some sense *against* normality, and yet each artist was called upon to return from outside the walls to the agora, to criticise how things are rather than to imagine how they might be.

This oscillation between outlaw and legislator, creator and critic, checking out and joining in, finds its social and expressive form in the tense familiarity of avant garde and bourgeoisie.[7]

II

Our political language has been so powerfully shaped by the French because theirs was the primary narrative of modern politics: the abrupt and violent overthrow of the ancien régime (another such key concept) by a new class come to consciousness of its insuppressible power, and offering to universalise its freedom in an equal settlement for all. Within four years of its Bastille moment (the place was in any case almost empty) those hopes had melded into the Terror, then into Bonapartism, and finally into the bathos of the Bourbons' return, and the coronation of the absolute bourgeois, Louis Napoleon, as constitutional monarch and genteel butler and ringmaster to the National Assembly.

Whether the revolution was worth it, was even necessary to bring about these changes, is not here of prime importance.[8] What counts is the vocabulary. The bourgeoisie won the day and appointed the avant garde as keeper of its conscience and scribe of those emotions likely to be stifled by the demands of moneymaking and the politics of appearance. Part resentfully and always uncontrollably, the avant garde signed the treaty. The new society busied itself about the making of its capital city and exporting its images and products to any city anywhere which aspired to be modern, prosperous, productive, leisurely, progressive—well, bourgeois; to these ends the avant garde would keep it on its toes, self-critical, futurist.

Paris became the centre of the new world. No doubt the rest of France was still living in (several) other centuries: in Gascony's remoter mountains, or the Jura, still in the seventeenth; in Brittany, living in a different country; in Occitan, Moors, brigands, corsairs remained in business as they had for four hundred years, and the stilted peasants of the Camargue were still crossing the salt flats on giant stilts at the speed of galloping horses as they had for centuries.[9] So Paris aimed her novelty and emancipation at London, whose place she had taken, and New York, which would supplant her.

Not that London was done for of course. And it is more than time that the parade of these capitalised abstractions—Liberty, Bourgeoisie, Art, and Lord Knows What—trampling the stage are again replaced by the solidities of character and corporeality. Our corporeal figure is admittedly fictional, but since it was Dickens who made him up, he is a lot more alive than most of us living.

A lot more alive, keenly living his most killing characteristics. Mr. Dombey, hero of Dickens's *Dombey and Son*, first published in serial form between 1846 and 1848, is as absolute a bourgeois as Napoleon III, and a good deal less likeable. He is perhaps the structural counterweight to the *avantgardiste*, inasmuch as he repels and kills by coldness all that art, imaginativeness, epiphanous beauty, may bring with which to emancipate human misery. He is a product of 1832 no doubt, but an immovable obstacle in the way of all its hopes.

At the same time, however, he is a product of the Romantic revolution in living straight from and never doubting his feelings. Where the game of deference and condescension was as we have seen it played, either timidly or cynically, in the London parks of the 1790s, the players (I contend) knew that what was at stake was the social order itself. If someone on the wrong, the lower, side flouted the rules of subordination, the offended rage this caused was not, so to speak, personal. It was institutional passion felt in defence of status, as Sheridan and Jane Austen bring out plainly. It is precisely new and socially shocking feelings which melt Mr. Darcy's pride and force prejudice to give way, against his positional will, to the truth of these new feelings. Anyone trying to ignore these social facts from either side of the barrier—the arrogance of caste or the necessity of respectfulness—could not find the emotional, let alone the actual, ground on which to stand and have things out.

The usual reach-me-down list of explanations will have to serve to fix the change in sensibility from Lady Teazle and Tony Lumpkin to the impregnable but novel pride which keeps Mr. Dombey so passionately hard, cold, and self-righteous. There was the softening power of new money pouring out of technological innovation and soaring land prices. There was also the weird anomaly that this money still left the nation steeply on the wrong side of the balance of payments: the only net exporting economy in the world was deep in the red. There was the fearful example of revolution across the twenty-one miles of Channel, a restless mob in the cities, rick-burners in the countryside, reduced by their panic-stricken dispatch across twelve thousand miles and eleven months to Botany Bay.[10] Lastly, there was the detonation of contrary ideas released, on the one hand, by the *philosophes* of the Enlightenment with their faith in instrumental reasoning and the compilation of the data, and, on the other, by the geniuses of Romanticism and their teachings about the inviolability of personal feeling.

At the further stage of these headlong forces stands the aloof, unshakeably self-satisfied figure of Mr. Dombey. History swirls through us all as both energy and matter. History had brought him money in large quantities together with the certainty that it was thus brought as a result of his own merits embodying, as they did, the merits of the house of trade which he represented. But his was not the old arrogance of caste and family. It was that same arrogance which the victorious bourgeoisie had so radically adulterated with its own coming-to-power after 1832. Mr. Dombey stands for and by the displacement of birth by money itself. Of course he inherits the values of continuity and bequest from the past: what else could he do—as we all do—but see his own life commemorated in the greater prosperity of his son in the future? When Dickens so poignantly causes the little old man of a child, the son Paul, to die at five or six, Dombey's own life-flow is stopped. Of course he keeps going in the old way, compounding his interest rates, and he stokes up hard his furnace of self-righteous feeling. When he marries the beautiful Edith, whose will to power (as Nietzsche taught us, the ultimate passion) is as ironclad (but as white hot) as his own, the stop in his life can only be unblocked, especially when she has cuckolded him in order to break his will, by that life tearing itself open to let the terrible passion drain away.

He has a stroke. He is struck dumb. He is humiliated and finds a dreadful kind of redemption in the care on his deathbed of his devoted, repudiated, wounded, and tenderhearted daughter, Florence.

Dombey was a leading victor in the 1832 revolution. The complex energies which flowed through the new rules of suffrage and recognition came to one sort of fulfilment in his passionate intensities: of money and the unassailability of those who possessed it and its magical powers. The same, as we shall shortly see, was true of the victors in the Parisian revolutions of 1848 and Louis Philippe's uncontested coup d'état (another essential French coinage) in 1851.

What Dombey dramatises in the hands of the great master who invented him and made him real (he still is; the world of today has lots of Dombeys mitigating the arrogance of money with the complacencies of modern hedonism) is the passion of pride. His manner is frozen, his certainties icily ablaze. He sets himself to live in a prison-house of tense formal rectitude and willed stupidity. He excludes his daughter from his vision as a worthless girl. Before the boy dies, he declares himself all the child needs, in order to ensure the continuity of the Firm.

> In the course of these remarks, delivered with great majesty and grandeur, Mr Dombey had truly revealed the secret feelings of his breast. An indescribable distrust of anybody stepping in between himself and his son; a haughty dread of having any rival or partner in the boy's respect and deference; a sharp misgiving, recently acquired, that he was not infallible in his power of bending and binding human wills; as sharp a jealousy of any second check or cross; these were, at that time the master keys of his soul. In all his life, he had never made a friend. His cold and distant nature had neither sought one, nor found one. And now, when that nature concentrated its whole force so strongly on a partial scheme of parental interest and ambition, it seemed as if its icy current, instead of being released by this influence, and running clear and free, had thawed for but an instant to admit its burden, and then frozen with it into one unyielding block.[11]

Dickens wreaks abominable revenge on his monster creation even though the moral is that love will conquer all. It is a leisurely vengeance, and its prime agent is Edith. She is the woman in the tale with the fight and the will not to refuse but to soil beyond cleansing the hideous role in which she has been cast—by her mother, by financial necessity, by the conventions of a society which looks to attach female beauty to successful money.

> "There is no slave in a market: there is no horse in a fair: so shown and offered and examined and paraded, Mother, as I have been, for

ten shameful years," cried Edith, with a burning brow, and the same
bitter emphasis on the one word. "Is it not so? Have I been made
the bye-word of all kinds of men? Have fools, have profligates, have
boys, have dotards, dangled after me, and one by one rejected me,
and fallen off, because you were too plain with all your cunning:
yes, and too true, with all those false pretences: until we have almost
come to be notorious? The licence of look and touch," she said, with
flashing eyes, "have I submitted to it, in half the places of resort
upon the map of England? Have I been hawked and vended here
and there, until the last grain of self-respect is dead within me, and
I loathe myself?"

These terrible sentences will leave their deposit in the definitions of celebrity, just as the iron will and self-righteous masculinity of Mr. Dombey
do also. The heartlessness of colossal wealth is not inevitable, we know, but
it is damnably likely. Sexual beauty in its female appurtenances is, however,
a prerequisite.

Mr. Dombey meets Lord Byron and is not fazed. Fame and money
come together in the awful figure of class respectability. The absolute
bourgeois then holds the stage until his pose is broken up by wars and
rumours of wars sometime in the 1920s. He (rarely she—there were not
many Ediths, as Dickens knew) was no doubt freely mocked and derided
to his impassive face by the avant garde. That was the very point of having
an avant garde, and thereby allowing old recklessness and Byronic desires
to irrigate the icy veins of respectable feeling. But the new bourgeois and
the old aristo kept an amicable peace for half a century or more. They
kept the peace by inventing a new kind of city, a two-level stage for the
enactment of desire: the long boulevards of apartments, banks, and offices
for the making and guarding of the money, and the great parks and the
playgrounds of the department stores for spending it and showing it off.

III

For this new pageant, only the French had the nerve and verve to do the
thing wholesale. They had made their violent break with the past in 1789

and clapped Napoleon as he brought the first manifestations of modernity—roads, a state bureaucracy, the Code, police—to the capital. In 1830 they had staged a reprise, during which it had momentarily seemed as though the draper or hosier, the skilled cabinetmaker or carpenter, the machinist and the navvy might make common cause to share the vote, to create a revolutionary fellow-feeling, to win the right to work, to control competition, to end poverty and have enough to eat.[12]

Good-bye to all that, when the dust settled and the corpses were cleared away. The city stewed in its own juice until 1848 when it boiled over again. In February the National Guard turned against the government and universal suffrage was decreed. It looked briefly and gloriously as though *les Travailleurs* had won by popular acclaim and Proudhonian socialism would be established.

By April Left and Right are again fighting in the streets at the first, almost only, moment of the barricades. The Right wins the vote in the National Assembly. In June there is a new, proletarian insurrection, put down hard. The bourgeoisie rallies itself. By November Louis Napoleon is elected president with draconian powers.

The troubles are not over yet. The following year there is another failed insurrection by the Left in June, and in October the future is made plain when Louis Napoleon dismisses his own conservative government and installs an unelected one of his own selection. Long ripples of discontent and resistance eddy back and forth in the *quartiers* of the old city, and the president abolishes universal suffrage in an act of astounding effrontery, then uncovers a conspiracy for a putsch in Lyons, calls a popular referendum to measure his support, and wins it overwhelmingly. At the very end of 1852, in a bloodless coup d'état, he makes himself emperor[13] and sets Paris to rebuild herself as capital of the world for the rest of the century, trifling interruptions like the Franco-Prussian War of 1870 and the Paris Commune of 1871 making no difference at all to the shaping of the new consumerism.

Louis Napoleon was bourgeois all through and even possessed the bourgeois taste, as Marx reminds us, not only for conspiracy (at which he was so brilliant) but also for "that confused, decomposed, floating mass the French call bohemians," and Marx added contemptuously, "the only revolutionary condition for them is an organisation adequate for conspiracy."[14]

The emperor saw them off while relishing the savour they gave to the city and the narrow streets of *pavés* which were their habitat.

Napoleon III appointed the Baron Haussmann prefect of the Seine, and as everybody knows, Haussmann set himself not only to build the capital of the world but also to open up and clear away those narrow streets, those jammed hovels and filthy workshops, the empire of the proletariat which could, in theory at least, shut itself off in its own fortress in a trice, throwing up a barricade in an hour or two, maintaining the terms of dark conspiracy quite out of sight of spies and class enemies.

There is, as T. J. Clark tells us, a good deal of mythicising in this history, and slum clearance as well as the construction of grand houses had been going on for some time before Haussmann arrived in his office.[15] He did not invent the park either; after all, the Tuileries had been there since Louis XIV's day. But it is impossible to withhold admiration from Haussmann's energy, vision, and sheer effectiveness as it is from the same qualities, exhibited in the same task by Robert Moses in New York after 1950. Certainly, Haussmann planned wide boulevards crossed at a clear right angle by service roads to ensure that the National Guard, once turned out, could get to the site of trouble with off-putting celerity. But the same boulevards had running beneath them the finest sewage system, paved, wide, odourless, that modern cities could show. Haussmann wrote in his memoirs of the building of Boulevard Sébastopol, that "it meant the disembowelling of the old Paris, the quarter of uprisings and barricades, by a wide central street piercing through and through this almost impossible maze, and provided with communicating sidestreets, whose continuation would be bound to complete the work thus begun."[16] He covered the canal which had once been a first line of defence for insurgent proletarians and built barracks close to all major crossroads. Wide roads ran to the railway stations ringing the city only a mile or two from its headquarters.

The working class was substantially expelled outwards to the new suburbs where Muslims nowadays congregate resentfully. The city was, as they say, rationalised, with grand apartments for the haute bourgeoisie, mansions for the mighty, building employment for both skilled trades and the unemployed for the rest of the century, the gradual defeat of cholera, and—in optimistic versions—a pattern of parks, green lungs with which to disperse the smoke and fog of the city, playgrounds in which the city could meet on easy, equal terms.

Haussmann may have ended up boss of the biggest bank in town, the Crédit Mobilier, as his reward, but both vision and achievement look pretty good at this distance. Counterrevolutionary no doubt, but who cares about that these days? Lots of people criticised it bitterly, for losing the old city's jostling familiarity, its picturesque decrepitude, its cosmopolitan colours, artisans of all sorts at work alongside market stalls, social classes intermingled and mutually recognisable, even greeting each other. The new city was bland and boring, they complained. But there's no pleasing some people.

The critics on the Left were right. "Streets are the dwelling place of the collective," wrote Walter Benjamin, pondering the meaning of Paris sixty years later. "For this collective," he goes on, "glossy enamelled shop signs are a decoration as good as ... an oil painting in the drawing room of a bourgeois; walls with their "Post no bills" are its writing desk, newspaper stands its libraries, mailboxes its bronze busts, benches its bedroom furniture, and the café terrace is the balcony from which it looks down on its household." [17]

This wistful recollection, sunnily ignoring cold or wet weather, is exactly what that ineffably snobbish duo, the Goncourt brothers, lamented about Haussmann's transformation. There is no denying that, in part unintentionally, Haussmann and his helots created the city defined behind its heavy rosewood doors as the capital of property speculation, and in its visible traffic as an Arcadian market place, where the delights of shopping were punctuated by those of taking coffee by the boulevard and listening to music, even dancing in the park. Gainsborough's promenaders in St. James's, those sharp-eyed, tight-mouthed girls keeping up their station, were replaced in Paris by a much more varied crowd, still minutely observing one another, keeping a total of the acknowledgements received and scoring them according to fame, fortune, or eminence, well aware that close enough beside them to be smelled were thieves, harlots, courtesans, hucksters, poets, painters, bohemians, all these alongside the complex ranks of the manifold bourgeois, checking themselves and others for fashionable correctness.

IV

The engine of reproduction for this mobile crowd, working away so hard at its display of leisure, was the new department store and its sacred nave, the arcade. In his repetitious and constantly rewritten notebooks on Paris in the nineteenth century, Walter Benjamin offers to catch the meaning and spirit of the new city in a brief series of images, the first of which is entitled "Fourier, or the Arcades."[18]

The arcades preceded Haussmann. They are the forerunners of the department store. They were made possible by the devising of iron girders capable of supporting the new invention of plate glass. They were the first public places to be lit by gas. Charles Fourier, a barmy utopian visionary, saw the arcade as "the phalanstery" (buildings occupied by a phalanx of progressives) of the future. They were gilded, marble-floored, fantasy avenues of the rich open to everybody to gaze into the shop windows and dream of unfeasible extravagance.

The remainder of Benjamin's images capture, one by one, the high romantic ambition of the designers of the new Paris to make it the city of *grands spectacles*, first in the contrivance and putting-on-show of the dioramas, detailed and elaborate toytown models of the whole city. The child in all of us responds delightedly to tiny but extensive models of places known to us; better still if models of the traffic can move, lights go on and off, images of clouds roll overhead. What one then sees as graspable and ownable is the city itself, and beyond the city (as Benjamin says) the green countryside, including (in the best dioramas) real water pumped along the river beds, perhaps turning a local mill and moving a miniature barge.

The full-scale counterpart of the diorama is the world exhibition. London had hers at Crystal Palace in 1851 (the biggest glass-and-iron construction in the world to that date); Paris followed in 1855. These huge palaces materialised the inauguration of the leisure industry on behalf of a whole nation (and in the case of Paris, thousands of British tourists also). "World exhibitions," writes Benjamin, "glorify the exchange value of the commodity,"[19] or in less *marxisant* accents, they display, for a kind of dazed and halfhearted desire in response, the triumphs of technology and the delicious enviability of luxury. Their success is judged by numbers. The more visitors turn up, the greater the success. The economics of the entertainment industry is born, whereby statistical totals become the commodity bought and sold. These are the first audience ratings. The new key concept is (as we have all learned since to say) the "specialty," and spotting with sharp inventiveness the opportunity, that amazing creation, the department store, followed hard on the 1855 exhibition.

The department store compresses the city into itself. It configures the comfortable interiors—sitting and dining room, bedroom as well—in a series of stage settings on different floors. A few discreet screens, and here is a shining, unused, seductively comfortable sitting room in which to rehearse one's imaginings of success, comfort, possession. The order is made, the credit obtained, and a way of being, an ontic reality, is boxed up at the warehouse, delivered in a week or two to the empty, echoing apartment, and asserts its inflexible terms for the kind of life which must follow. Not that the whole magical business is bullying or oppressive; on the contrary, and quite without irony, it brings instant satisfaction, often happiness and fulfilment.

Home, Philip Larkin wrote a century after the department store came to fix things up for us all, is "a glorious shot at how things ought to be." It all began, as good stories should start (and this one has turned into legend), when a Parisian draper called Aristide Boucicant lost his way in the middle of the 1855 Grande Exposition.[20] He was ravished not only by the gleaming goods, but by the artistic surprises and vistas which the design of the place created with such variety. Boucicant was a very wealthy trader. He went home to his successful Left Bank store, which sold *specialités* for sure, and an old-fashioned and tremendous jumble of hardware and furniture, took upholstery commissions, made up curtains, dispensed *tabac* and chocolates at the front of house. He hired the supreme glass-and-iron architect of the day, Eiffel of the eponymous Tower, who designed him his amazing new premises for Bon Marché, first department store of this or any capital.

There had been more diminutive forerunners[21] at Bainbridge's in Newcastle's Grainger Market, and at Kendal Milne's in Manchester, but these were essentially much enlarged drapers' shops. Bon Marché was unprecedented. Boucicant had grasped and Eiffel had mirrored the window-shopping experience. They designed a vast shop-warehouse, crammed with luxury and *specialités* for every aspect of private life and to provide for every room in the house. They then released their putative customers into this palace and left them to browse, to buy if they chose, to gaze if they did not.

This was the really audacious move. Hitherto shop assistants had been trained, like Kipps in H. G. Wells's novel, to solicit, to show zealous and deferential attention, but to crowd the incomer into purchase. Only the lordly old class had the nerve to dismiss Kipps's hand-rubbing servility; the anxious new class, buying its furniture for the first time and its household style with it, bent their necks to Kipps and his unspeakable boss, or never went near the shop in the first place. At Bon Marché you did not have to buy a thing; you could give yourself up to the gaze, to envy, desire, and the haunting dissatisfactions of fantasy. Idling, browsing, gazing, *flâneant* (Baudelaire's untranslatable verb, meaning "idling," "strolling," "musing," "observing") were the rich pleasures of this amazing dream-palace, and these were rewarded by the splendours of the spectacle in the shop. Eiffel had devised an exquisite framework of slender iron columns roofed with glass which made not only for the pleasure of sunlight illuminating the displays, but also for maximum flexibility in putting the goods on show. The slow throngs of visitors could move easily through the large, open spaces as if through the interlocking courtyards of a hygienic, well-lit, always surprising city.[22]

The model for the place was the Exhibition. Its lines of display were planned to draw people on, to discover the surprises, to admire the effects, to crave possession. Advertisements pictured enviability and desirability in their flat two dimensions. Bon Marché dramatised these qualities and made them three-dimensionally present to the senses. The regular expositions (after 1855, others in 1878, 1889, and 1900) pulled in attendances rising from sixteen million in 1878 to forty-eight million in 1900.[23] Bon Marché imitated first the form, then the numbers.

Not that Boucicant was left unrivalled. As soon as the word was out, Printemps built a competitor on the Boulevard Haussmann which opened in 1865, and Samaritaine opened by the Pont Neuf (still there) in 1870. Galeries Lafayette, also on Boulevard Haussmann, became the fourth great power among such stores and settled the Parisian triumph in 1895.

The triumph, I suppose, was that of the newest and wealthiest of the bourgeoisie. These gigantic emporia could only have fitted into the kind of long, high, and crescented façades Baron Haussmann's new Paris made available. (Easier by far on the grid plan and in the riotous competition of New York, where Macy's set up a hand-to-mouth arrangement in a jumble of houses on Sixth Avenue in 1870, before screwing a cast-iron front onto them to unify the effect.[24]) The store in Paris was precisely adjusted by Boucicant and his imitators to the *arriviste* bourgeoisie which was making big money as northern France caught up with the technological revolution, competed with Britain for empire in Africa, the Middle East, Indochina, and equipped itself with the weaponry it was going to need in assorted wars due in the coming half-century and beyond.

Luxury, specialty, display, finery, swank: a new class system was fashioning itself over just a few decades out of these sumptuous abstractions. The city multiplied its population by five to 2½ million during the century, and, prompt and shrewd as ever to chart the progress of venality, exploitation, and misery within its protean geography, Emile Zola published *Au Bonheur des Femmes*, his department store novel, duly equipped with a wretchedly put-upon store girl, puffed-up manager, vain and haughty customers.

Vanity and haughtiness were to be expected in such places, in Bon Marché and La Samaritaine, outside on the boulevards, and then, at leisure— leisure for showing off and looking at (the ferocity of those prepositions!), for putting on (style, effect, manner), and for (contemptuously) stripping off, off with a sneer, a grimace, a "cutting dead" by looking glassily through.

The thing that brought everyone of these showpeople up short was, as Clark puts it, the illegibility of the city.[25] You never knew where you were with people, whether new money or old, good birth or parvenu, plain scandalous or just vivacious, sincere or false. "The world," complained the politician-poet Lamartine, "has jumbled its catalogue," and as a consequence knowing what to make of one another, how to condescend and when to defer, whom to cut and whom to fawn upon, how to *classify* and therefore to understand, was all damnably difficult, had to be done invisibly (give no game away) and at top speed (keeping the advantage thereby).

So it is no surprise that it was the strange *flâneur*, the demon idler, Baudelaire, the eager beaver naturalist-novelist, Zola, and the painters— the crowds of the painters, a dozen of them geniuses as it turned out, with their impressionist impressions of the crowds, bars, balls, bedrooms,

Music in the Tuileries Gardens, 1862, by Edouard Manet (1832–1883). Oil on canvas. National Gallery, London / The Bridgeman Art Library

boulevards—who taught those crowds how to recognise themselves and classify others. Renoir, Manet, Vuillard, Degas, Seurat, Monet, Sisley, Pissarro, Morisot, and all, these caught the attention then and now, long before one reached the second and third raters, turning out society portraits and softly pornographic nudes with their own stories to tell about the new bourgeois man with his trousers off.

Telling the tale of the city and telling it kindlily, truthfully enough, these men (and one woman) became famous also in themselves, accrued stories to their name and charged accordingly, placed their friends to advantage in their paintings. When Manet painted *La Musique aux Tuileries* in 1862, he put his friends, relations, and himself in prominent positions in the picture: himself bearded and bareheaded standing at the table on the right, the writer Gautier, well-known commentator of the day on art and fashion, the painter Fantin-Latour, the English milord Taylor, diplomat and clubman, splendid in white trousers and topper just off centre foreground, and of course Charles Baudelaire, for some time already notorious

A Bar at the Folies-Bergere, 1881–1882, by Edouard Manet (1832–1883). Oil on canvas. © Samuel Courtauld Trust, The Courtauld Gallery, London / The Bridgeman Art Library

for the impeachment of his poems, *Fleurs du Mal*. Yet what will probably most strike us now is the smallness of this literary and social circle, the short circuit of fame.

This is so. These are local and early processes in the industrialisation of celebrity. At this stage, if not a cottage it is hardly more than a workshop industry, manufactured by word of mouth, gossip, and commonplace sightings in the park or at the bar. Many of the paintings, as we know, took the form of Pissarro's *Avenue de l'Opéra*, done (or rather begun) on a sunny winter's morning in 1898. The painter has positioned himself, like a sniper, high above the view, able to see all the way along the avenue, and to situate the massive solidity and respectability of the architecture, five storeys up to the mansard, as bulking over the busy little figures and their conveyances darkening the long line of shop fronts and awnings down to the embarrassing new Opera House with its crazy medley of styles and its embonpoint. This is what the new city means to the tourist: a magnificent advertisement.

When the tourist moves in closer to the foreign bodies of the city, however, Manet takes him or her (in 1882) by the arm to *Un Bar aux Folies-Bergère*. There, behind the champagne, the rosé, and the Bass, the tourist encounters a dashingly dressed young woman, velvet choker, lace ruff and posy decorously enhancing her décolletage, figured velveteen waistcoat, her undoubted prettiness clouded by abstraction, by a touch of unhappiness at her beautiful mouth, by her not quite meeting anybody's gaze. Behind her in the mirror we can see the place is packed, packed with a far more varied, lecherous, wild, and drunken mixture of people than turned out for genteel music in the Tuileries. Some of the same people are there—Manet for one, and he of haut-bourgeois extraction, as well as the gentleman in the topper weighing up the bargirl.

The crowd is here for the *café-concert*, a music-hall menu of raucous songs and piano-bashing, patter-comedians, and, if you were lucky (at the Alcazar for example), a small chorus of girls dressed as *bergères* in early versions of the leg-show. But the place was a café, not a theatre.[26] People went to eat, drink, smoke, and chatter. The atmosphere must have been as thick as an old duvet, brown, palpable. If you went there as and with the respectable classes, you ran the risk of mild offence, of coarse mockery, even of flagrant sexuality, and of course that was the point. There were some exclusive corners—the best places like the Folies-Bergère had boxes like a proper theatre—but essentially the point of the café-concert was to enable a far more multitudinous mingling of all classes than you could find in fresh air. The *flâneurs* and the bohemians turned up for sure; it was their kind of place exactly because it was everyone's kind of place—and so did the working class alongside the bourgeois men who had come to find sex perhaps, but also clamour, colour, fast food, heavy drinking, off-duty fulfilments in which direct desires could find simple expression. What Baudelaire found was ennui, life's repetitive tedium, as so did thousands of other sportsmen. But then, any number of others, from all classes, found the rough trade of this hearty, horrible marketplace just to their taste—a taste for a bit of danger, a dissolution of their respectable selves, the simple pleasure of breaking their awful social training. Men only, of course, but for the men not democracy (no call to get sentimental) but equality of opportunity, the pursuit of some sort of happiness.

V

As part of the developing machinery of celebrity production, the café-concerts functioned just fine. They provided a rendezvous for a rare mixture of social classes and gave their tense hostilities, rivalries, and convivialities safe but noisy expression. On that edge stood Baudelaire, and packed into his rather brief life and long, meritorious immortality are most of the conflicting representations of the new Paris, the century's capital. Baudelaire was idling his time away, strolling, observing, desiring, self-loathing, on the very crossroads of all the latest systems of production, exactly where the traffic hurtled past in its frenzy of moneymaking-and-spending, and the tireless energy it put into its self-display. Work and the hard work of leisure were alike objects of scorn to the *flâneur*-poet, but he missed nothing in either. What made for Baudelaire's singular niche in the pantheon of national celebrity was the deadliness with which he pierced boisterous conviviality and insisted on the desolation it concealed.

"Une nuit, quand j'étais près d'une affreuse Juive ...."

The horror of sex—which was to kill him over twenty years by way of syphilis—he veeringly balanced against his tenderness and fidelity to his three long-lasting lovers, Marie Daubrun, a sexy actress, the rich and voluptuous Apollonie Sabatier, and Jeanne Duval, a mulatto woman, at the end a wreck whom he fed and protected until he died, while she pursued him in extreme destitution. In contemplation, he watched over the roofs of the *faubourg* and gave the cityscape its exquisite quietus:

Il est doux, à travers les baumes, de voir naître
L'étoile dans l'azur, la lampe à la fenêtre,
Les fleuves de charbon monter au firmament
Et la lune verser son pale enchantement.

Only since Romanticism have poets coloured everyday townscape with their signature concepts. Thousands of people in France, and then, by way of T. S. Eliot, in Britain, learned the imagery of the new city from Baudelaire without ever reading him. The mist, the window lights, the street lamps, the empty, shining pavement, the temptations of the dark canal and the lonely prostitute, a solitary cat, the moon glimpsed through the iron of a fire escape, these became the signs of what Baudelaire, in another untranslatable concept, called "*Spleen*" as it drifted towards "*L'idéal*." Alongside the painters, who had on the whole to stick to a cheerier semiotics, Baudelaire taught, as much by fame as by being read, the inescapability of city boredom, the delights and beauty of solitude, the bitter self-conflict intrinsic to pleasure, the grim necessity and brief satisfaction of sex, the pull, the pull of opium, the dissolution of self in its sticky reek.

He turned to opium not out of any commitment to *spleen* or playing the part of *poete maudit* (the popular designation he wore like a badge[27]). He took it for years in laudanum, a mixture of honey, opium, and warm water which acted as an analgesic upon the agonising stomach cramps brought on by syphilis. But he later smoked hashish as a cure for ennui or accedia, the medieval sin of meaninglessness from which only the promise of travelling—towards the distant ocean, to the other side of the mountains—retrieved him, even though he hardly left Paris. His imagination was his prime refuge from ennui—the hard work and pure exhilaration of a good poem, escaping from self-loathing and the torment of contradictory feeling by catching and holding these awkward, private passions in a line.

When this medicine works, Baudelaire turns away from the fog and mist, the dark city and its solitaries, and finds himself inwardly, charmed out of himself by visions of fountain water falling on alabaster, crimson and azure birds in oriental trees, the "verdant perfumed paradise of childish loves."[28] These clichés he shored against his ruins and handed over to buy fame as the author of everybody's favourite images of freedom, insouciant travel, the utopia of the perfect holiday.

Mr. Dombey turned the Romantic passion into the cold intensity of social pride, the savagery of rage when crossed or affronted, the stiff pleasure of receiving deference. Baudelaire taught the new sensibility and its expression. An honest man must see how frightful the world is in its commonplace squalor, its demeaning desires, its revolting hypocrisy. But no one can live in a state of continuous moral repugnance (Baudelaire contemplated suicide for many months in 1860 but rejected it as cowardly and ignoble, saving himself by writing furiously.[29]) As a consequence he was stuck, veering between *spleen* and *ideal*, beset by ennui, not knowing what to feel but feeling it nonetheless with an extreme intensity, clarified only in a poem. The only feeling on which he could count for solace was nostalgia, the yearning for what, in a recollection reestablished only in the poem, seemed so wonderful because now it is lost. Its lostness is the source of its overwhelming affect. In his loveliest poem, *Le Ballon*, Baudelaire recaptures the power of lostness in an elegy to a lover and has no way to finish other than by bidding "Those vows, those fragrances, those infinite kisses" farewell. Perhaps nostalgia is his first passion—nowadays it is a term only used disparagingly, as something not to feel yet felt everywhere—and his bequest to modernity.

Until the last five years of his life, Baudelaire was, in the subfusc fashion which came in with the Victorians, a well-known, leanly attired figure along the café tables of the Boulevard St. Michel. The censor's action over *Fleurs du Mal* gave him notoriety, the poems themselves commanded the respect of the youngsters, the smallness of literary and artistic circles, their propinquity to and contempt for the respectable, well-off bourgeoisie, all ensured his visibility. His appalling honesty about his way of life as well as his gaunt white handsomeness and black threadbare suit gave him his fame as the very image of demonic heresy, its attractiveness and its doom. Edmond Goncourt, for forty years the snobbish, social-climbing, malicious, and all-seeing diarist of literary Paris, once wrote:

> I was thinking, last night, that one of the reasons for the implacable literary enmities that I encounter was the decency of my life. Yes, there is no doubt about it, this is an age which has a liking for unsavoury conduct. Who, after all, are the idols of the youth of today? They are Baudelaire, Villiers de L'Isle-Adam, and Verlaine: three men of talent admittedly, but a sadistic Bohemian, an alcoholic, and a murderous homosexual.[30]

Goncourt knew what he wanted; he belonged to the generation before he was born; he wanted a life of quiet cultivation, social recognition, malicious gossip—the life of London and Paris before the balloon went up. Baudelaire's life's work was to see through Goncourt's "decency," to catch new feeling as it flitted by, to face up to the terrible ambivalences of the city, to both horror and desire, and to find and name feelings which would do justice to the heroes of circumstance. Just where these worthies would be found—in which social class, which café, *quartier*, or dingy bedroom— was what kept his great poems down to such a low score.

Manet, born to a comfortably-off family and swift to find amenable success, turned to the same questions and painted the barmaid and, in 1865, *Olympia*, which he well knew would cause the terrific commotion it did. Between them, Manet and Baudelaire embody by dramatising the deeply derided psychoses of their day. The new world wanted to spend its money on a good life (where good includes badness) in which respect would be assured, happiness simplified, desire gratified, envy dissolved, appetite matched precisely to expression. Poet and painter would show how this was to be accomplished.

Poet and painter showed them only contradiction, calculation, disappointment, ambiguity.

VI

The establishment of the middle-class family as the moral centre of the nation was pretty well complete in France and Britain by the second half of the nineteenth century. The line between public and private life was drawn in black by the novelists, the idea of domestic respectability, single-minded fidelity, parental authority (father for power, mother for care) was confirmed by the queen herself and her respectable consort, and the bohemians set up camp outside the walls of home and its sanctity in order to confirm its fixity by a delicious demonstration of how not to behave properly.[31]

Within the family, as Freud was the first to see, these new, strict rules had their lethal consequences, especially for women. The moral and market premium put upon virginity, purity, and girlish inexperience as necessary conditions for eligibility sorted ill with the parallel expectation (or hope) that the eligible girl also be spirited, resourceful, assured in social life, cultivated in artistic expression. The crux in all this was, to be sure, regulating what feelings were permitted visibility at home, and what feelings were allowed out of the house.

There is a danger at this distance of the free spirits of today scoffing unbelievingly at the repressions of upper and lower fractions of middle-class Victorian society. Those free spirits—you and I—are deeply shaped by that history. Our own emotional and moral development is its direct descendant, as the lives and characters we require of our political leaders testify. What the Victorians were trying to puzzle out was the two kinds of conduct which belonged to the two sides of the line between public and private lives.

In public, the well-off Victorian was, if a gentleman, buttoned into a pressed dark suit, tight collar with cravat, close-fitting boots, heavy overcoat, buttoned gloves. Imagery and actuality alike were eloquent of constraint, unbendingness, expressionless as to features and colour, as motionless and unexcited as possible. "Good form" taught the suppression of gesture ("Latins" were scoffed at for their excitability and demonstrativeness) to men and women alike, and when it came to women's "correct" attire when in the open air, their bodies vanished, as Sennett reminds us,[32] inside an exaggerated and unhuman profile of bulging petticoats, grotesque bustle, and poke bonnet, the only curve provided by the heavy pressure of the corset.

Sexual display was allowed out on fixed occasions—the ball, the theatre, the reception, the wedding—but even then the rules were strict about exactly how much spine or cleavage may be permitted, and how the licentiousness of a lady's hair should be pinned back and tightly held, with the barest hint of the voluptuous relief of its being allowed to tumble down. In secret there were surprising excesses to reassure today's handful of puritans that things have been bad for a long time. Nipple-piercing was not unknown, earlobe-piercing usual once girls put their hair up at the awkward age,[33] and even in public, as a sampler text of 1880 reminds us,

My great-aunt Prue
Was a modest dame,
But she wore lipstick
Just the same.[34]

The tense contradiction held in by these clothes was between the secret release suppressed but implied by the showy dress and muffled suggestiveness of the ball or the theatre bar, and the rules of expressionlessness in public—the tightlipped formality of greeting and smiles, the immobility, the correct vacuity of the conversational exchanges. Beside Mr. Dombey, we may set the professional chaperone (the officer in charge of inhibition), Mrs. General.

A cool, waxy, blown-out woman, who had never lighted well.

Mrs. General had no opinions. Her way of forming a mind was to prevent it from forming opinions. She had a little circular set of mental grooves or rails on which she started little trains of other people's opinions, which never overtook one another, and never got anywhere. Even her propriety could not dispute that there was impropriety in the world; but Mrs. General's way of getting rid of it was to put it out of sight, and make believe that there was no such thing. This was another of her ways of forming a mind—to cram all articles of difficulty into cupboards, lock them up, and say they had no existence. It was the easiest way, and, beyond all comparison, the properest.

Mrs. General was not to be told of anything shocking. Accidents, miseries, and offences, were never to be mentioned before her. Passion was to go to sleep in the presence of Mrs. General, and blood was to change to milk and water. The little that was left in the world, when all these deductions were made, it was Mrs. General's province to varnish.[35]

This contradiction, site of God knows what neuroses, is nonetheless the tight knot of our own emotional inheritance from the Victorians, and the radioactive deposit which was to burst out in a hot glow, first in the person of the star, and second, much more explosively, in the person of the political leader of mass politics.

The knot was tied between personality and solitude. Baudelaire may not have brought this to realisation, but he intuited it. The point of Courbet's endearing painting of 1848, *The Meeting: "Good morning, Monsieur Courbet,"* was to repel *both* quantities. The picture shows the itinerant artist with his wide-brimmed hat, his painting gear and his pipe in his mouth, genially greeting two local people, who recognise him friendlily and suppose him to be about his proper, useful labour. Courbet wanted the artist to stand as *the* type of free citizen, unencumbered by either propriety or personality. The Victorians cast him quite otherwise. The poet, the painter, the pianist, the conductor, above all the actor and actress were assigned to create and express the forceful feelings which constituted personality, and to do so on a special stage from which the spectators withdrew into the dark, leaving the personality to do his or her ardent feeling under the dazzling lights.

Gradually, across the middle decades of the century, the theatres and concert halls darkened except for the bright pool of light over the performers. At the same time the audience began to quieten down. In Garrick's day, or Kean's, the flares of the house burned equally on either side of the stage, and the audience, as we heard, shouted out at will at the performers, pushing them in and out of role. Nor was ordinary chat suspended in the concert hall, or only for sacred music. From 1840 onwards, however, as the drama of the street, whether in Paris or London, Norwich or Bath, became more and more illegible, even when, perhaps most of all when, it broke out into violence, the stage and concert platform became the experimental laboratory of feeling and of the genetic recoding of personality.

The extraordinary originality of the dramas of Ibsen and Chekhov was that, in withdrawing the "fourth wall" of the living room, so that the audience sitting in the dark could eavesdrop on the private life in front of them so stringently hidden away in actuality, they exhibited and anatomised the struggle for freedom, self-expression, for a soul to call one's own, which the audience was at such pains to conceal. Hence the shocking nature of *Ghosts* or *Hedda Gabler*—of its being quite clear that what is wrong in Hedda's life is thwarted sexuality, that the secret of Oswald's life is the worst secret in the world, the most terrible thing laid bare.

It may be that Sennett, in his contention that the theatre itself helped generate the new cult of personality and then tilted it towards politics, overdid things a bit.[36] Personality as a new social force had been stoked up with rocket fuel by the Romantics, by Byron, by the hedonists at the court of the Prince of Wales, by the leaders of street fervour like Fourier and Blanqui, and most of all by naval and military heroes and villains, by Nelson and the old curmudgeon, Wellington, and by Bonaparte. But it cannot be doubted that the new star system of theatre and concert hall as it picked up speed towards 1900 caused an acceleration in the huge wave of expressivism as well as in that countercurrent sweeping individuals to solitude and desolation on the urban beach. On the one hand, the thunderous applause from the dark greeting Liszt's bravura virtuosity under the lights; on the other, Degas' lonely absinthe-drinker, a shabby, not-elderly woman staring at her own blurred misery.

This is the twistpoint of the new consumerism. On a good day the virtuoso won hands down. For he or she (pianist or actress) had been appointed public demonstrator of the passions. The audience watched in silence, the performer threw her- or himself into the excesses of visible, barely harnessed feeling. At the end, performance melted into applause and personality shrank back into person, perspiring, smiling, glimmering, and going dark.

What the great actor and performer did—"great" because appointed to the office—was teach the inimitable attainment of expressive genius. The artist was to be a rare, an incomparable kind of person, such as one cannot emulate (and, mostly, would not want to, being oneself respectable). Nonetheless, his and her powers of self-expressiveness, of creative insight into the possibilities of life, show the public what it cannot have but contrarily longs for. The feelings fired up in the concert hall fade in the rain outside; they are a token of how life might but will not be. "Being" on this scale must be hired out to the performer, but ratified by his or her public. Hitler and Mussolini intuited, as we shall see, the significance of all this.

The performer must remain aloof when off duty. Solitude is the condition of artistic genius. The virtuoso, whether instrumentalist or conductor, actor or director, plastic artist or dancer, possesses such intrinsic powers of passionate expressiveness because of rarity of talent and character. Above all, *they knew what to do* when on show. One obvious product of the exclusion of the public from significant political action which was the result of the creation of the benign, surveillant state was that significant personal action shrank to the zone of the suburb.[37] It was entirely unclear how to be a manly man or womanly woman, especially when held by the wooden conventions of immobility and unfeeling. The performer showed what it should be like to act significantly, and this was to be largely a matter of arousing and displaying, with passionate sincerity and clarity, the very centre of meaning, the passions themselves.

At the same time, as is always painfully clear, the narrative form of drama or symphony moves towards resolution, the knots untied, the mystery disclosed in peripeteia. The virtuoso can then appear to the crash of applause, but as we say on the way home, "life's not like that." We are back with the old irresolution, looking for a stab at the awful daring of a moment's surrender.

If things were easier in the eighteenth century—setting aside the brutality, the ghastly play of caste arrogance and grim privation—it must have been because human nature was a bit more in the open and readier in response for those with the money to make leisure, plenty of such people not city folk at all. The thrilling liberations of feeling brought by the prophets of Romanticism were apt to lead to a dead end. What shall I feel? What shall I do to create feeling? These are still dismal and familiar questions. As for the Victorian audiences, the best they could manage by way of feeling right-enough-to-get-along-with was the *flâneur*, keeping to himself (the girls would have to manage for themselves), observing the world with as much noncommittal irony as can be raked up, and roused to inexpressible enthusiasm, briefly made visible, in the brief release of acclamation, by the performer's performance. The self, wry, unself-assured, timorous of what other people were making of it (what they make of us, makes us), dissolved willingly, self-recognisingly, into the action over there, in the light on the other side of the dark. The cinema would complete this process. It would bring to an impossible closeness the very lips and eyes of the actor, but those near, familiar features would only be in actuality the play of a million shadows on a flat white screen. There, each spectator, sitting alone in the dark, could weep real crocodile tears over the well-known, unknown features, without fear of being laughed at for childishness.

By 1890 the performer of art therefore had come to occupy a focal place in the strict drama of Parisian, London, and New York life. The city of the spectacle, with its parks, promenades, dinner tables, and theatres, arranged itself so that in its leisure it could puzzle out what was going on by showing itself to itself. No doubt this is to speak in too unitary a way: the city was a mosaic of fluid classifications. That is why it was such a puzzle.

The department stores were put at the service of this delicious and macabre dance. They provided the arena in which the competition of appearances was played out. Revolution? 1830, 1845, Louis Napoleon's coup d'état, the terrifying shock of the Paris Commune in 1871 notwithstanding, the new model army of both *haut* and *petit* bourgeoisie marched victoriously on, invincibly snobbish, racked with self-doubt. Duelling with their rivals and carrying the weapons purchased from Bon Marché and La Samaritaine, they played the game not of condescension and deference, but of a heavily armoured and taciturn exchange of unconcessive formality.

The revenge of the psyche was taken out on the performers. Their display and their fame were forced upon them by the lonely crowd.[38] The performer might be artist or musician or national hero. As I suggested, Admiral Nelson was an early one such, especially when he took up with Lady Hamilton. As the naval officer in Robert Graves's poem puts it at Nelson's funeral,

> The most bird-witted, unaccountable,
> Odd little runt that ever I did spy ...
> By his unservicelike, familiar ways, Sir,
> He made the whole fleet love him, damn his eyes.[39]

Nelson's oddity made him an early celebrity in a special guise: heroic rescuer of national pride. By the end of the century the longings which settled on Nelson out of chauvinism had been rewritten for quite another treaty. Its factions were in part engaged in the silent struggle of the classes; they were also the shadowy projection of divided selves, as each new urban individual battled to resolve the demands of self-expression and the passions, as opposed to seemliness and propriety. The performers of the action were rewarded by celebrity, and the money that went, while it lasted, with it. But they could not call their souls their own. That is the point. Ask Sarah Bernhardt.

VII

Even now, the name retains an electric charge. She gathered to herself a dozen currents of feeling flowing across Europe and released them into the international theatre which was, by 1880, the incandescent crucible for the hectic desires created by new money, old snobbery, the competitiveness of fashion, the hotpot of sex. As genius will, she sucked these forces into her skinny body topped with her amazing, springy, red-gold hair, concentrated

Sarah Bernhardt (1844–1923), 1862. Philip H. Ward Collection, Rare Book and Manuscript Library, University of Pennsylvania. Photographer: Félix Nadar (1820–1910)

them as personal passion, and let them pour out over audiences in countless American cities—ninety-nine on her final tour in the United States in
1915, aged seventy-one—the first world star.

The story of her career is, like all the best celebrity biographies, irresistible. (That is one firm point in this book: stories about celebrities must and
should grip us; fastidious distaste will not do; these people have things to
tell us about the meaning of our lives.) Sarah Bernhardt was born perhaps
illegitimate in 1844 to a German-Dutch family living in Paris, rejected
by her mother and brought up on a remote farm in Brittany, Breton her
first language.[40] She became an actress when one of her courtesan mother's
many protectors, the duc de Morny and Emperor Louis Napoleon's half-
brother, obtained her a place at the Paris *Conservatoire*.

The duc had noticed his protégée's amazing voice—pure, clear, thrilling—and perfect elocution. It took some time and luck, naturally, to make
her a success—behind every celebrity lie the dead bodies of their sometime
rivals—but in 1872 her performance in Victor Hugo's colossal romantic
melodrama, *Ruy Blas*, brought her first stupendous success and a love affair, among hundreds, with Hugo himself, forty years her senior.

She was beautiful, sure, in her ashen-faced pre-Raphaelite way; she had
her wonderful voice, she was anorexically thin, she was necrophiliac (sleeping from time to time in her special coffin), she was reckless and passionate
and impulsive and ... all the excessive things Romanticism taught as attributes of the distinctive and creative personality. She invented grotesque
lies about herself without shame, retelling them brazenly in her autobiography,[41] claiming in one choice example to have saved the life of Lincoln's
widow while at sea in a storm. It was Henry James, of course, who immediately took her moral measure: "[She] has a perennial freshness ... [and]
understands the art of motion and attitude as no-one else does, and her
extraordinary personal grace never fails her. Her Andromaque has postures
of the most poetic picturesqueness—something that suggests the broken
stem and drooping head of a flower that had been rudely plucked."[42] With
his usual confident genius, James foresaw that "She is too American not to
succeed in America. The people who have brought to the highest development the arts and graces of publicity will recognise a kindred spirit in a figure so admirably adapted for conspicuity." James went on to use Bernhardt

as his model for his heroine, Miriam Rooth, in his novel *The Tragic Muse*. (Now there is lasting celebrity for you!)

It cannot be doubted that Bernhardt had colossal genius as an actress. What she also embodied, and transmits to subsequent epochs with all her powers of electrifying conduction, was life as role. Always sincere, she was always acting. Always acting, from 1880 onwards she acted as single controller of all her performances, often her own producer, always commissioning for herself stage sets, lighting, cast, managers, and schedule (above all in America). She made nine tours in the United States, and wherever she went she stopped the traffic, jammed the hotels, dominated the newspapers, living with glorious fidelity to her mysterious, anonymous, voracious self. She led a scandalous love life (horrifying and hypnotising American sternness in such matters), hopelessly spoiling her illegitimate son Maurice. She travelled crazily, accompanied by pet lynx, alligator, python, she made death on stage her tour de force. Perhaps most singular of all, she staggered her audiences by taking the parts of male leads with complete poise and conviction—her Hamlet perhaps her greatest triumph, but her whole style a rejection of stagey melodrama and overacting for truthfulness to self, declarations of sincerity, the display of unforced passion, all the key values of the new ethics of personality and honest feeling.

She gave form and flesh to the actress as celebrity genius, and the conscientious citizen-dames of the present still pay handsome tribute to the kinds of life she enabled them to create. Moreover she also created (like Byron) a new role for herself and later celebrities as national heroine, turning the Odeon into a hospital during the Franco-Prussian War, capably nursing wounded soldiers. In the great anti-Semitic scandal of the Dreyfus affair, she comes out in support of Zola's famous letter to the government, *J'accuse*, and finally chooses amputation of her own leg after decades of agonising pain in her knee on and offstage. This at seventy. Then off she goes on her ninety-nine-city lecture tour of America.

"I've always acted," she wrote, "I never stop ... I am my own double." She hands this on to the developing industry of fame. Her attributes were real and palpable, her genius undisputed, her intelligence acute, and her life true to her inexpressible ideals (her personal motto, *"Quand même"*).

So she's a test of authenticity in her heirs; she is one of those figures in this weird history who provides us in the middle station with a touchstone of worth, of the goodness of celebrity.

Her history in her day uncovers a useful contrast, illustrating the unlikely pleasures of phoniness as well as launching us across the Atlantic to attend the dance of colossal wealth and that "highest development of the arts of publicity" which Henry James foresaw as his nation's contribution to culture and politics.

Lola Montez (our contrast) was not Bernhardt in diminuendo. She was an ungifted, tarty fake who, without any insight into what she was doing, intuited how to make herself into a celebrity while lacking talent, opportunity, birth, and money. She is therefore an object lesson, briefly to be noted, scoffed at, indulged not without affection, in that substantial fame factory which somehow takes the talentless on their own inflated valuation and projects them violently onwards until they land onstage and onscreen and are just as violently destroyed.

She did it mostly with sex. "The splendour of her breasts," one admirer wrote, "made madmen everywhere."[43] She made and lost a prodigious fortune as a dancer, which she was very bad at, jeered and laughed at and pelted with rotten fruit (smelly but soft) until she turned and furiously berated her all-male audiences. They then stopped hooting and cheered. The joke was amply that she was a terrible dancer, a sort of stripper (especially in her dire tarantella), obliterated (by her abuse of her detractors) the distance between stage and pit so effortfully defined by Garrick, and somehow commanded by her crass performance of "womanly" wiles a long line of admirers who kept her in the high style.

Born Elizabeth Gilbert in County Sligo sometime in the early 1820s, she gradually transformed herself into Donna Maria Dolores de Ponis y Montez, and by judicious displays of her frontispiece and tumbling etc. ringlets, eventually and after many predecessors, entranced King Ludwig of Bavaria, tearing open her décolletage to his goggle-eyed gratification. Thereafter she was made, and made big (ten thousand florins a month). She became of course notorious *and* famous, dancing her clumsy, stomping way around America and Australia, sanctimonious, shameless, hooted, cat-called, and impregnable. She died of religious mania, immodesty, opium, and drink, aged barely forty, old Ludwig faithful to the last.

She serves to confirm that necessary mixture of cynicism and nausea with which we have to behold at least half our subject matter. Lola Montez is one unattractive version of that familiar and endearing figure in the novels of P. G. Wodehouse, the sweet-natured and pretty young chorus girl who is the young heir's choice of fiancée, to the horror of his snobbish and titled family. Even by Wodehouse's day in the 1920s she was an anachronism, but in the real life of Lola Montez we can see her as intuitively catching up and playing to an unsavoury brew of crude sexual desire enacted very publicly and in the days of its formal repression, allied to a raucous misogyny blowing its top off on the lads' night out, given its arbitrary occasion (they had to take these appetites *somewhere*) at the best-known show in town.

She was an inane and lucky accident of a kind the celebrity machine was beginning to engender. Somebody had to play her part; there were very few vacancies; she filled one. Bernhardt was no doubt a great actress, but Lola Montez was cut from the same cultural cloth. Sex is intrinsic to art, and with increasing flagrance for two centuries, publicity must needs adorn them both.

Chapter 5

New York and Chicago: Robber Barons and the Gossip Column, 1880–1910

Paris has been capital of the nineteenth century ever since Walter Benjamin said so; it had the money, the shops, the new boulevards, and the Bois de Boulogne; it had a few picturesque riots and mythic barricades to remind tourists that history is the history of class struggle; and it had Americans trooping from the gangplanks of the liners moored beside the Channel at Calais and Le Havre, and rattling into the Gare du Nord in hundreds every day of summer, come with dollars to burn, love affairs to consummate with Frenchwomen, paintings to buy, and novels to write.

The Americans came to find what they did not have at home, and take it back as souvenirs, above all on canvas. By 1890 every picture Monet painted was promptly purchased by an American for between four and six thousand francs; there were well over a hundred big dealers, led by the biggest of them all, Ambroise Vollard[1] of the Rue Lafitte, toadied, cajoled, and bargained with by the ineffable soon-to-be-Lord Joe Duveen, with cheques in his pocket from Frick, Morgan, Hearst, and all. Paris was *the* type of what a capital should be, and leading characters, pumped up larger than life by their emblematic status as artists, actors, poets, novelists, musicians, 0and, of course, as representatives of historical families and resonant titles, became the sights and statuary the Americans came to see.

Numerically, the tides of travellers ran westwards. Millions were migrants, destined for the interminable procedures of Ellis Island. But sitting, according to social class, in the first- or second-class lounges of Cunard's liners were all those already famous as well as those ambitious of fame, sailing to the crazy Byzantiums of New York and Chicago, in a trance of hope and greed, imaginations addled by tales of the wealth in the streets waiting to be picked up. And when they got there, after they sailed up the Hudson to the massive wharves protruding from the west side of Manhattan, with the stupendous backdrop of the city before them, they found, in the words of J. K. Galbraith, "that it was not enough to be rich; the wealth had to be celebrated ... the Gilded Age was, very specifically, a world of competitive ostentation."[2] Good old Galbraith goes on to say that from our historical vantage point we can only contemplate the mad excesses of the super-rich in Newport, Rhode Island, with "gentle ridicule ... sometimes on the brink of derisive laughter." As people say, "I wish." But due social democracy is now and once again swamped by money worship, and even if the colossal display of the high society mansions is no longer thought tasteful, the money which bought it is enviable and its makers silently applauded and consecrated.

To catch hold of this crucial link in our story between mere wealth and contentless fame, you only have to walk the tourist trail round Newport. The place started life as a seaport for a bunch of Puritan colonists from Boston in 1639. As such it thrived for a century and a half, opened up trade with the Caribbean, renounced anti-Semitism, permitted quaking Quakers, built well and durably, and after the 1776 Revolution turned itself into one of the first American seaside resorts, with ornate pseudo-cottages and the busy literary-artistic set which soon springs up in holiday towns.

Towards the end of the century, as the new multimillionaires built gigantic fortunes, they spent the stuff on the mansions of Newport. Between 1978 and 2009, in a new epoch of capital accumulation and the rapt worship of money, we became accustomed to the league tables of mammoth individual wealth and the brutal discrepancies between chief executive officer and staff. But it is worth adding that, in 1890, the Vanderbilt fortune, while at present equivalent to about £3.5 billion, enough to be going on with, was untouched by income or corporation tax. It could be spent on consumables amongst which a Savile Row suit to be shipped from London would cost Cornelius, head of the family, only $20 and his new yacht a mere $250,000 (God knows what a palatial yacht costs today but at least $60 million). Meanwhile one of his full-time chambermaids was paid $12 per month.[3]

The money poured in such a torrent from real estate speculation (the Astor family had, for instance, bought up at knock-down prices the farms of mid-Manhattan); from the doubling of railroad track in the last decade of the century, moving bulk wheat and meat at unprecedented speeds to the cities while the railroad owners (Stanford, Vanderbilt, and, for steam ferries, Fulton) charged what they liked for freight; from oil (John D. Rockefeller), its piecemeal exploitation and crazy market (still true) once its new technological importance was realised; from steel (J. P. Morgan, Andrew Carnegie), from coke (Henry Clay Frick, wooden and militant strike-breaker, fourteen union men killed by Pinkerton detectives in a lockout). Henry Frick became a celebrity for the rich themselves and in a very straightforward way when attacked by an anarchist Russian immigrant who shot and stabbed him. Frick, in his forties, mute and inexpressive as always, fought back, held the killer down, and wrenched out of the man's mouth the capsule of mercury fulminate intended to blow the pair of them to shreds. Then he went back to acquiring the most amazing collection of paintings any one man has ever had his agent assemble and arranged them around his Fifth Avenue shrine.

This register of the rich—a dozen unmentioned still, Guggenheim, Goldman, Sachs, Ford, Mellon, Hearst (we shall go back to him), Burden—rolls on, like a ground bass in the cacophonous symphony of celebrity. Everyone knows the names as the eponyms of wealth, even if they do not know how they made the money. They know the phrase, half admiring half dismissive, "robber barons," and they vaguely know the particular course of a piratical life from young privateer to grand old philanthropist. New York's greatest streets are lined with their memorials—Waldorf-Astoria, Carnegie Hall, Frick Collection, Guggenheim Museum—and these dark materials daily reenact the celebrity of their owners and donors.

They present the official masks of the power of money. Their unofficial features, no less public, are most readily to be found in the holiday mansions of Newport. For it is part of the strangeness of celebrity that the uncelebrated masses who do the celebrating insist on searching for the man (and woman) behind the mask—Carnegie Hall is a piece of sober, splendid, and chic architecture; the Frick Collection, compact, classical, domestic, even lovable in its way, is impassive, clad in dress clothes, reticent. "What were they really like?" people ask of themselves. The gorgeous palaces reveal (in the untrustworthy verb so important to gossip) only banalities.

Nowadays those same palaces provide the tourists with sights to see after they have docked at the marina and before sampling the little shops. At its peak, there were scarcely any hotels in Newport; only the very rich went there with their crowds of invisible servants, one to every two guests at the hundred-cover banquets, and if you had not the money to rent one of the elephantine "cottages" or to build your own mansion, you were not rich enough to go in the first place.

The Breakers and Marble House were from the first publication of the planned buildings the premier showplaces in town. Both of them built by Vanderbilt brothers, William K. at Marble House, an anniversary gift for his wife, Cornelius II at The Breakers, ostentation being at its most rivalrous inside the family, both designed by Richard Morris Hunt, prince of fashionable architects, in the dizziest styles of the day. Marble House is a neoclassic pavilion with echoes of the Trianon at Versailles,[4] clad inside and out with Sienese marble, and entered by a towering classical portico mounted on a sweeping plinth of a driveway with marble balustrades set off with coiled gothic six-lamp standards. Inside, the ballroom, gilded from floor to ceiling with sumptuous gold mouldings and choirs of golden cherubim blowing tiny trumpets from the vast chandeliers, received five hundred guests for the glittering betrothal party given by Mrs. Vanderbilt to celebrate her daughter Consuelo's being affianced to the ninth Duke of Marlborough. In this symbolic union, the heir of the Churchill family and of Blenheim Palace in Oxfordshire, gift from a grateful British nation and finished in 1722, joined blood to money, lineage to arriviste.

By the time of the great ball, Mrs. Vanderbilt had divorced William without scandal and in the affable American way. She dressed her servants in Louis XIV kit, released hummingbirds and butterflies into the garden, served a twelve-course dinner with four hundred different birds in the game dish, and set the mark for all such subsequent occasions.

Nothing could upstage such a performance, but Cornelius II outbid the family scenery by building The Breakers, also with Hunt as architect, this time in his Renaissance Italian and baroque style, but with those influences vastly magnified to fit the huge limestone bulk of the building, punctuated on its famous eastern aspect looking out oceanwards by two storeys of col-onnaded loggias, heavy scrolled buttresses, hipped roofs, classical piers be-neath ornate balustrades, further colonnaded loggias flanking the massive

The Breakers. Shutterstock © TravelBug

wings. In both its actuality and its symbolism, the building declares wealth
and exudes power, each at their simplest and most American. It borrows
historical longevity from the style book—Medici bulk and opulent brutality, Athenian grandeur and commoners' democracy, baroque display and
ornament—much as sister-in-law Alva bought it from the Churchills' title;
but there is no touch of cultural cringe anywhere. The house, with its enormous spaces, sweeps of staircase, priceless carpets, and exquisitely copied
Louis XIV furniture, its marble panels and Byzantine enamelling on every
inch of wall, serves as a touchstone of what celebrity, first in America, then
in the world, would mean and does from then till now.

"If you seek his monument, look about you" reads Wren's plaque in St.
Paul's; if you want to understand not just American wealth and power, but
the public and visible dance of its enacted meanings, spend a morning at
The Breakers and Marble House. The very rich allowed the crowd a lot
nearer than was usual in Europe. You could not gatecrash, but you could
get close enough to gaze, to disparage, to envy, to puzzle over their like-
nesses and differences to yourself. The dramas of these houses when empty

for the tourist (all that gilt is now, significantly, a bit dulled, the high ceilings echoing emptily) is now retrospective, however compelling. That way of affirming power and wealth is over for a season. But the meaning of the balls, the receptions, the weekending, the weddings, and the welcomes to visiting dignity of an equal sort lives on in the moral imagination of the present as what celebrity confers when it lives long enough and accumulates the money which grounds status on marble staircases and the blasphemous mimicry of cathedrals with coffered ceilings and Wedgwood tondos in the spandrels.

For there are distinctions to be made here. The houses of the Gilded Age were built by businessmen, and business, as countless Hollywood movies remind us, has spellbinding force in the American political vocabulary. The fame brought by business success is still dark-suited, its dramatis personae a bit distant, composed, constrained, correct. The portrait of Henry Frick in his museum or the photograph of John Jacob Astor IV with his second wife in these pages are together eloquent of this suppressed and formal eloquence. To be a celebrated businessman is to be self-possessed, accessible but only on official affairs, to be rich and getting richer, to be expressionlessly mature and poised in the boardroom, on Fifth Avenue, a man of fortune greeting heirs, as Wallace Stevens, poet of the rich, imperturbably puts it.

Wealth and magic have always been near allied. The ancients, so the story goes, attributed magical powers to gold and precious stones because they believed the source of light, the sun itself, had been fragmented and then trapped in the metal and stone. "As radiant things give up their magic claims, renounce the power with which the subject invested them and hoped with their help himself to wield, they become transformed into images of gentleness, promises of a happiness cured of domination over nature. This is the primeval history of luxury, that has migrated into all art."[5]

The rich man wins the gold and diamonds out of the ground. He transforms them into images of gentleness by giving them to his wife and mistress. They adorn themselves and their home with the precious objects which, glowing with their locked-in power, hold out the promise of the happiness of immunity to time and chance and the sickness unto death. This is the perfection of luxury, and it is implied in all art. Newport's balls, picnics, polo, paddling, tennis, riding, all conducted in the right, the

Madeleine and John Jacob Astor IV with their dog, Kitty. © Brown Brothers, Sterling, PA

elaborate, wardrobe, were shows of class power, naturally; but more than that, they were the rituals which showed that their actors carried off their unassailable magnificence as token to the world of their gentleness as well as their permanence. The fête champêtre was a living work of art (bad art, often; vulgar art almost always), proof that luxury and art together are the highest forms of universal fulfilment.

II

These marvellous effects were certainly effective. Original Puritanism and the melting pot of mass, impoverished migration notwithstanding, the very rich embodied and dramatised America's solidary myth of wealth achieved and its perfect freedoms. The presentation of self this took was inevitably much contested, even bloodstained. The formation of the "Metropolitan 400" is well-known, the phrase and the accompanying directory being the work of a creature hanging on to Caroline Webster Schermerhorn, wife of William Backhouse Astor Jr. This thing, one Ward McAllister, remarked that "There are only about 400 people in fashionable New York. If you go outside that number you strike people who are either not at ease in a ballroom or else make other people not at ease," and he duly prepared an exclusive list for his hostess's use, a list instantly promulgated by the press and approved by all those who were on it.[6]

These were the ways of an unformed society piling up its loot and trampling on the fingers of anyone trying to pick some up for themselves. Something of the same kind happened in eighteenth-century London, and to an even more marked degree in Paris after 1848. But in the European cities, applications for membership in the ruling class were strictly regulated by the old noblesse, and mere longevity of status trumped sheer money any day, until (in France and Britain) just yesterday. Things moved far faster in the States, especially in New York and Chicago, and, as the centre of world production and capital accumulation moved westward across the mid-Atlantic, there was a new kind of class struggle to determine not rule—the Constitution had done that—but regard, prestige, preeminence; deference, sure, but of a democratic kind; above all, admission ("will they let me in?"), alliance ("can I marry her?"), permanence. In his caustic and excellent history of America's stinking rich (as class warriors used to say), Gustavus Myers wrote: "The class which had the money arrogated to itself all that was superior and it exacted, and was invested with, a lordly deference.... Surrounded with an indescribably pretentious air of importance, it radiated tone, command and prestige."[7]

McAllister's rule was that old money (preferably of three generations' length) was senior to new, but lots of money will always be admitted. Family line and pedigree retained prestige until, say, the end of the First World War; by the time the films *High Society* (1956) and *Easter Parade* (1948) were made, pedigree had become a nervous joke ("the Vanderbilts have asked us out to tea," sang Fred Astaire and Judy Garland, dressed as hoboes). Status struggle remained, however, a fact of historical life and an engine of social change. After McAllister's efforts, *The Social Register* was published (in the 1880s) with ineffable cheek, by a bachelor listing nearly nine hundred families of the "socially elect," with addresses, schools, telephone numbers, and clubs.[8] Hard to tell the anonymous author's exact criteria for admission, but these were the people, in his words, "naturally included in the best society."

C. Wright Mills reckoned that the period 1890 to 1920—pretty well the period marked for our interest by the present chapter—was the defining three decades for entrance to the magic circle. As a measure of the contrast with the present, those ejected from *The Social Register* suffered dismissal because of "unfavourable publicity ... anyone who keeps out of newspaper columns—whatever his private life may be, or clandestine rumours may report—will not fall foul of *The Social Register*."[9]

This is not quite right, we already know. Publicity is the water which wealth must swim in, but for society to keep itself at a sufficient height, the water (until 1920 or so) had to be kept clean. This was the chlorinating effect of nineteenth-century Puritanism on the American rich. In London in 1820 everyone knew and was careless of Byron's mistresses and bastards; in Paris in 1848, they were instructed perforce and in print by the poet himself about Baudelaire's partners in bed; in New York in 1900, against a backdrop of ruthless financial piracy, brutal suppression of industrial dissent, police protection rackets, and the acknowledged enlistment of big-time criminals in both political and business competition, the families in the *Register* maintained an immaculate conception of private life. "Conspicuous consumption," in Veblen's famous phrase, was accompanied in the domestic realm by blameless respectability.

For several decades celebrity and *The Social Register* were more or less the same thing. Hollywood changed all that irrevocably, but even before *The Perils of Pauline* made the first world-famous film star out of Mary Pickford, the scaffolding of celebrity raised in London and Paris required those socially registered families, in particular their doyennes, to feel the spur of fame pricking their flanks, urging them on to the next dinner party or debutantes' coming-out from the awkward age, the next charitable ball or race-meeting.

In café society, Mills says, the major inhabitants of the world of the celebrity—the institutional elite (corporate rich, leading politicians, warlords), the metropolitan socialite (functionless moneymakers old and new), and the professional entertainer (stage and screen actors, certain kinds of sportsmen—racing drivers, aviators, explorers, sailors)—mingle, publicly cashing in on one another's claims for prestige. He goes on: "It is upon café society that all the spotlights of publicity often coincide, spreading the glamour found there to wider publics. For in café society glamour has become a hard fact of well-established business routines."[10]

Glamour, let us say again, is enviability made flesh. What is glamorously enviable in a society is a medley of values fashioned into a living work of art. The work of art will probably be vulgar, saccharine, meretricious, but it will have the properties of art: imaginative power picked up by its audience, a gleaming unity conferred in this case, perhaps, by youth, health, beauty, but in any case by *success*. Success is then the public and visible attainment of status and recognition. Different kinds of status retain recognition for varying periods of time; plenty of celebrities vanish overnight. Success shines with glamour only when it is held up with completeness and composure. The rules of glamour require impregnability.

I suggest, in the aftermath of these ruminations, that the hard exterior of success and the bright shine of glamour are the result of a blend fused in the collision of the socially registered and the new celebrities emerging in New York after 1900. The new stage for their action would, in a couple of decades, become the beach, the yacht, and the night club, not the Newport garden party nor the gilded ballroom. But the new compound carried off from Newport, from the Waldorf-Astoria, from the right Episcopalian churches and the best men's clubs—Boston's Somerset, Philadelphia's Racquet, New York's Knickerbocker and Brook—a dress code, a handbook of manners, tastes in food and drink, rules of self-presentation of both body and soul, a list of the preferred passions out of which film stars and newspaper barons could make, as they say, a lifestyle and a culture.

My history is neither a structural nor a narrative history. If anything, it is the social history of distinct stages and geographies in the growth of an industry. As such, short biographies of key industrialists have their explanatory place.

It is obvious that for the energy and insanity of American capitalism to work as it did, it had to create the newspapers and magazines with which to tell itself what was going on and how things ought to be. A poor little rich boy[11] arrived on cue to provide the necessary newspapers, to connect them as instruments of social machinery and the generation of money, certainly, and of success into the bargain, to the cinematograph, and to compress these complex processes into the mad fable of Xanadu, all to be played out forever by Orson Welles, as Citizen Kane.

William Randolph Hearst inherited the fortune his oldtimer father in a black slouch hat had made in the golden lodes of the Californian Gold Rush of 1849. That same high wind blew him into a seat in the Senate and a mansion beside the Golden Gate. His son was sober (drank only Coca-Cola from a silver mug at fifty), silent, iron-willed, truculent, thrown out of Harvard for sending each of his professors a chamberpot engraved with their portraits.

He asked father to buy him the San Francisco *Examiner* and turned it into the prime low-life newssheet by way of his sharp, streetwise young men and his own keen nose for a prurient populism—antitrust, dish the dirt on the stinking rich he knew personally, fix a gaolbreak for a beautiful Cuban revolutionary called Evangelina; then in his most famous coup he butted into America's short, pointless war with Spain by landing himself at Manila Bay carrying a Colt 45 and capturing a bunch of unarmed Spanish sailors.

This was the Press Baron played as buccaneer-democrat. Hearst had bought three newspapers in New York before he was thirty; he had his only rival, Pulitzer, rattled; he was tirelessly energetic; he married a girl in the chorus legline of *The Girl from Paris*; he made it to Congress. His papers opposed the war. By 1919 he believed he could run for president as Woodrow Wilson's health failed, his papers stood out against corruption in public life (Standard Oil bribing politicians) and for revelations from the sex lives of the rich, vilified trade unions and the Left by reflex, found much to praise in the new Chancellor of Germany in 1933. In a spectacle to match the Newporters, he built his Andalusian mansion at San Simeon, overlooking the Pacific and finally died there in solitude.

At fifty, however, he took up with another twenty-year-old dancer (from Ziegfeld Follies) and carried off his liaison with silent aplomb. By now, his terrific energy and malign vision were directed towards the movies, and he had purchased both the manufacturing company and the global distribution of *The Perils of Pauline*. Gore Vidal calls Hearst "a mindless genius, or an idiot savant";[12] for us he assumes a central position as supreme lord of the press just as the press assumed power on a worldwide (that is, American-dominated world) scale for the first time. Hearst was therefore the first such figure to attain world fame, and it was Orson Welles's genius in *Citizen Kane* to grasp the epic proportions of the story and turn it into tragic myth, of a man with a decisive genius for landing himself (well equipped with the necessary cash) on the intersections of political power and the roar of vulgarity, of sentimental narrative and the waves of history. Hearst had grasped that the important thing in the weird, unprecedented world of American moneymaking and power-broking was not to be right but to be audible, not to lead but to be *seen*.

The new city press in America took its subject matter from the amazing city itself, and it was a feature of those cities to be utterly distinctive, a distinction conferred partly by the characteristic production of each— timber, meat, grain, money, movies—and partly by the clamorous friction of its ethnic neighbourhoods. In this clamour, which had so scared the Londoner Charles Dickens, the new newspaper reported, and at times explained, the city to itself. The headline had to be noisy enough to catch attention over the din of the street; the vendor's ritual shriek and, until quite recently, his own shouted version of the headline had to cut through the same clatter and racket. The American paper shone with the glittering novelty of all that cities promised. Its pace ("the latest news," "stop press"), its compression of big events into simple headlines and brief reports, its ease of access, its dependable dismissal of boredom, its putting-you-in-touch, and its mastery over the force of circumstance all commended themselves to the (mostly) men for whom success in the city was the acquisition of these qualities. In Europe and the United States, *men* went in hats and out to work and filled the streets, and men first adopted the habit of reading the daily newspaper.

If that newspaper were to contain such a jostling and scattered plenitude of facts and fictions, it would have to classify specialisms for its reporters. Sense of it all had to be made in time for the next edition.

This was a messier and more urgent matter for the American than for the European editor. In Europe, the recognisable stories would be tied to politics, even if politics were to be turned into commercial packages. In America nobody had very much idea how to wring any sense out of this extraordinary new society, but if they were going to sell newspapers they would have to do so every day and with sufficient consistency to keep the readers happy.

To bring off this balancing act, editors and reporters between them had to improvise a variety of ways of doing the job, which was to say, ways of working and writing which would match the mixture of voices needed to fill the saleable list of contents in each daily. No wonder that those doing the improvisation in the city and then in the columns, and doing it in a way which would keep the peace between owner and editor, looked a shifty bunch and could find for many years no fixed abode in the social structure. They had to hunt out the news, and the news had to be new. Novelty-as-value is a creation of the novelist and journalist alike, and both as city-dwellers. The legendary "nose for news" of the reporter meant having the gift to sniff out those situations which would fuse briefly into an event capable of shock. Such an event, shaped by the reporter's way of seeing, must be brief, encompassable in a single silhouette, dramatic, "humanly interesting," at once recognisable *and* exceptional.

It is a tall order to find such contingencies every day. The only way one could anticipate such a sequence of necessary surprises would be to have at hand a pretty straightforward set of narrative classifications: of place, time, plot, and character. Exceptionality and abnormality as framed by "newsiness" became the speedily spotted signals of what the journalists were looking for. Since such attributes turned up frequently in the law courts and the police stations, those became the haunts of journalists and lent them at the same time their air of raffishness. Lawyers, with their high tone, manner, and handedness, commanded such places; policemen in the uniform of the state patrolled them; journalists hovered and sneaked in them, looking neither for retribution nor for justice but merely for that low thing, a story, a story to sell outside as cheaply and brazenly as possible.

So the offices of law and order became classified by the news industry as places which provided the facts for its fictions, and the "assignment" system began.

The second absolutely dependable source of stories was money and those who were known to possess it, the more so if they also displayed it and became thereby that quite new sort of character on the city stage, the celebrity—a creature partly self-made in eager response to the celebrity-making machinery of the city, partly made out of nothing much by that same machine in order to feed the insatiable, clattering presses.

Power is one source of celebrity, although some of the powerful are at pains to avoid it. In any case, power works in mysterious ways, and our attempt to catch it in action, whether we are journalists or citizens, is not helped by the crude way we have of understanding power as either "the great beast" of coercion or a bad smell ("old corruption"). Power for journalists is mysterious and alluring. The journalist hovers as close to it as possible, but even at those points at which he (and, as I remarked, in the late nineteenth century it was almost entirely "he") unmasks the ordinariness of the powerful, their power is enclosed by an estranging, glamorous, unanalysed aura.

Power attracts and repels. In the manufacture of news it first drew the reporter to itself to celebrate itself. The robber-barons encouraged journalists in this. But they also encouraged them in the exposure of power not their own. This sorted happily with those strong drives in American life and Constitution which counterposed power to freedom and independence and for which one way of keeping power down was to show up its quotidian frightfulness and cruelty.

Hence the journalism of revelation, exposure and "muckraking" (the new term supposedly coined by Teddy Roosevelt in 1906). If American journalism had no party politics and started out as strictly commercial, it came to politics by way of exposing the mighty on behalf of the ordinary, putting down their pretensions to probity and philanthropy by raking through the muck of their money and showing how inherently dirty was the business of making so much of it.

Muckraking went along with what came to be called reportage, which meant a plainly factual but humanly sympathetic storytelling about all those singular neighbourhoods, districts, and downright slums in which the new Americans battled to make themselves the life they could not make in old Europe. These pieces, often series of articles in journals such as *McClure's*, *Everybody's*, and *Collier's*, carried such classics as Lincoln Steffens's *The Shame of the Cities*, in which one of the big, flaring names on the staff documented the graft, corruption, and worker exploitation he found in St. Louis, Minneapolis, Cleveland, Pittsburgh, and Philadelphia as well as in the great wens of Chicago and New York. At more or less the same time, *McClure's* ran Ida Tarbell's influential series on John D. Rockefeller's Standard Oil. The stories she told, after four full years of her investigation, undercover and above ground, into crookedness, bullying, murderous brutality in the workforce, bribery and venality in the topmost circles of American fame and power, fuelled the successful campaign for antitrust legislation. In a similar vein, *McClure's* had printed Josiah Willard's "True Stories from the Underworld" and "In the World of Graft" (Willard's own coinage, they say) which, like Steffens's work and Lewis Hine's remarkable photographic exposure of ten-year-old children working in coal mines, combined reportage with *outrance*, careful social-scientific objectivity with a social conscience to match.

Muckraking lasted only ten years in its original form, although there were over two thousand essays in the genre. But it set a seal on the constitution of journalism, and however differently they wrote up their revelations, later journalists felt that old radical energy running through their bloodstream, earthing itself in their own lives. Muckraking gave its practitioners and the history of their profession a populist and progressive politics. It provided the profession with one of its most unkillable superstitions: the honest, small-town reporter who, in simple pursuit of the facts, mortally wounds the enemies of the people, city bosses, robber barons, king gangsters, and such. In truth, the muckrakers won reforming victories. As a question in the uses of literacy, it may be that revelation of big graft on the part of Mr. Big did him no harm at all, and that the local readership enjoyed the local gossip without drawing either progressive or reactionary morals. Maybe Mr. Big himself thrived on publicity, and maybe even the cleaning up of city shame would have come about without the press. However all this may be, the crux for us is the journalist-investigator and the powerful biographies this character added to the stock of liveable narratives in the trade.

Hearst, Pulitzer, in Britain Northcliffe and Beaverbrook, possessed vast wealth, and they loosened its grip on social structure. They did much, therefore, for better and worse, to replace old money with mere money; to break off longevity and tradition, and replace them, with chance and chancers. These men and the many like them stand at the main gate of modernity. In their curious way they understand it well. Intuitively, we shall say by way of explanation, they felt strange currents pass through them and found a way, a partial and extravagant way, of harnessing those energies.

They felt the stirrings of vast masses of people who had never known how to speak in public about anything at all, and certainly had not been asked. They sensed that the moment of the demagogue, armed with God knows what ideological rant, had come and thrilled at the thought. They saw that this weird new confection, the newspaper, made a headlong world briefly intelligible to the unprecedentedly great expectations of poor, free people determined to hand prosperity to their children; their imaginations seethed at the sight, and they found they could speak strange tongues. They saw that they could cause wars or peace, and they loved it. So they fired and hired, bullied and hustled, drank and fornicated, becoming legends in their own minds and for the space of brief times.

III

The piratical entrepreneurs of the press had set themselves to capture unprecedented new audiences. As the states united themselves along a frontier further and further westwards, the small, insistently local newspapers found themselves, for all the strong American allegiance to localism, without the staff or the reach to keep their readers up-to-date about the doings of the mighty which had such consequence for their lives. Pulitzer was quick to syndicate his best-known columnists; the telegraph was sending the essential news from Wall Street to hot and tiny offices in Montana and

Arizona; the local paper had to thrive on its necessity to *be* local, to hold up a neighbourly and a prairie pride against the great cities which would dispatch their tales of fame and fashion, of meat and money and new technology so unstoppably down every little Main Street.

Sheer wealth was what commanded attention, and although it might be made anywhere in this amazing land, as soon as it was, it fled to the biggest cities, New York and Chicago above all. There the Gilded Age began and put on its airs and graces with astonishing speed and resourcefulness. In no time, the fashions of the Galeries Lafayette, themselves copied and mass produced from the leaders of haute couture Paris (the phrase, Larousse tells us, dates from the 1840s), appeared in the windows of Macy's and, slightly more expensively, Bloomingdale's.[13] When they did so, when they joined the Easter Parade, Pulitzer's men and women, and those of the rivals—James Gordon Bennett, William Randolph Hearst—were watching.

The reporters watched and reported the fashions within the frame of a simple, telling sociology. For owner and journalist alike were clear that what counted in this headlong and unfabled economy was the man who made it work for him, and the stories which gave off the glow of cash or cow, iron or railroad, ships or wheat, were the stories which gripped the imagination of their readers, themselves piling off the immigration boats in order to pile into the scrum where fortunes were made. Naturally, the stories on the flipside were those of failure, of fortunes lost and opportunities missed, of criminal daring and its rewards punished, of virtue and hard work disregarded by fate.

The lead stories were success stories, and success was found in making fortunes. So the newspaper owners sent their men, and later their women, to conduct "interviews" (another neologism) and write "profiles" of the successful. A well-off man of letters called William Dean Howells, editor of a sound literary magazine, a capable novelist, friend of the James family, wrote an illuminating novel about this sort of encounter and, indeed, about the nature of robber barons. In *The Rise of Silas Lapham*,[14] the journalist Bartley Hubbard writes a profile of Lapham, a paint magnate, and tries to take the moral measure of a man standing astride a ruthless economy, but not without complexity, cultivation, an ironic sense of what he has had to do to win his victories and enjoy his wealth.

Irony, of course, is of its nature self-exculpating. To be ironic at one's own expense, as Silas Lapham is, is still to leave one's interlocutor paying the moral bills. But Hubbard in his profile has grasped something of Lapham's necessity in such an era—in a way Henry James failed to do with Adam Verver in *The Golden Bowl*, exactly because to be the millionaire he was, Verver would also have had to be, on his day, hard, cruel, and piratical rather than, as he is pictured, wise, gentle, and compassionate. Very rich or powerful men keep their lives in tight compartments, one is told; but not that tight.

Bartley Hubbard tells rare truths in his article. The actual interviewer-journalists were probably not as acute, and in any case were sent out, as a memorandum of Pulitzer's to his editors put it, to connect the colossally wealthy to a vast and scattered readership, half of it speaking American only awkwardly and not when at home, split into Germans, Italians, Irish, Norwegian, English, Scottish, Poles, Russians, Greeks, Chinese, each national group divided and opposed within itself, all alike seized by the passion to make of their own lives a lesser but sufficient version of the huge biographies, J. P. Morgan, Andrew Carnegie, Philip Armour, John D Rockefeller, Henry Clay Frick.[15]

Pulitzer wrote: "Please impress on the men who write our interviews with prominent men the importance of giving a striking, vivid pen sketch of the subject; also a vivid picture of the domestic environment, his wife, his children, his animal pets, etc. These are the things that will bring him more closely home to the average reader."[16]

Mostly the style of the profiles of the rich was respectful; only gradually did the writers conduct the interviews with a view somehow to compromising the subject, to winning embarrassment from a remark, admission of failure or (better still) of enmity and dislike for a rival. These banal kinds of conflict have, a century later and more, become the very structure of interviews with the famous, especially the politically famous, and the public figures themselves quickly learn to bat away any probes with a dangerous point to them.

Yet the early profile-writers could not and would not simply write of the rich as enviable. The strong strain in American popular culture resentful of any assigned superiority on the part of others, and a still rigorous

Episcopalian and nonconformist tradition of a plain-living distaste for mere wealth and its showing-off, united in a sharp qualification of vulgar money-worship allied to a sound suspicion of power itself.

This transpired from two veins of journalism opened up after 1900 or so and allowed to bleed plentifully across the columns of both "the muck-rakers" and "the sob-sisters" (excellent blunt names, both of them). The sob-sisters, led by Adela St. Johns ahead of Winifred Black and Nicola Greeley-Smith, made rather more extended "home visits" than there was room for in a daily. They wrote for *Munsey's* "In the Public Eye" column, for *McClure's*, *Collier's*, the *Saturday Evening Post*, and the *Ladies Home Journal*, and their subjects were more likely to be the wives than the robber-barons themselves, and their material the taste, the attractiveness, the in-telligence, the possessions, and, if possible, the human interest of their subjects, plainly understood as forgivable misdemeanour, slight personal weakness, and, best of all, family tragedy or, at least, domestic (but not marital) mishap.

To our eyes now, it was patball. Yet like all discourse formation, its his-tory is easy to read in the present. When Adela St. Johns interviewed Clara Bow, she was (typically) intent upon presenting the actress as having "a strange and complex nature" which "slips through your fingers like quick-silver,"[17] and a little later, at the very start of Katharine Hepburn's lengthy career, was at pains to present that formidable woman in the pages of *Lib-erty* as a combination of "iconoclast" with a "modern marriage" along with a "maternal soul just like her mother's."

Gossip columnists had to pay on both sides; they did so in virtue of the social values which, collectively enshrined in the mind of their times and its frame of feeling, held both participants in the interview together and transmitted its force to the readership.

This was no less true of the muckrakers (it is platitudinously true of a whole society). When Lincoln Steffens and Ida Tarbell wrote their "expo-sés"—another important coinage, along with the workload put upon the verb "to reveal"—of corporate corruption, a heroic moment in the history of journalism, they spoke precisely to and for that strong tradition of local and upright domestic dignity and churchly rejection of extreme wealth which characterised so many aspirant Americans of 1900, and did so in their own idiom. That idiom was homely enough, but plain, unmalicious, sentimental, raucous on occasions, its desires shaped to an image of the self not congruent with French or English readers at the same time.

Across the Atlantic, as we saw, not without repugnance, *all* social attitudes and the feelings which propped them up were suffused with social class: with its resentments, its exclusions, its cruelty, and its soft blandishments. In the United States, there was certainly a class structure consolidating itself fast, but doing so around new wealth, refracted through the imagery of *success*, a curious value in itself.

For success was not just to be measured in mountains of dollars. The tides of Romanticism had also rolled across the Atlantic, leaving behind most of Mr. Dombey's deadly coldness and unbending hauteur, but sweeping with them plenty of the turbulence of acquisition, aesthetics, showmanship, and, above all, the new doctrines of selfhood.[18] These counselled the successful, if they were men, to be strong-minded, ruthless in business, physically fit and adventurous (handsome, too, if it could be arranged), "colourful" (a keyword) in manner and turns of phrase, humanly accessible, varied in taste and response to the world ... anyone can extend the list; we live by it now.

Their womenfolk (in the phrase) were to be complementarily soft, gracious, amusing, talented (cooks, pianists, water-colourists, with an eye for dashing dress and striking coiffure), ardent, good-looking, shapely, piquant, faithful ... these were demanding terms; no wonder they led to tears and the green sickness upstairs. For in the hands of the profilers, gossip columnists, and sob-sisters, they were magnified and projected upon the huge invisible screen towering above the rapt faces of both high society and all those who took their lead, sprinkled with salt, from the columnists' "People Often Talked Of" and "In the Public Eye."

Henry Pringle's profiles in *Collier's*, the *Ladies Home Journal*, even the (tonier, by far) *New Yorker* held his readership for thirty years, as did Adela St. Johns in Hearst's *Herald*, also in the *Ladies Home Journal* and in the *Saturday Evening Post*, where Norman Rockwell's icons (it is for once the right word) so regularly defined the nation's levelly sentimental image of its best domestic parts. It was not until the advent of Walter Winchell that the terms of reference began to include a more bitter, rat poisonous taste.

Winchell, in his horrible way an astute and creative kind of Tartuffe, reinvented the gossip column as a subtle tissue of malignant innuendo, genuine and truthful discovery, systematic denigration, and old-fashioned toadying. He was the prototype for the loathsome figure played by Burt Lancaster in the happily named *Sweet Smell of Success* (1957) and counts for much in this corner of our story because, unlike even the great muck-rakers Ida Tarbell and Lincoln Steffens, who pretended to the status of tribunes of the people, he pushed his way into the closed circles of the very rich, into the principal offices on Capitol Hill, and juxtaposed in his column the high, the mighty, the downright shady, and the appalling little tarts and hangers-on (like the ghastly parasite played by Tony Curtis in *Sweet Smell of Success*).

Winchell announced, even caused, that strain in the manufacture of fame which strives always to damage, disgrace, humiliate, or merely em-barrass the mighty, and trip them up. The stuff of this was sex, on the ethics of which the rich, successful, and attractive elite is dependably to be caught out if not in duplicity, then (which is just as tasty) in intimacy. For the society shaped by London and Paris and then transmuted in New York marked a strict boundary between the public persona and the private self. Admission to private selves and their world was just what the first gossip columnists had to obtain and, once through the door, respect. Only as they acquired their own fame (as in the case of Walter Winchell) could they administer any moral tonic or a shot of cynicism.

IV

Bitterness, malice, spite, envy, these savoury unpleasantnesses could be given freer rein at the lower level of the celebrity hierarchy which so quickly established itself in the gilded age. After (or alongside) the business rich, the politicians; after them, however, an uncertain medley, comprising new heroes and heroines of high technological travel (racing car drivers, aviators, yachtsmen), who joined the established elite of artists (always on the edge of rebellion) and the leading exponents of recently professional-ized sport.

This is not the place to go into the invention of sporting celebrity. I try that out in more circumspect detail later. The point at this stage is to fix the outline of the gossip columnist's ideal character, specific no doubt to each social type (businessman, wealthy wife, sportsman, actor) but overlapping in certain important repetitions. So the ideal sportsman remained, in the antique designation, true to sportsmanlike values. That is, he (and until Suzanne Lenglen came along in the twenties, it was only "he") resisted the idea of winning at all costs, of not playing for the team but for his own greater glory, of acquisitiveness. The good sport was modest, encouraging to youngsters, accessible to passers-by, a family man, a law-abiding player and citizen, apolitical. Occasionally, in the individualistic sports—boxing—he might be "colourful" like Jackson or "rugged" like Jack Dempsey, but if caught out drunk, or living it up too high at the gaming tables or among fast girls, then the columnists wrote, more in sorrow than smirking, about "letting down the fans." They could not speak well enough of Bobby Jones, the amateur gentleman-golfer from the South, who won the Grand Slam but always, as Paul Gallico put it, "wanted golf to remain a beloved game."[19] These accents still touch one's heart when one contemplates the ruin brought to sport by the globalisation of capital.

I suppose it was the film stars on whom the columnists could really spread themselves in the United States, after about 1916 or so, by which time Hearst had bought and circulated *The Perils of Pauline*, the silent thriller-serial in which Mary Pickford was left, each week, tied helplessly to the railroad as the Silver Streak hurtled towards her.

But both diction for and judgement on actors had been formed around Sarah Siddons and David Garrick back in the 1770s, and the latest gossip lived on and off much the same dualities and contradictions: proprietorship and adulation; well-dressed public figure and bare forked animal; envy and malice; applause and the raspberry. A veering tone was written into the rhythm and has only become a deeper and more sickening swell ever since.

Which is not to say that there was not plenty to feel queasy about, nor that the celebrities at once self-made as well as confected, as you might say, for public consumption, were not subjects ripe with ambivalence and damned hard to evaluate. Our realisation here must again be that *they were what there was*. At our very beginning, when we looked over the shoulders of the crowds in Cheapside, pledging themselves to Queen Elizabeth I, receiving in return her pledge of herself and her blood and body, bedecked in the magic of gold and jewels, we were watching the public drama of political power subtending its best picture of itself. In the same way, a wholly different politics and its means of cultural dramatisation is enacted in the interplay of columnist and celebrity. "A constellation of ideas," in Geertz's all-inclusive phrase,[20] makes itself visible in the public conversation about greatness, its virtue and viciousness.

V

As always, that conversation turns on what it is to live a life worth living. As I have suggested several times already, the great novelists of the period between 1860 and 1920 or so both reflect and bring about certain key changes in this gripping topic, the very heart of all lives.

They alert us, just as the journalists do, to the vast power intrinsic to the Romantic doctrine of self-expression and self-fulfilment, and they render on the page the bafflement experienced when turning this magnetic possibility into action, an action which must remain true to the discovered self. Making money *tout court* will hardly do, and the acquisition of blank power has neither destiny nor destination. That is the trouble for a tyrant; his imagination has nothing to work on but the retention of power. Apart from that, the only narratives at hand for such a limited purpose are warfare or the orgy.

The American heroes and heroines of Henry James, William Dean Howells, Edith Wharton, theorists of the leisure class (as Thorstein Veblen called his vinegary classic of sociology[21]), addressed the question of how to live well when you made your fortune in the America of the period, when you *could not* have made it without cruelty, ruthlessness, pitiless self-regard. No doubt many of those qualities were needed by British and French imperial chancers, but for the American writers, whether popular or populist, European brutality was mitigated by tradition, longevity, a settled landscape, and a noble house—all the subtle stuff of manners and action whose absence James himself famously lamented in Boston: "no state, no national name, no sovereign, no court; no aristocracy, no church, no army, no diplomatic service, no country gentleman, no palaces, no castles, no manors, no old country houses, no parsonages, no thatched cottages, no ivied mills, no cathedrals, no great universities, no political society, no sporting class ."[22]

Americans wanted all this, all right, but they also wanted their free-and-easy democracy, their colossal geography, the thrill of lawlessness in the Panhandle.

So the question of what to do to make a virtuous narrative was a tricky one. Even in England, by 1900 it had been borne in upon the cultivated classes that their comforts were dearly bought at other people's expense, and even that those other people might have, as Dickens had told them, manners and graces unknown to cultivation in its more expensive attire. In France, of course, the same perception had led to blood in the bucket, yet the good life as equipped for taste, dress, property, art and its objects, and the laden table, still won out and hands down.

So social action for the novelists and the journalists alike justified itself in private lives and conspicuous leisure. Sure, the money had to be made, but its blossom was made manifest in such fruits of the spirit as (and supremely) works of art, exquisite but unassuming dress, careful and uncondescending courtesy, the reticence of high, withheld intelligence, discreet but massive generosity towards the nation, a complex and interestingly ironic attitude to life.

Against these grand, middle-aged, and bounteous qualities, exuding the certainty of success, the narratives of spontaneity, passionate (probably erotic) expression, vivid impulsiveness, hot allegiance, financial insouciance thrust themselves forward on the side of youth. Calm and fulfilled marriage on one side, the reckless love affair on the other; this is the twist-point of value as the First World War trundled over the horizon, and it was in these terms that celebrity was called onstage to enact the constellation of ideas.

Drama thrives on the collision of values in which either the admirable or the hateful is destroyed. In this short fresco of American life culminating in 1920, the gangster as celebrity is one favourite such action, particularly in the United States where social forms were so plastic, and success so defined in terms of physical action and sudden reward—gold mines, railroads, herds of cattle, newspapers, murder. So the ambiguous dramas of Al Capone, John Dillinger, the Pinkerton agency, and the grisly escapade in a garage on St. Valentine's Day have a brightly lit corner in the moral imagination of the epoch, and in ours, its inheritor. What makes Francis Ford Coppola's masterpiece trilogy, *The Godfather*, into America's *Henry*

IV and its *Coriolanus* is the vividness as well as the steady pace with which he melds the gangster and the businessman, Eros and Nemesis, the bandit and the patriarch. The success of the movie, its promotion to a classic of world cinema, is a mark of a universal recognition of its truthfulness *and* a response to the pull of its Nietszchean ethics. (Remember how satisfying it is when Robert Ryan as the crooked cop is shot across the pasta and in the head by Pacino in the restaurant?)

Accordingly, it serves as vividly re-creating not so much our accurate memory of either 1920 or 1946 (though no one doubts its fidelity to appearances) as the thrilling, forbidden alliance of daring crime and business ethics, of murder and fidelity, of the contradictory authority of law and lawlessness, greed and courage, in American definitions of success.

Insofar as the plain, blunt reader comes from Hume's "middle station" in life, he or she would be right to sup holding a very long spoon with the characters enumerated in this chapter. But it is hard to withhold both awe and fascination at quite such a display of bright colour and dark energy, such *suffisance* and address, such will-to-power and conspicuous generosity. Thinking along these lines, one might come to ruminate that there are worse ways than those of American celebrity in the first twenty years of the last century to put on show the meanings of our lives.

PART III   The Past in the Present

Chapter 6

The Geography of Recognition:
Celebrity on Its Holidays

As folk history and the advertisers never tire of reminding us, Thomas Cook arranged his first excursion in a treasured haven of temperance and the family. He chartered a train on July 5, 1841, which was to take a medley of citizens and their children away for a day from the dangerous licence of industrial Leicester during a public holiday to Loughborough, not twenty miles away, a little market town without a public house.

In no time (that is, by 1869) his business had run away with itself, and he was organising tourist cruises to the pyramids and was patronised by the still-powerful forces of aristocracy and the dependably indiscreet and tubby form of another Prince of Wales, who only became a rather hapless Edward VII in 1902 and after a deucedly long wait.

The holiday was another conspicuous product of the changes I have recorded in Paris, London, and New York between 1860 and the outbreak of the First World War.[1] The industrial working class in Britain had fought for and, very gradually, won extensions of leisure time which expanded the old Wakes Week from northern cities nationwide and made the seaside holiday in Blackpool and Scarborough, Margate and Brighton, available to men and women who had never seen the sea.

Meanwhile, the middle classes, in their endless, silent competition, had colonised and reinvented le Touquet and Deauville, Bournemouth and Atlantic City, for the venerable pastime of showing off at leisure. The capitalism of the department store and the travel agent was quick to spot a new correspondence between the structure of middle-class feelings, the margin of disposable income, the orderings of time and the spending of its freedoms, all together with the arrangements of an accessible geography.

The vacation predicates time and money to be spent finding the right place to have the best feelings. Rightness will combine ruggedness with luxury, self-improvement with self-gratification. The holiday is to provide easy and adventurous travel; it will be punctuated with art and historical instruction, which are always good for you in modest doses and which had been written into the syllabus by the Romantic poets and painters; it will encourage a taking off of city uniform and a putting on of holiday gear: boaters, blazers, light organdie dresses, with ribbons and sailor suits for the children; all this abandon and insouciance will also, it was to be hoped, sweep holidaymakers off their feet and into sex.

It is hardly surprising that the place which best gave rise to all this was the north Mediterranean littoral. Those seas, rocks, groves, columns, and sands, amongst which lingered the delicious echoes of classicism, of Nausicaa and Icarus, Andromeda and Hercules, gathered and intensified the images of leisure, luxury, and freedom. It had been just those poems and that architecture of the small city-states which, two and a half millennia ago, gave birth to the first rough ideas of beauty, selfhood, and human flourishing.

That, at least, was the folk history which led the imperialists of the holidays to the Mediterranean. All that went under the name of vacationing was turned by capitalism's alchemy and its house magicians in the advertising agencies into a world whose roots were in the Galeries Lafayette and Selfridges, as well as in the parks and riverside walks of the capitals. But the Mediterranean seaside world offered a fulfilment always stretched a little too far, its aspiration always tilting down at the last towards disappointment. It is a world immaterially materialised by the new value, glamour, which we may think of, as already suggested, as the untouchable closeness of luxurious enviability. After Hollywood began its necromancy, the glamorous figure appeared as intimately known but inimitable, quite without physical blemish, smooth and swift and shining as a seal, past us on the other side of the barriers in a flash. The experience of seeing the star glowing with glamour lends itself to the Mediterranean holiday; it is no accident that the Biennale came to be held in Venice and the Film Festival at Cannes. The holiday is the world of spectacle, time a sequence of foreshortened moments caught on camera, pleasure a work rate (one cathedral, one master fresco, one celebrity, one glass of Brunello is a memorable day); leisure pays its dividends and the hours spent lying in the sun pay for the golden tan.

II

The rich we always have with us, and the realm of their leisure expanded, as usual, well ahead of everybody else's until they came up against the peculiar excesses of late twentieth-century acquisitiveness, whereafter, for a time, avarice and stupefying wealth, taken together, will not let their owners rest. The strange new international elite who thus combine glamour and overwork, greed and asceticism, will figure as ominous omens of a postmillennial irresponsibility when we come to the doors of the future. In the meantime the creation of leisure and the competition to buy and sell it are best understood as a history of how to feel, how to imagine, how to yearn, and how to go places and do nothing.

It was in our beginnings in the 1760s that the great German tastemonger, Winckelmann, reaffirmed antiquity as guide and tutor to the young blades and middle-aged scholar-sybarites of the Grand Tour and taught them of the lavishness and grace of old Italy. Admiring the paintings of Claude and Poussin, they drank copiously from the Pierian springs. In visiting the excavations, at Pompeii and Herculaneum as well as in Rome, they rediscovered the power of the old poets whose lines they had learned by heart painfully to analyse and construe in the long drudgery of ruling-class education in the eighteenth century. Behind them, in turn, stood the great fortresses of Renaissance learning built out of the materials of rediscovery, when the intellectual riches of Catholicism were first broken open by the Italians, the Germans, and finally the Dutch and English, and the new humanism was effected from the union of classicism and Christianity.

New culture grows out of old residues. Boswell and Lady Mary Wortley Montagu doubtless knew much of Virgil by heart, but plenty of those grandish tourists who solemnly visited Avernus just north of Naples, where Aeneas escorted Virgil down to the underworld in order to meet the shades, did not. Nonetheless, their little outing, presaging a large picnic, was tribute paid to those who *did* know the old poets by heart, and their brief moment of indifferent attention to the dark lake acknowledged the presence of the Mediterranean in their formation.

The Mediterranean meant, and means no doubt, much more than the imagery of the Latin authors. But the poets fixed up the first views of its geography. We owe to them, just as we do to Poussin, Claude, and company, our familiarity with olive tree, cypress, and vineyard, white marble and quiet water. We owe them the very idea of *belvedere*, of a view opening gradually beyond the slopes and coppices which frame it into the largeness of distance and the curves of the horizon. We even owe them the plans and poetics of the houses from which we shall see these views. It was the Augustan Romans who invented the country villa and its direct descendant, the holiday home, and the classier kind of seaside hotel with its courtyards, balconies, and poolside greenery.

After 1900 or so, modernity swept in through the Straits of Gibraltar, and on its irresistible tide was also carried the flotsam of meanings which make for the other side of tourism. So far, I have spoken (from the bottom of my heart) for the noble settlement and sediment of Mediterranean life in our feelings and values. But here come the others, the boisterous, the gluttonous, the lecherous, the sociable, the reckless, and the free, come, as the slightly priggish narrator in *The Great Gatsby* himself put it, "with a simplicity of heart which was its own ticket of admission" and "after that conducted themselves according to the rules of behaviour associated with an amusement park."

Until, let us say, the 1890s, the male halves of the haute bourgeoisie on tour had made no distinction between those places in which they would be assiduous in scholarship and culture, and those places where they would misbehave themselves with women, wine, and a general class propensity to throw things about and break them. Tintoretto and Cicero, swimming or riding, and falling in love with married women went together just fine for Byron and Boswell.

That strain in the complex interminglings of the tourist's values which pulls our heroes towards tasty licentiousness began, towards the end of the nineteenth century, to find for itself a separate zone of practice. The undoubted attractions of fun and games had been happily indulged when the grand tourists arrived in Florence and Naples, for they had not looked around much on their condescending way through Provence. If they had, indeed, there was little enough for them to see: evil lodgings, wretched fishing villages, a mere glimpse of the Romans at Orange and St. Remy, nothing of the magnificence with which they associated antiquity and its Renaissance restatement and would find in the fountains of Rome. News got back home about their antics, of course, and angry fathers paid off betrayed mistresses, met the cost of breaches of promise, and closed down allowances to their prodigal sons. But misdemeanours of this sort went, as they say, with the territory, and the territory in question was the big city on the tourist trail; Paris first no doubt, but above all, Italy.

Capitalism in general, and railways in particular brought a new moral tone to tourism. The respectable middle classes were on the move south, and while self-improvement by judicious contact with uplifting master-pieces was very much the point of the trip, drunkenness and fornication were not. Though there is no doubt from all they wrote that the young men and, beside them, the young women of the travelling bourgeoisie found the whole adventure to be, when the moment was right, exhilarat-ingly free and reckless, they were easily and, so far as one can tell, nonsen-sually satisfied. The tougher eggs among the women—someone like Mary Kingsley, for instance—had stomped off into the wilderness to see (and understand) what the natives were up to.[2] But for her sisters, to whom such travel was new, the excitements of art were quite thrilling enough. Lucy Honeychurch in 1906 and Forster's novel *A Room with a View*, in spite of her deep respectability and a temperament capable when things went wrong "of joining the vast army of the benighted, who march to their destiny by catchwords," is swept up by the appeal of young Mr. Emerson to freedom, to spontaneity and the wise recklessness of the heart.

As her class emerged from its shabby *pensione* with its Cockney-Italian landlady, so it brought to birth, as we have seen in the Bois de Boulogne, the new social group, so distinctly the progeny of the bourgeoisie, so dog-gedly braced against it. These *épateurs* began to invent the uniform of the Bohemian regiment, and to imply that life be best understood and lived as a permanent vacation. Baudelaire, doomed poet, and his brother artist, the free, the dashing, the radical and unrespectable Gustave Courbet, turned *outrance* against a daily working schedule into a way of life.

This class fraction led the way in restoring an agreeable licentiousness to being away from home, and sex being what it was for respectable Vic-torians, its members made much of breaking the sexual rules. Being an artist and sleeping with people to whom one was not married went happily together. The scenery of *La Bohème*, of not having any money and living in a top-floor attic studio, comes from the same moment of fin-de-siècle as does Gilbert and Sullivan's sardonically named *Patience*.

There are always plenty of people, however, eager to join in a little self-indulgence and flouting of convention quite without the prior qualification of artistic talent. The enthusiasm of the appropriate segments of the ruling class for a high old time was hardly diminished by the arrival of the censorious bourgeois, and indeed may have been confirmed by it. The rich were becoming, in this unprecedentedly moneymaking and mobile society, not only enviable but emulable. Plenty of novels and moralising anecdotes of the 1880s warned of the debauchery of younger sons wasting their fathers' new-made fortunes.

So there was a mutual pull towards one another of raffish aristocracy and artists. The division of labour being what it is, artists sought out other artists to talk to. Now that the art patron had disappeared and stately old genre painting gone down before this new impressionist stuff, artists needed dealers, buyers, and markets just as they urgently needed good light and cheap lodgings. Paris was expensive and rainy. The place to go for the light and the colours as well as much cheaper rooms to rent was the South. Van Gogh wrote on his arrival in Arles to his brother Theo: "One night I went for a walk by the sea along the empty shore. It was not gay, but neither was it sad—it was—beautiful. The deep blue sky was flecked with clouds of a blue deeper than the fundamental blue of intense cobalt, and others of a clearer blue, like the blue whiteness of the Milky Way."[3] He painted the bright yellow lights of the café, and the amazing blues, at midnight and midday, of the Provençal sky. And he painted the sun and its flower.

This was a new kind of painting, familiar, domestic, cherishing the small details of sunlit life in the South. Cézanne had been down here forever, doing the same thing of course, and together they established a local subject matter—pine trees, fruit, chairs, unguarded, off-duty human bodies—which drew other painters, world-famous ones, after them, Bonnard, Matisse, Picasso. Quickly and involuntarily, the South of France became a place to play the new game of art-celebrity-spotting.

It was not the artists who invented the Côte d'Azur. (The phrase was coined by a guidebook in the literary manner published in 1887.) Money had to do it first. But as money did, it brought its different flush of colour to the Mediterranean passion. This was the moment of the invention of the seaside. People with money and political power also took themselves away from the cold Parisian grey and, like Napoleon III's prime minister, Ollivier, built themselves Plinian villas in which to write and become leisured scholars and sages. For a long time Nice had been an anomaly, geographically in France but belonging to Italy (Garibaldi was born there), speaking neither language The chief ports of the coast had always been Genoa and Marseilles, and it was not until 1860 that Cavour and Napoleon III struck a deal, the Niçois voted "yes" in a referendum, and Nice, having always been either Provençal or Italian, became French.

More to our point, once the railway had arrived from Marseilles in Nice in 1864 and one François Blanc, a hugely successful casino owner in the German spa of Bad Homburg, so oiled the wheels of railway development with cheap and enormous loans to the French exchequer that the trains from Nice began to arrive in Monte Carlo by 1868, within two years visitors to Monaco totalled 150,000, and in 1875 celebrity-spotters were gratified by the arrival of the then Prince of Wales, a presence certain to encourage all big spenders, stout parties, and genteel adulterers.[4]

The colossal success of the Casino at Monte Carlo and its lesser imitator down the railroad at Nice meant that the money pouring into the South of France had an agreeably risky, raffish, chancy savour to it. It lent the Côte d'Azur more of that daring perfume which separated it from the classical itinerary of the Tour and made this a place not only for *outrance* but also for gay abandon, kicking over the traces, sowing wild oats, all those touchingly dated phrases with which to name the delightful risklessness of holiday impudences so easily deleted from one's resumé when one gets back home to work.

The mixture was well brewed by 1890. Monte Carlo for the gambling and the celebrities; St. Tropez and Cannes for the artists; Nice for the lavish hotels and the Promenade des Anglais—the splendid palm-clad seafront, overlooked by all those priceless, bulbous, palazzo-style hotels, dominated by the Palais de la Mediterranée; lastly, Menton for the hypochondriac, the convalescent, and those dying of tuberculosis. All those hotels sprang into such solid and towering reality in the same two or three decades as everywhere else, but on the Côte d'Azur, of course, they were covered in dazzling, icing-sugar-white stucco, still the ultimate sign of a Mediterranean and Victorian luxury borrowed from Brighton. The Promenade des Anglais is one long line of opulent wedding cakes, this one with a timely touch of Moorishness, that one pure Victorian Gothic, here a little further east, the arcaded, pillared, stained-glass monster casino, the palais itself, completed in 1929 as it were from the picture-palace recipe books, Odeon, Regal, Granada, of the day. The casino at Monte Carlo, antedating it by half a century, is a different sort of monster, colonnaded, domed, crenellated, minaretted, every kind of sumptuous ornament in and out, and surrounded by elaborate tropical gardens, but still sedately of its day, the home of the *haut ton*, king, electors, princes, counts, taking the kind of time out they would have called "naughty."

The new class of high livers had a short enough day beside the sea, dressed in the new clothes of glamour. By the time the Second World War came and the Mediterranean closed for a season, glamour had become the key commodity of this weird new *Stand* (Max Weber's word) whose outline one can see in Nice, Monte Carlo, St. Tropez and Bandol by the late 1930s, and which now occupies so much of our publicly imaginative life.

A *Stand* is a subclass, and the members of this one were the smart set, the *demi-mondaines*, the Bright Young Things, the Idle Rich, the fashionable writers, artists, film directors, aristocrats, quondam princelings, bankers, playboys, millionaire titans, and their innumerable hangers-on and *vivandières* who flocked to the strip of beach, seafront, main street, and scrubby hillside which was the Riviera. Scott Fitzgerald apostrophised them in *Tender Is the Night* and saw, with bitter regret, how the Beautiful People turned flabby and mad, the devastatingly good-looking ingénue boiled hard, and the brilliant pyrotechnics burned out. Maybe Fitzgerald himself was much too apt to flourish his own metaphors—ones like fireworks cascading and fading into darkness. It is a tonic instead to hear Martha Gellhorn tell Mary Blume roundly that when she hitchhiked there to stay with a college friend in 1930 (it was a student destination even then): "I just knew it was no good—a bunch of crooks and loonies, low-class American expatriates and filmy people like the Dolly Sisters. We went one night to the casino and I saw those claws coming out covered with rings and I thought thank God, I'm young and poor."[5] Applause for that. When you look at the rich vacancy, the preposterous nothingness of the life led on the Riviera by the Duke and Duchess of Windsor in amongst all those other deposits of the belated end of absolutism and anciens regimes, then you think, serve them right.

Yet that pointless, self-celebrating way of life made something enduring—horrible in itself, perhaps, but still fascinating us. It assembled the culture of glamour, cut its uniform, wrote its schedules, planned its manufacturing procedures, weighed its profits. The Côte d'Azur was, with Hollywood, a showcase for advertising and what was soon and well called show business. Indeed, Nice and Cannes and the rest, warm and splendid as their front-of-houses are, became the lens through which we could see really close up the stars who make fashion and turn the wheels of its industry. The celebrity mixture of the 1930s—out-of-work royalty, film directors, film stars, gamblers, artists, and gangsters, the awful motley of the international rich—prepared the ground for the big occasions of the postwar boom to be thoroughly institutionalised. The centrepiece festival and fashion shows, the countless minor self-displays of related industries, fix the French and Italian Riviera in a crucial spot for the functioning of the cultural industries by 1930, as everyone now puts it, at the cutting edge of capitalism and an unignorable presence in its international politics.

The metaphors for such life lie ready to hand: "frothy" maybe, "scummy" even. One can only turn away in disgust at what all this parading and photographing and crowding-round-to-get-a-glimpse-of-the-star does to people on either side of the camera. When Roger Vadim made in 1957 his utterly harmless little movie about the prettiest girl he had ever seen, *Et Dieu Créa la Femme*, Brigitte Bardot lost any chance of living a happy or even a sane life, and St. Tropez finally lost any chance of remaining the neatest fishing village on the coast.

It will not do, however, just to wag one's elderly head over the deturpation of things. Movies are seriously judged at Cannes, paintings at Venice. Indeed, the Côte d'Azur is still a magnetic geography for painters joining the great, living tradition of impressionism and modernism. After all, Mont St. Victoire stands exactly as Cézanne painted it so many times. Matisse settled down there for the second half of his life, paid little attention to the Germans after 1940, found his red room and his headland, painted the big pines overlooking the Cap d'Antibes, and faded quietly away in the plain house with peeling shutters behind the closed iron gates. Their mighty paintings, rooted in that ancient land, serve to remind us that great art retains its power, and so does a beautiful coastline, whatever the rich do to them both. Moreover, people will always conceive new places for new self-conceptions. As vacations, holidays, and tourism exploded into the vast new leisure industry of the postwar Western world, the Côte d'Azur offered itself as the ideal spot to try out self-indulgence, excess, prohibitions, recklessness, all in the name of the hoped-for happiness and excitement this novel sort of excursion could bring.

III

Hidden in Scott Fitzgerald's two masterpieces, *The Great Gatsby* and *Tender Is the Night*, is, as there is in any novel, a theory of the emotions. In 1925 Fitzgerald saw what was plain enough north of Long Island Sound and on the beaches of the Baie des Anges, the composition of a new elite the point of whose leisure was to be beautifully visible and exclusive. They would be watched but not joined.

It is well-known that he found a curious magnetism in the very rich. Hemingway is always awarded the prize in their famous exchange: "The rich are different to us," "Yeah, they have more money," but Fitzgerald was intent on finding and rendering the thrilling alchemy which (he believed) courses along the veins of the stupefyingly wealthy and glows with a radioactive flush in the heat of their harmlessly empty endeavours: shopping, dinner parties, cocktails, sex, sun, sand, sea, snow, all tinged with a little art. The Riviera in summer, Chamonix in winter, became the stages on which the rich made themselves watchable and sovereign over other people's desire, and, as Fitzgerald's dramatised theory of the historical development of the emotions implies, the 1920s provided the moment at which old English formalities collided with and gave way before new American excitement. The settled power of class and property and prose disintegrated under the detonations of liquidity, freedom from dreary old politics, the public enchantments of and with youth and sex and physical prowess.

No doubt Fitzgerald is complicit in this. His plangent prose bewitches the utter banality and pleonastic freshness of the film actress in his novel, Rosemary Hoyt. It lends the commonplace domesticity of sunbathing on what was then the empty beach along from the Promenade des Anglais and the ordinariness of lighted dinner tables en plein air on balconies above the Mediterranean a sorcerer's magic with which to conceal the coming disappointments and transfigure an enviable experience into a purchasable commodity.

This is the psychosis of advertising, come to fruition after 1918. Like all psychoses, it is circular and unstoppable. It moves through longing to envy, to acquisition to disappointment to rage or resignation, and back to longing. Fitzgerald re-creates the power of the psychosis in his prose. But he is in thrall to it, and his vision of happiness and fulfilment belongs to the irresistible travel brochures, the painterly advertisements for Cunard and Pullman, the magic labels on the brown leather suitcases.

He sees, nonetheless, how celebrity will constitute the elite hereafter. His motley assembly of artists, writers, rich Americans, film star, racing car driver, brutal mercenary, minor royalty, and Italian princeling, money piling on money of itself rather than by way of work, career, production, completely presages the power elite of C. Wright Mills's day in 1956 and our own. Their pastimes were formed and dictated on the French coast between 1920 and 1939. The leisure ideal was of a festival of excitement.

> There were fireflies riding on the dark air and a dog baying on some low and far-away ledge of the cliff. The table seemed to have risen a little toward the sky like a mechanical dancing platform, giving the people around it a sense of being alone with each other in the dark universe, nourished by its only food, warmed by its only lights. And, as if a curious hushed laugh from Mrs. McKisco were a signal that such a detachment from the world had been attained, [Dick and Nicole] Diver began suddenly to warm and glow and expand, as if to make up to their guests, already so subtly assured of their importance, so flattered with politeness, for anything they might still miss from that country well left behind. Just for a moment they seemed to speak to every one at the table, singly and together, assuring them of their friendliness, their affection. And for a moment the faces turned up toward them were like the faces of poor children at a Christmas tree. Then abruptly the table broke up—the moment

when the guests had been daringly lifted above conviviality into the rarer atmosphere of sentiment, was over before it could be irreverently breathed, before they had half realised it was there.[6]

This is magical art,[7] in the technical sense that emotions are conjured up in order to be discharged into action elsewhere. The thrill of happy excitement with which Fitzgerald enchants us takes its power from childhood, when the unknown possibilities of a party with its compression of exciting moments, its swings of mood, its prizes and surprises, fill the expanding sensibility of the innocent thirteen-year-old with a barely containable intensity and expansion of feeling.

Just as the child comes off the bend and out at the finish, so the adult resumes normal being, and tastes, as Fitzgerald's last sentence so beautifully conveys, the bitter sweetness of loss and the luscious push of longing for a past only just over. This is the rhythm in which holidays instruct us, but in the company of the rich and famous it seems as if one would always be able, amid that infinite plenty and the free time so extravagantly paid for, to live on its swooping circuit, to take one's energy straight from one's best feelings, anywhere and without concealment. Then one would have and be a personality, just as Dick and Nicole invent and confer such a thing on their guests.

Dick Diver is a professional psychiatrist married to a beautiful but deranged millionairess. The young film star falls, of course, hopelessly in love with him. He sees one of her movies, and at "a lovely shot of Rosemary and her parent united ... Dick winced for all psychologists at the vicious sentimentality."[8] There is no distinction for Fitzgerald's hero, nor for Fitzgerald, between moralist and Freudian; in this, the novelist presages his century and the new epoch it entered after the First World War and declares his national identity. When Nicole turns abruptly away from Dick and his moral and medical authority, there is no recrimination or pleading. She is going to live with the hard-bodied soldier of fortune; Dick judges nothing, can do nothing (he is right about that), drifts into solitude and drunkenness, his career broken. Not knowing what to do or feel, he does and feels nothing.

This is life after celebrity. Unbound by any strong ties of friendship or durability to his rich elite, he and they turn away their faces in a kind of shame, easier with the techniques of avoidance and nullity than the wild pains of regret. The rich have more money, and they can use it to magical effect if they have a spellbinder on hand. Indeed it is a useful gift for those who make their living writing up the imagined lives of the famous to be able to spot the house spellbinder. There is no assigned space; the spellbinder may be a hireling or courteous sponger, he or she may be the leader of a group. But without some such magician, the worked-up activities of the off-shore, off-piste rich elite—yachting, skiing, climbing, shooting—will lack the glamour they must have for its members in order that they can radiate it to their spectators.

With the right magician, the simplest of the new wealth-displaying activities will do. The department stores taught the universal fulfilment to be bought by just doing the shopping—or rather, not *the* shopping, you understand, but luxury shopping, watched with envious admiration by the many separate shoppers in the store:

> She helped Rosemary choose a diamond for her mother, and some scarfs and novel cigarette cases to take home to business associates in California. For her son she bought Greek and Roman soldiers, a whole army of them, costing over a thousand francs. Once again they spent their money in different ways, and again Rosemary admired Nicole's method of spending. Nicole was sure that the money she spent was hers—Rosemary still thought her money was miraculously lent to her and she must consequently be very careful of it.
>
> It was fun spending money in the sunlight of the foreign city, with healthy bodies under them that sent streams of color up to their faces; with arms and hands, legs and ankles that they stretched out confidently, reaching or stepping with the confidence of women lovely to men.[9]

Fitzgerald saw, but was made dizzy and helpless by, the negotiated interplay of such transient desires. The Romantic tradition had blended with the Christian ethics of emotion in putting all the moral weight on solidity and continuity in feelings. If they were going to matter so much, feelings had better be determinate and dependable. Once, however, feeling was released from the stout frame of convention, and once the field of social action shrank to the store, the bedroom, the children, the flames of the feelings still flared up, but they were flickeringly detached from the force of circumstance. Henry James's characters spent gripping pages in trying to catch hold of their elusive light and heat for long enough to make them trustworthy. The beautiful and damned (Fitzgerald's own title, of a different novel) found their delight in the succession of beautiful moments, inaccessible, one assumes, to the poor, the ugly, the old. In the generation between James's *The Ambassadors* in 1900 and Fitzgerald in 1930 in the South of France, heroic emotion had moved pretty well out of reach. As I have already put it in chapter 2, Henry James shows us the diffidence as well as the tenacity with which hero moves between an evaluation of feelings, a correction of the evaluation, an aligning with these of his or her tentative judgement about each, and a pause while indistinct entities swirl together and commend to him or her a possible course of action, perhaps never to be taken. By the time we come to Fitzgerald not so many years later, like Virginia Woolf at the same time, we find him giving life, in *Gatsby* and *Tender Is the Night*, to people whose emotions have disintegrated into moments of pure consciousness, divorced from the productive world, unavailable as guides to what one should actually do, and not even considered for that purpose. The point of the novelist's reflection is to watch how feelings gleam and flash and dislimn into subsequent feelings. The only significant action is the love affair. Excitement replaces moral purpose; sexual attractiveness substitutes for character and presence. So: "She smiled at him, making sure that the smile gathered up everything inside her and directed it toward him, making him a profound promise of herself for so little, for the beat of a response, the assurance of a complementary vibration in him. Minute by minute the sweetness drained down into her out of the willow trees, out of the dark world."[10]

The psychologising moralist, Fitzgerald, and his semblable and hero, Dick Diver, do not know what to feel about the beautiful rich people. (Once they were old, Martha Gellhorn knew all right.) When they are horrible, they do not repel him; when they are attractive, he finds them irresistible.

That goes for us now, I suppose, at least until one bumps into celebrity at its most crude and infantile. Judgement comes hard, not only until we (observers at the scene, social historians perhaps) understand what is going on, but until the monads or atoms realise to what degree they are complicit in the action. "Do you really *want* to be attractive?" the advertisement asks.

IV

By way of an answer, we can counterpose a different novel from the same historical moment. The hard-hearted, soft-centred glamour of Fitzgerald's playboys and -girls was close enough to the reality of the Côte d'Azur between the wars. On more crowded beaches, now in the Caribbean, it still is; his art performs, as it should, its signal task to discern the future in the present.

The same task was undertaken in a much more caustic, nonchalant tone, caught from the very beginning by Evelyn Waugh's sardonic quotation in his terse title. *Vile Bodies* came out in 1930; the novel ends on a ruined battlefield with the exhausted hero asleep in a smashed-up staff car, while the fat general and stray but still bright young thing share champagne on the front seat. Plenty of people feared the return of pointless warfare in 1930; Waugh's war is typically arbitrary and directionless.

The sounds of battle returning "like a circling typhoon" are, however, no more than the novelist's characteristic grace note. The novel takes as its theme the emergence of the same postwar generation as Fitzgerald's, here stripped of all pretension to fine feeling, whose lifestyle is to drink hugely, to vomit copiously, to live it up. In the tolerant, derisive phrase of the time, these were the Bright Young Things, which is to say, heartless hedonists in whose soft bosoms and hard-boiled shirts appetite replaced desire, and mere impulse ordered conduct. The older generation—British landowning aristocracy and fatuous politicians—is made by Waugh to gaze with uncomprehending indifference at the endless, drunken parties, the sudden wagers and loss of fortunes, the frivolous marriages and the absurd, comical, P. G. Wodehouse jargon, running unstoppably on through sudden death, casual racism, and flagrant betrayals.

The thing is done with Waugh's singular combination of tearing high spirits and black misanthropy. Its point for our purposes is the invasion and demolition of the old order and its needful conventions by the runaway tides of, in particular, American money and the eager scrapping of anything like responsibility and modesty by the venal hordes of young hedonists whose only concern is to win access to the money and then shower it on drink, sex, movie-making, and competing for the prizes in the race of fashion.

Indeed, there is an early sighting of our pet word "celebrity" on page 126 when Lady Circumference and Mrs. Hoop have a fraudulent vision of a nobler past. After the halfway point in the novel, when most of the grisly, contemptible, and ineffable cast has been assembled—Lady Throbbing, Mrs. Mouse, Lord Monomark, Miss Runcible, Mrs. Ape (an American evangelist), Mr. Outrage, you get the idea, this is Ben Jonson country— the action is impelled largely by the fictitious column written by Adam Fenwick-Symes, the vague, more or less decent hero.

Waugh gives Adam a job on the *Daily Excess* as the house gossip writer, and mostly he simply invents, that is, *makes up* the news. In this démarche he foreshadows much in such mendacious magazines of today as *Hello!* whose pages we turn with nauseated reluctance in a later chapter. The difference is now that people have learned both scepticism and indifference. The reader response to *Hello!* is superficial; attention drifts over the page until the end of the commuting journey. Adam's column in the *Excess* was a matter of life and death to the appetites of those who followed his tips to gas-filled dirigibles, seedy hotels, and derelict bars, or who tried to find the latest starring figure in the rout of partygoing who was one of Adam's many inventions.

Fame in this delirious whirl is to be mentioned in the column. Adam's most important creation proved to be Imogen Quest, whom "he put down one day, quietly and decisively, as the most lovely and popular of the younger married set."

And from the first she exhibited signs of a marked personality. Adam wisely eschewed any attempts at derivation, but his readers nodded to each other and speedily supplied her with an exalted if irregular origin. Everything else Adam showered upon her. She had slightly more than average height, and was very dark and slim, with large Laurencin eyes and the negligent grace of the trained athlete (she fenced with the sabre for half an hour every morning before breakfast). Even Provna, who was notoriously indifferent to conventional beauty, described her as "justifying the century."

Her clothes were incomparable, with just that suggestion of the haphazard which raised them high above the mere *chic* of the mannequin.

Her character was a lovely harmony of contending virtues—she was witty and tender-hearted; passionate and serene, sensual and temperate, impulsive and discreet.

Her set, the most intimate and brilliant in Europe, achieved a superb mean between those two poles of savagery Lady Circumference and Lady Metroland.

Soon Imogen Quest became a byword for social inaccessibility—the final goal for all climbers.[11]

The gossip column has come a long way to this from its laborious beginnings on Pulitzer's and Hearst's staff. Waugh's breezy and sardonic cartoon catches one version of the good person and her ideal personality which it is the social meaning of the celebrity to incarnate. Or rather, this is the meaning, impossible to live consistently, which the celebrity-manufacturers assemble on behalf of the public, and against which the actual life of the chosen victim is measured, and the inevitable discrepancy then used viciously as an instrument of redress.

This is the spite to which envy and disappointment turn in vengeful satisfaction. The beautiful Mrs. Quest expresses the perfect personality as envisaged by a century of white heat in the Romantic crucible; "she is witty and tender-hearted, passionate and serene, sensual and temperate, impulsive and discreet." All beautiful rich women must possess these qualities of feeling; the social beauty derives her distinction from her sensibility, not her actions nor her accomplishments. She can be paid on both sides by a public struggling in crowds to catch a glimpse of her, and then smirking with satisfaction (these are passing feelings, not passions of the soul) when the gossip-writer catches her out and, on our behalf, does her down.

There is in all this, as in all mass emotion, much that is phoney and rotten, and the cultural industries thrive on such sentimentality and its aesthetic form, kitsch. At the same time, these are living ideals of sensibility. In our society then as now, women aspire to express these feelings and, even when defeated by the inevitable shortcomings of face and body, shortage of money and position, by the laughable impossibility of carrying all that impulsive serenity about, the ideals still hover in mid-air, immanent and sort-of-holy.

V

The gossip columnists have a lot to answer for, although answering *to* the strange viruses in the body politic from which they must catch an infection and work up a temperature. Waugh's novels are sprinkled with the new, horrible peers of the realm, the press barons. Lord Copper in *Scoop* finds all of life's fulfilment "in the pleasures of monolocution," and Lord Monomark hauls Adam in to praise his page "as peppy, plenty of new names ... and ... the intimate touch I like,"[12] but to forbid him to mention the latest fashion accessory, a prank of Adam's, the "bottle-green bowler."

The newspaper owners were to teach the great dictators a thing or two about demagoguery. They too were in their business to create a mass audience out of sheer circulation. Their prime concern may have been money, but the commodity was inseparable from power.

Everybody notes about the coming-to-prominence of mass-circulation newspapers the degree to which they throve on the day-to-day invention of novelty. Adam Fenwick-Symes holds his readership by making up half or more of his characters. So the editors, with their vain and watchful bosses on the floor above, urgently needed spotters of novelty out of which to fashion new celebrity.

They found it in the activities produced and rapidly perfected by wartime technology and then turned into instruments of play by the rich, thereby into objects of leisure attention by the crowds who could not afford the lethal toys but had the time and money to spend watching them. Waugh includes a wonderful parody of the conversation of fast-car addicts, and the Monte Carlo rally (where else?), the Dolomites 500, Goodwood, and, a bit later, les 24 Heures du Mans, turned the racing driver at the centre of his team of mechanics all dressed in the chic white overalls into one of the sporting elite.

So too with Charles Lindbergh and Amy Johnson. Like the racing car drivers, the trade of aviator shone with the glow of heroic action, solitary, determined, flying through the worst the weather could do. Unlike the mass spectator sports of cricket, baseball, football whether Association or American, the drivers and the pilots needed either private money or rich backers. Donald Campbell, world land record holder, whose death on Lake Windermere going for the world waterborne record confirmed him so satisfactorily as an immortal celebrity, was a wealthy regular on the Côte d'Azur. Lindbergh, to begin earnest in promotion not of himself but of the machine, found his backers for his lone, astounding flight in the single-engined aircraft, *Spirit of St. Louis*, across the Atlantic in 1927 and was then swamped by the acclaim and rewards which followed.

His life was inflated out of all recognition by the pitiless pursuit of the journalists. Politics, in the way it has, sucked him into its orbit and then, when he so injudiciously gave an ignorant endorsement to Nazism, flattered by lavish attention from Goering at the head of the Luftwaffe, spat him out. It is a paltry, piercing tale. His fame brought abductors to his door on the four-hundred-acre estate in New Jersey which success had bought him. They kidnapped his two-year-old baby son from an upstairs bedroom while his wife and the baby's nurse were downstairs in the kitchen. Ten weeks later, the decomposing body of the baby was discovered by chance in the New Jersey woods. A doubtful victim, a German immigrant and ex-convict, was executed as guilty after a six-week trial lit glaringly throughout by the daily press. When Lindbergh's wife, a high-society daughter of the U.S. ambassador to Mexico and a best-selling writer, became pregnant with a second child, Lindbergh took his family in 1935 to live for a while in southeast England, all in order to escape the ceaseless importuning of journalists and photographers. They stuck to him, and he repaid them.

Lindbergh was more than just a pilot. He knew aerotechnology intimately, he understood aeronautical design. When the U.S. military asked him to visit Germany to inspect aircraft development, he went gladly. He attended the 1936 Olympic Games as guest of the Nazi authorities and had a medal pinned on his chest for his pains. He spoke admiringly in public of Hitler's achievements, while writing in 1939 in a grisly disregard of what was already happening in the Reich, of the need to "guard ourselves against ... dilution by foreign races ... and the infiltration of inferior blood. Aviation is one of those priceless possessions which permit the white race to live at all in a pressing sea of Yellow, Black, and Brown."[13]

As one would expect from this, he expressed cautious but firm anti-Semitic opinions as well—"A few Jews add strength and character to a country, but too many create chaos. We are getting too many."

Mrs. Lindbergh topped the best-seller lists with an antiwar, neo-Fascist sermon, *The Wave of the Future*, while Lindbergh himself, pressed by some to run for president, pulled enormous crowds to hear him take Germany's part and to urge the United States to stay out of the war in which Roosevelt at the time was doing everything to help Britain and France, apart from joining in as a belligerent. The political organisation which most eagerly recruited him, America First, was vehemently against intervention, undoubtedly racist and anti-Semitic, and called out very large audiences. Lindbergh was their trump card. They arranged a huge meeting in Boston to follow the smashing success of the rally in August 1941 in Madison Square Garden, when Lindbergh addressed 25,000 people, and the audience acclaimed him as the next president. The Boston rally was due on December 10, 1941. Four days earlier, it was cancelled by force of circumstance and Japanese fighter-bombers, and America First subsided with a vast exhalation of hot air.

Lindbergh is an example, of which more will appear, of a celebrity whose peculiar achievement and the energy of fame propelled him across usually impermeable boundaries. By flying nonstop for thirty-three hours from New York to Paris, he signified the advent of world air travel, whether for business, bombing, or vacationing. His action demanded plenty of courage and cool determination, as well as advanced technical knowledge. On a miniature scale, these are the military virtues. Projected onto the global screen of politics, his confidence undiminished either by fame or by tragedy, Lindbergh showed himself for the cheap rube he was. Celebrity gave him presence; the mass audience saw in him what they wanted, and that in turn corresponded well enough with what he was.

Thus it was that he passed through the separations which more or less keep apart, in civil life and the exertions of power, the politicians from the entertainers, the idle rich from the world movers, the soldiers from the civilians, the sporting set from the intelligentsia. An implicit sociology permits them all onto the same beaches, yachts, and ski slopes, as we have seen, but those same structures strictly regulate the public passages from one group to another. Presidents learn how to carry off and exploit celebrity from the film stars, but film stars can become presidents only after lengthy enough service as jobbing politicians.

VI

The new racers were, however, as far as our vacuous, hard-edged concept is concerned, minor fractions in the sum of things. Far and away the biggest screen of the twenties and thirties was the literal screen in the cinema. When Hearst bought into the movies he condemned all newspapers to a century-long struggle to ward off their own demise. The words Gore Vidal makes Hearst, grim old genius that he was, speak seem well chosen. He says to a rival newspaper owner:

> "I think movies are the answer."
> "*To what?*"
> "The world.... The beauty of the movies is they don't talk. Just a few cards in different languages to tell you what the plot is.... Everyone in China watches my *Perils of Pauline*, but they can't read my papers there."[14]

Then he adds, "Distribution companies, theater chains, those are what matter."

The First World War had ended with governments confidently directing and unconsciously directed by their new instruments of propaganda; as I said and everyone knows, over the same years the momentous invention of Hollywood brought to birth the sacred infant of the century, the star. The new media of film and radio, working to restore immediacy and intimacy to human narrative when everything in city life seemed so anonymous and fragmentary, imbued the stars with magical emanations. Cinema stars, like the political leaders who made themselves into similar stars, offered the reassurance of individual recognisability at a time when that was proving increasingly hard to find. Hence, whether you were a politician in 1919, or merely a millionaire investor in movies, you could have no doubt that these dazzling new media would do everything for your power or your pocket.

To say it again; the tale of the twenties and thirties is first of all, therefore, a story of how the great dictators and indeed the everyday victors of electoral politics—Mussolini, Hitler, and Stalin, along with Franklin Roosevelt and, eventually, Winston Churchill (without electoral victory)—made themselves into stars on the world stage of politics and corralled the public spectacles of celebratory propaganda—the rally, the armaments parade, the Olympic Games, the Cup Final, the tickertape drive through Manhattan, the state openings, the royal weddings, the Mayday march—which then became essential adjuncts of power. All such occasions lent themselves, with the help of newsreels and hugely amplified martial music and megaphone rhetoric, to the public dramatisation of power. The mass political spectacle, no less sumptuously orchestrated at the 1937 coronation of King George VI than at Nuremberg—marching men, drums, banners, horses, and the mute power of the crowd—is *the* feature of political life between the wars. It affirms for each society some of the most important of the social values and traditions and makes the small public figures at the centre of such vast attention uniquely recognisable and still sacredly remote.

This is the powerful contradiction at the heart of our phenomenon. I repeat what I said for clarity and emphasis. Celebrity after 1918 combines knowability with distance. Political leaders or cinema stars are intensely familiar (one of the family) by way of the cinema screen, and (at first) by way of their voices on the living room radio, but physically and in terms of how we all need to feel the directness of experience, they have the remoteness of the supernatural. This is the compound which makes for the sacredness of celebrity, and may suggest the reason why people both worship *and* vilify the famous. The invention of stardom and the instantaneous mass publicity it released by way of the new media from 1919 onwards twined together in a strong rope of meaning some of the strongest and strangest passions of modern society. The irresistible shine of money was added to the new emphasis given by the advertising industry to physical desirability and youthfulness. The industrialisation of leisure offered new locations in which to display its conspicuous consumption—holiday attire, seaside games, expansive freedom, informal intimacy, all as watched by the envious and their hired eavesdroppers, the gossip columnists and photographers.

The site of such sightings was nonetheless the picture palace, the only palace the countless audiences of the poor had ever entered. When Hollywood industrialised itself, it did so by way of the so-called "studio system," which everyone supposes still to be functioning. The studios made the movies and paid the actors their wages (large enough once the actor metamorphosed into the star—Hearst bought and sold Mary Pickford for a million dollars). A small team of writers, directors, camera operators, publicity officers (crucial), and supporting players were circled around the "star," and the movie was made in terms of her and his image.

The easeful moment of stardom, which I would place between the late thirties and late fifties, awaits us in chapter 8. Here it will do to say that the studio assembled their kitsch-and-cliché narratives and then rented them out to the distribution chains of theatres. When they were rented out across the Atlantic and the talkies became the rage (Hearst's problem was easily solved by separate magnetic tape-recorded dubbing), 40 percent of the British people went to the cinema every week. Large crowds went to the football, the *palais de danse* were full on Saturdays, but the cinema audiences took in the entire population.[15] The music hall faded, the theatre wilted. The movies poured out in dozens, the stars worked round the calendar; Cary Grant made twenty-four movies in five years before 1940, Bette Davis made fifty in twelve.

The idea of the star has somehow retained its freshness and cleanliness. Celebrity, as this history shows, is always an ambivalent designation, the feelings it engenders at once bilious and rapt, envious and dismissive. In what I call the easeful period of stardom, the stars looked down, with something like compassion, and the vast crowds, silent and solitary in the packed palaces, looked up and *loved* what they gazed at.

Chapter 7

The Great Dictators

It is hard to recover, after fifty years of universal home television, the extent to which Hollywood saturated the moral imagination of all nations with at least two picture-houses in the smallest town after 1918. But it is obvious how a quite new kind of celebrity saw the fact straight off and bent its form, especially in the irresistible novelty of the newsreel, to the gross magnification of celebrity until it aspired to enclose the being of the nation.

Post-1918 brought to birth the moment of mass politics. War and revolution had vastly enlarged people's sense of what could be done by and done to sheer masses of men and women, and I think it is fair to add that the cinema had helped bring that sense of themselves to popular consciousness. Certainly mass politics did not survive the decline of the movie house and the victory of a small, domesticated image on television. In 1918, and for fifty years thereafter, politics took its enacted drama to school with, first, the mass-circulation newspaper; second, the nationwide newsreel (worldwide when it got away with the reels); third, the mass attendance in adulation of the man high on the platform before the banners. He is the startling apotheosis of the star system as we saw it generated by the nineteenth-century theatre and concert hall.[1]

For the great dictator also had to learn the lessons of sincerity and authenticity.[2] He felt intuitively—this was the genius of Mussolini and Hitler, though they were sent crazy by their gift—that insofar as he aroused belief in his audience in himself, they lost their own hopelessness, their sense of themselves as trapped and helpless. "Instead of judging him, his listeners want to be moved by him, to experience him ... they focus on who he is rather than what he can do for them."[3] This formulation is right, but only half-baked. The dictator's audience do not, as Sennett puts it, "lose a sense of themselves"; rather the special nature of the mass audience causes the crowd to *find* in him what they want to feel about themselves, if they are suitably prepared as the Germans were for Hitler in the 1930s. They were made ready by defeat in 1918 and humiliation at Versailles, by the failed insurrection of the Left in 1919, by the long list of national catastrophes from inflation on a crazy scale to the nerveless failures of the Weimar Republic. In 1914 Admiral Tirpitz had provided them with an invincible navy. The new nation with its Prussian lineage was up in arms. This glowing and swollen self-image was still strong and recent in the national memory when Hitler came to power in 1933. His audiences looked to him to express their muffled and confused feelings and longings, to sort them into a programme for action, certainly, but above all to bring them enlightenment about feelings and their direction: whom to hate (not themselves); how to justify their self-pity; how to restore self-respect by going back to 1919 and putting all the wrongs right, which was to say reaffirming the greatness of the nation (and incidentally restarting its economy) by the usual methods—weapons, armed forces, the racist reinvention of national membership as the *Volk*, mammoth public works, architecture, roads, trains, railway stations, airports.[4]

So although there was no doubt that Hitler offered to his huge numbers of listeners the experience of himself as moving his audience's strong, obscure feelings into an immediate direction which they could follow with passionate assent, he could bring this off only by proving the link between passion and policy. Those same policies did not need to be rational, let alone just or legal. When his regiments of hired thugs, killers, and hooligans, the *Sturmabteilung*, went out of control, hysterical with their early successes in Jew-murdering and bullying, Hitler first vacillated then struck. Their leaders were shot without trial, just as were the left-wing trade union leaders who had so put the terror of Communist revolution into German hearts.

The comprehensiveness and brutality of Hitler's methods are part of our folk history (horribly true for all that), and their timbre is here to be heard in the nerve-grating rhetoric with which he addressed the Reichstag in July 1934 after his purging of the *Sturmabteilung* (as an inconvenience, once his instrument of terror): "Mutinies are broken according to eternal, iron laws. If I am reproached with not turning to the law courts for sentence, I can only say: in this hour, I was responsible for the fate of the German nation and thereby the supreme judge of the German people.... I gave the order to burn out down to the raw flesh the ulcers of our internal poisoning and the poisoning from abroad."[5] Parliament and country bayed in approval.

II

The dictator is no doubt the supreme celebrity; he bends all his efforts to become so and continuously so in the sensibilities and the minds of his supporters. "Supporters," however, are exactly what they must be; they lift him and salute him thunderously—as we shall find Leni Riefenstahl showing us so unforgettably in the two movies *Triumph of the Will* and *Olympic Games 1936*—because he expresses himself precisely as they want to express themselves.

There is the danger in all this of sliding into a sort of slack-jawed functionalism, whereby *any* celebrity can be taken as a useful necessity for corroborating the relevant social meaning knocking about the culture and looking for a significant person to embody it. Maybe the chanciness of the celebrity process, particularly with regard to political celebrity, no doubt the humanly most important kind whatever may be the popular derision of politicians just now, is best illuminated by the extraordinary career of Hitler's rival in dictatorial fame, Benito Mussolini.

Mussolini was not just chancy, he was self-ignorantly certain but, in the end, lethally irresolute, contradictory, volatile. For sure, the Italians focused on who he was, but not at the expense of what he could do for them. As Paul Ginsborg points out, there are marked similarities between the weird, protean, kaleidoscopic character of the indestructible Silvio Berlusconi and Mussolini, and it is true that Mussolini is not remembered in Italy as a figure of national disgrace.[6] What he did was single-mindedly to establish himself in popular consciousness as through-and-through a strong, passionate, and commanding Italian male, where maleness was inseparable from both military uniform and the body.

Maleness was also sudden, authoritarian, capricious. Here it is difficult— never more so than when trying to connect the approved character-forms of the famous to the everyday desires of the unknown people—to avoid lapsing into cartoons of the labile Latino. One has to risk saying that

Italian fascist dictator Benito Mussolini (1883–1945) leads his officers in a spirited run in full military regalia. Photo by Keystone/Getty Images, photographer: Keystone/Stringer. Hulton Archive, Getty Images

stereotypes are categories, and that national characteristics are changeful but categorical. Mussolini was certainly fractious and captious; he contradicted his own orders the longer he was in power; by 1929, after seven years as prime minister, he had taken to himself chairmanship of eight of the main committees of government, including Defence, the Council of State (the Cabinet), and the Court of Accounts (the Exchequer).[7] He appointed nonentities, cowards, incompetents, and scarecrows to ministerial office, and when he was away from Rome, the administration just stopped.

The inadequacy of his insubordinates did not matter because he took so many major and minor decisions himself (the number of buttons on a dress uniform, which days the band should play at the Lido in Venice,[8] punishment for any civil servant not at his desk by nine o'clock). He established the criteria of totalitarianism: absolute command over the press and radio; an efficient network of goons, spies, informers; the appointment of sycophants as his inner circle, the purging of the party of all rivals or dissenters, executing them when he thought it necessary and denying that he ever gave the order for capital retribution. Above all, he ensured the universal visibility of himself while at the same time only going out in public surrounded by up to two dozen armed bodyguards and never meeting the citizenry unrehearsed.

These are the dictatorial methods so marvellously parodied in Chaplin's great movie.[9] It is perhaps banal to add the theoretic rider that all these manifestations came dressed in Italian rhetoric and uniforms. Ginsborg suggests, and Tim Parks concurs even about the present,[10] that ever since the unification of Italy in 1870 regional identities and regional governments have counted for more in Italian politics than Rome. Parks also speculates, with amused distaste, that after years of political instability and the fall of many governments, Italians live at a much further remove from formal politics than the next four or five neighbours to the northwest. The infamous obduracy of its bureaucrats, the political venality, the inadequacy of its welfare provision, the chaotic economic planning, and the endless procrastination of its legal procedures, all these permit the citizen in part a mocking distantiation from political rule, in part a quick-eyed readiness to turn that rule to personal account, to dodge taxes and circumnavigate planning laws.

If feelings of a political sort were different in 1929, as it has been my purpose to insist, it was still the case that for all Mussolini's ubiquity—in the press, on the radio, in school textbooks, on the hoardings—and for all his mass support, a strong residual cynicism, an irony compounded with dislike (all bursting into flames with the northern partisans after 1941) kept his celebrity status in equivocal readiness for the dreadful photograph of Il Duce's corpse suspended upside-down from a street lamp in Milan, beside that of his mistress, Clara Petacci.

It is a savage memento mori for all those greedy for fame. Envy turns to disappointment as the sparks fly upward, and the exasperated spirit will wreak its revenge. But the sociological truism stands: the character of the celebrity makes and is made by its audience; in the end, they do with it what they will (in the case of the huge German Army, they kept ultimate faith with it, even as far as the ruin of the nation). So Mussolini's fatuous boastfulness (pretending he knew by heart great tracts of Western litera-ture—the celebrity as aesthete), his histrionic switches of mood from bel-lowing anger to silent menace (he would practise his platform grimaces and melodramatic gestures in front of a mirror), his insufferable conceit (photographed running a kilometre uphill in full dress uniform alongside the *bersaglieri* mountaineer infantry[11]), his everyday irresolution and his truckling to stronger men (anxious to please and be liked by Hitler, Stalin, even Lord Halifax, who was, after all, peer of the realm)—all these inani-ties and pitiful weaknesses were tolerated, admired and despised accord-ing to taste, geography, and social class in Italy. Yet this ridiculous figure remained in power for twenty-one years. The quavery, rotten old state lived off his fame.

III

We are hoist with the truism that cultures colour the constitution and presentation of celebrity, and in the case of political celebrity between the wars, in very strident colours. The national leader up above the masses had to discharge the force of his personality into his audience, and they had to be ready to receive it. It was as though the dictator was conductor of a load of very high-tension electricity and his audience a series of receptors in low tension waiting for the switch to be thrown and power to thrill through it.

The parallel with the virtuosi of the theatre is clear: they too prepared for such theatricals right down to the frame of feeling waiting to be charged. It is as well, however, not to become too sombre about the structure of these historical moments. Mass politics is more or less over, although presiden-tial elections in the two halves of the American continent often replay the old imagery. Television reduces the noise level of celebrity; rock musicians have to sit still and talk ordinarily in the studio. What television has done is further to personalise achievement, and where the achievement in ques-tion is political power, then it must be carried off personally.

The readiest and most reassuring way of putting this may be to say that Stalin, Mussolini, and Hitler so impressed upon subsequent genera-tions their awfulness and the hysteria they orchestrated so deliberately that some societies at least would never tolerate such displays of egoism and demagoguery again. Not just so, at any rate. But the evil trinity left deep deposits in all cultural sensibilities; the crowd remains an active and unpredictable force in politics, and the single, celebrated politician still thrills and is thrilled by the acclaim of the populace, physically gathered in one place to cheer, to be heartened, to be roused and merged in one feelingful entity, not so much freed from self as released into a destiny in which that same self, ineffectual and tiny, is joined and enlarged by thousands of others all directing their will to the single figure, emblem of their hopes.

The history of celebrity has therefore much still to absorb from Hitler's hideous strength. A rock concert or even a crowd protesting against a rigged political election is not a rally at Nuremberg nor a Mayday parade in 1930s Moscow. Only when social order breaks down are the firm boundaries and hierarchies which keep the different carriers of fame apart broken open, and rock singers, footballers, professors, film stars act not on the professional but the public stage. Mostly what happens is that the politicians use the glow and glamour of lesser power to reflect gleamingly upon their own. One cannot doubt, however, that Hitler's public method left its deposit and did so because of its appalling success. He caught up and expertly compressed the ardour of thousands in a single expression of passion. It is not that he told the fair-haired young men and women saluting and chanting in front of him what to feel, it is that he gathers their feelings and aspirations, half-formed and unvoiced, into a vision of action in which they can realise themselves.

Crowds of a certain kind can do this, but only if they have the right conductor. (There are many different kinds of crowd.[12]) Nor can all celebrities bring off such an effect, even if they are crowd-pullers. But leadership of a political kind will not last if this magic is missing. Magic is the right word. The leader speaks the magic words which rouse the feelings he or she needs to discharge into the action he or she has planned.

Hitler, like Stalin, persuaded his people that he was indeed "father of the nation." Mussolini never brought off the same trick. The working class of Turin, Genoa, and Milan failed to turn out and roar for him. Hitler, who took twelve years longer than Mussolini to establish himself as Führer after 1921, was much more completely ruthless in eradicating dissent and opposition than the Italian. In the star system, whether of actors, concert pianists, or dictators, there is no room for competition. Popular sentiment in Germany was bitterly hostile to communism, which had so let down the people in 1919, and perfectly ready to give the führer leave for murder and banishment without benefit of the courtroom.

On his way to absolute power, Hitler wrote a striking memorandum for the organisation of the Nazi Party (Italian fascism being a much more ramshackle affair, for all its genius in designing its dress and insignia). He wrote:

> The basis of the political organisation is loyalty. In it is revealed as the most noble expression of emotion the recognition of the necessity of obedience as the premiss for the construction of every human community. Loyalty in obedience can never be replaced by formal technical measures and institutions.... The aim of the political organisation is ... the maintenance of the life of the nation as well as the will that serves it.[13]

Not an efficient bureaucracy nor a coherent set of policies, nor even allegiance to principles, beyond the principle of party loyalty and the patriotic will (the "will" being Hitler's preferred instrument in politics). His fame and the feelings which sustained it rested upon the kind of man he presented himself as being, and it was such a man which the people readily persuaded themselves (once they had him) they needed. What they experienced as Hitler was an enormously magnified version of the good leader, and that leader would, first, have aspects of their own character much more ideally developed and, second, connect them to something transcendental, in the case of Nazism, the nation-as-community, for it is a definition of community membership that it is exclusive. Hence the essential quantity, an inimical, resented, menacing minority, the Jews.

Propaganda as black magic must be kept separate from the propaganda of kitsch and uplift. Moreover, "kitsch" itself may seem, in such a book as this, too briskly censorious a word. Kitsch, according to the sternest critics of modernity, especially Theodor Adorno, is the product of transformations in the cultural realm by the interests and instruments of capitalism, whereby popular art is turned into the sweet opiates of solace and delusion.[14] For Adorno and the toughest eggs of cultural criticism, the only antidote to this pervasive sugaring of art was to make it as difficult and unyielding as possible.

However this may be, it is certainly true that the accoutrements of fascism as designed in Italy and Germany were characterised by terrific *style*. This expressed itself, on the one hand, by such flashy details as the big, contrastively coloured lapels of senior officers' greatcoats, their polished riding boots, and their bowed riding breeches; on the other, this dandyism was placed beyond criticism by the brute power and mass of metal and thunderous noise commanded by the troops of tanks which were overture to the appearance onstage of the single, solitary, and heroic leader. The quotation of horsemanship (nobody ever saw Hitler on a horse) was enough to summon up antique echoes of imperial statuary—the emperor on horseback leading his victorious armies; the historical phases then modulated into the absolute brutality and gigantic indifference of the tank, emblem of modern political violence.

These were, at times still are, the trappings of power and the expression of the leader's will. No one could fail to see both the slight effeminacy as well as the undoubted chic of the Fascist uniforms, but no one could be but struck dumb and awed by the bannered theatre of death-dealing technology.

At its centre, under the lights, stood The Man. In Leni Riefenstahl's amazing work of kitsch and art, *Triumph of the Will*, she presents the 1934 Nuremberg rally as a theatre of the people's will, concentrated in all humility as well as arrogance in their single, chosen instrument. It is worth adding that, for all Adorno's attribution of blame to capitalism for the invention of kitsch, the Stalinist theatre of power and political celebrity was much the same as that of the Third Reich. True, the uniforms weren't so well cut, and the cold in Moscow, even on May Day, meant that the Little Father's fur mittens were less elegant than the Feldmarschall's leather gauntlets, but the podium was as high for the nation's parent, the tanks as terrible, above all, the soldiers' goosestep was the same in Russia as in Germany—a march, as George Orwell said, "*consciously* symbolising a boot coming down on a human face."[15] At Stalin's seventieth birthday extravaganza in 1949 in Moscow, the leader's face was projected as an image played upon by two dozen searchlights in the sky high above a packed Red Square. No doubt some of the detail was more demotic for the benefit of communist beliefs than the much dressier Fascists, but the essential dramaturgy was the same.

Triumph of the Will is of course a deliberate and shapely work. It lasts over two hours. But it serves our purpose here as a textbook study in the invention of that peculiar form of celebrity created specifically for the mass politics of a totalitarianism now more or less vanished from the world but still present and vital as deposits in the quite different circumstances of politics and popular culture eighty-odd years later. Those visible traces in contemporary Democratic or Republican conventions in the United States would surely, were they to be pointed out, unsettle today's dark-suited candidates; but the staged applause, the happy crowds, the lights, balloons, lapel buttons, and teenage majorettes in boots, perky caps, and nylon-fur-trimmed miniskirts, join the long march of the spectacle of power which wound through Nuremberg in 1934. There are hints of the same origins in the opening displays of all Olympic Games.

It is not only the thoroughness of the Nuremberg theatre which retains its force—that is, after all, the merest byword for all German administration—it is also its representativeness or, as people say, its inclusiveness. Everyone gets a role. Instead of the standard-bearer being singled out as leading part of the procession, banners of, naturally, an archaic Roman kind have been liberally distributed. To each section of the march its emblems of honour, and no party too inferior to be shut out. The very pioneer force tramps by, shouldering its spades and mattocks. The whole people is on parade, and above all its youth, golden-haired, good-looking, skimpily dressed so that its handsome bodies and well-proportioned torsos and legs may be seen to best effect.

The *point* of the procession, to which this grand spectacle leads both spatially and temporally, is the leader. He or she is the tip of this gigantic, blood-and-iron pyramid. But of course it is also a crucial part of a spectacle that it be watched, and watched by not just a sufficient but an excessive crowd, and such a crowd must feel equal as well as happy.

[T]his, precisely, is what happens in a crowd. During the discharge distinctions are thrown off and all feel equal. In that density, where there is scarcely any space between, and body presses against body, each man is as near the other as he is to himself; and an immense feeling of relief ensues. It is for the sake of this blessed moment, when no one is greater or better than another, that people become a crowd.[16]

The crowd must not be permitted to become bored or it will leak away. Anticipation generates its own happiness so long as it is fulfilled in time. Riefenstahl ensures that we see first a crowd happy in its newly cherished gregariousness, in its glad anticipation, and then with its gaze brimful with realisation: with the procession, the bands, the massed men (and some women), the wondrous vehicles, tanks, armoured cars, soldiers of iron, the long, orderly marching lines played over by the rippling banners. Her crowd gathers high and low; the windows of Nuremberg's tall medieval terraces are as packed as the pavements below, faces gay and open and un-afraid. This is a festival of confident national pride and easy independence, as it is of sheer plenty.

The procession winds its way into the vast stadium. Those who were the spectacle now become the spectators. The only subject of their gaze is now their leader, and whatever it is that "charisma" can be said to mean—it has a number of appearances still to make—it must indicate at once a quality exuded by the charismatic, *and* a corresponding excitement in the sensi-bilities of all those who are its subjects. In everyday chitchat, "charismatic" turns out to mean little more than that a strong personality in a prominent position has caught and held the attention of a large number of people. "In the general psychologism of the age," as Clifford Geertz remarks, "so well remarked by Philip Rieff, the study of personal authority narrows to an investigation of self-presentation and collective neurosis; the numinous aspect fades from view."[17]

Hitler, however, like any other political leader, must embody the nou-men, which is to say, the unapprehensible mystery of his own authority. This is the moment as well as the fact of charisma, and it is less a psycho-logical than a cultural quantity. Hitler's charisma (and Mussolini's, Stalin's, and, as we shall see, John Kennedy's and Mrs. Thatcher's) was rooted in his symbolic importance and his position at the very centre of the social order.[18] At that centre, his society's dominant beliefs, ideas, and allegiances coincide with its paramount institutions. The space he commands is where what matters is enacted. It is the social heart.

The passions such a figure arouses as well as those he (in Hitler's case) may himself exhibit are, to put it a bit blankly, peculiar to the history and geography in question. At Nuremberg, the audience was first happily expectant, then rapt, then abandoned in a tumultuous applause expressive of gratitude, a melting of the self into the single identity of the crowd, above all of mutual recognition, recognition of the sacredness of the sovereign and of his acknowledgement of those who put him in his place.

All this is much more than a simple tally between the dictator's presentation of himself and the popular psychosis. Nor was Nuremberg—or Stalin's Moscow, Mussolini's Rome, assorted presidents' ticker-tape cavalcades up Manhattan—crudely to be interpreted as a big masquerade put in front of the true business of raw power. Celebrity of this kind needed to embody and enact itself according to these spectacles and performances. These were not the adjuncts and externalities of power, they were as much Fascism in action as beating Jews in the street and fixing louvres to the tail-fins of Stuka fighter-bombers so that they howled when diving.

Hitler himself, therefore, as (in a very strong sense) centre of attention, had to be in uniform, of course. As Riefenstahl shows us, he is unbending in manner, expressionless of feature (no smiles), saluting not waving, receiving homage not with humility but with a grave propriety. When at last he addresses the hushed multitude, the only strong feeling he allows himself to express in public is anger—anger at those outside Germany's borders who deny him the legitimate demands he is making on behalf of all Germans. For the rest, his manner and features are settled in impassive severity, softening only, as required at the numinous centre, when greeting children, off his eminence and on their level. It should be added in this brief analysis of the Hitler noumen that the demeanour and the emotions he showed in public should never be thought of as merely external and somehow shallow and insincere. That is the error against which our very short history of the feelings is intended to warn. Everybody outside the Reich made a joke of the *führer's* ungovernable temper (never inside, obviously; none of a tyrant's people may laugh at him unpunished). But the public manner—calm, stern, removed, imperious, and so forth—was not only how the German masses wanted to see him. It was *what he was*.

IV

It is part of the self-congratulation of the self-styled liberal democracies to suppose that the days of the great dictators in the quondam totalitarian states are over, and that their leaders were defeated by the open societies and their principled absence of performance, spectacle, flummery, and all that. Even the British now suppose that their ceremonial and bemedalled displays in the capital—the occasional royal wedding or funeral, the opening of Parliament, all that Walter Bagehot called the "dignified" as opposed to the executive arm of the state—are no more than historical residues mainly of interest to the financially essential tourists. An accidental rip in the fabric like the death of Princess Diana in 1997 gives the lie to this supposition (as we shall see), but the tear is soon mended and British, Americans, and West Europeans all happily assume that the symbols and theatre of power have dissolved into ordinary and everyday behaviour.

On the contrary, all such behaviour is patently symbolic and historical. It is not heavy-handed, it is matter-of-factual to say that, in this crucial instance, the making of the concept of celebrity into the value and meaning it now has (and which will gradually change into something else) partook in its time of the fabulous showmanship of the worst the last century could do by way of tyranny.

The contrast with the way things were done in London and Washington as opposed to Berlin and Moscow was both useful and customary. When the British Prince of Wales known to his family as David became Edward VIII (in 1936) but was determined to marry his twice-divorced American mistress, Wallis Simpson, he was replaying the familiar role in British society of royal sexual notoriety. What he failed to do was to confine his love affair to the conventional limits of scandal, the royal bedroom; he pressed for the respectability of marriage. Unlike his predecessor and grandfather, Edward VII, who was twice scandalously cited in divorce cases, let alone "the Prince of Whales" (and Mrs. Fitzherbert) in Brighton in the 1800s, Edward VIII was resolved to press his suit until it tore apart, apparently in the vain effort to prove himself a serious lover to his people.

Indeed there was general sympathy for the far-from-youthful couple (the new king was forty-two), and some support for a king's party. In the terms in which we are at present discussing the symbolics of ceremony (in this case the ceremonious meanings of no slight thing, the appointment of a new head of state), Edward VIII was attempting what turned out to be a premature change of meaning. That he was forestalled by the ruling elite and its class battalion does not tell us much except that they could do it. The Tory prime minister, old stager Baldwin, concluded that the titular head of the Church of England could not marry a divorcee, and the party, at that date still absolute, concurred. The wretched Edward's attempt to share the commoners' privileges went smartly down. All that was left were the games of beachball on the Riviera at which we glimpsed him in chapter 6, and the post of wartime governor of the Bahamas.

The stain of divorce proved too visible on the royal tabard. It was too glaring for the other values a king had then to carry to be able still to shine out. It is a commonplace that numinous power is hypocritical, but the hypocrisy must be, so to say, allocatable.[19] A sovereign ruler, even one as helplessly constitutional as the British monarch, cannot flout certain ultimate conventions which prove to him, her, and society the definitions of relevant propriety. No room here for the ethics of existentialism and the doctrine that one may just refuse, as bad faith, determinate conditions in a social role. Or if you do, as Edward tried to, you lose your job; if the going is particularly tough, you may lose your life (some tragic heroes, celebrated enough—Antigone for instance—concluded that they had to do exactly that, in the very name of a higher value).

Against his will, Edward did his bit towards the upkeep of traditional order and masonry. His brother, nervous, stammering painfully, hating the prospect and practice of being king but doing it staunchly, completed the restoration. Indeed, the seemly, modest clatter of his coronation in itself confirmed that restoration. A ruling elite rules by way of such rituals; they do not adorn, they *express* that rule. It was Max Weber who taught us that we discover the authority of the state at the point at which it exerts the force of legitimate violence, and this is so. But we also find the state in action wherever the symbols enact the tale of authority and status. For sure, soldiers and policemen play their plentiful part in the ceremonious tale. When George VI and his pretty wife trundled through the crowded streets of London on a pleasant summer day in 1937, the decorous, cheerful multitude waved their little Union Jacks from behind the helmeted policemen and saw their monarch in his heavy gilded carriage escorted towards Westminster Abbey by the cavalry of the Household, clad in the formalised helmets, polished breastplates and glossy boots of a light operatic Ruritania invented by the genteel George IV after he abandoned his dissipated princedom.

The dramatic point of the cavalry is, however, not to pretend the monarch is ever a field commander, but to bestow a contrived historic continuity upon him, to affirm the longevity of the "dignified arm" of national power, and to lend it a worshipful gravity. Thus and thus the heavy weight of carriage and horsemen smoothed the passage of the new king onto his old throne and brushed aside the slight detritus of his brother's attempt at self-definition. So he and his queen waved graciously to their people and smiled the faint, removed smiles which expressed both their remorse and their accessibility, and which their gentle and kindly audience ratified as how royalty ought to be.

The king, queen, and his two young and pretty daughters may certainly be thought of as celebrities in their day. They picked up without even wanting to the burdens of tradition, and because the nation was steadier then, less torn by rage and rivalry, more settled in the calm of class differences, they looked without rancour for their titular head of state to reciprocate, in his station, their own best meanings: family unity, friendly courtesy, dutiful decorum. It was not an exigent code, but it had to be made visible on a national stage.

V

Europe was caught between the new imagery of its awful weaponry and the man who dominated it, and the rival order of archaic ceremony and quiet domesticity. Power in America had its own fluid and protracted dramaturgy. Two presidents serve here to configure it.

Franklin Roosevelt was jostling for the position of what was the most powerful man in the world even in 1913 when, at thirty-one, he became assistant secretary of the navy. He learned by heart a dictum of, surprisingly, his predecessor Calvin Coolidge, who got the job from vice president when Warren Harding died in office in 1923. Coolidge decided to serve only a single term; on being told that he had died, Dorothy Parker asked, with her usual brutality, "How could they tell?" All the same, it was Coolidge who observed, "In public life it is sometimes necessary in order to appear really natural to be actually artificial," and this tortured admission catches something important about popular sentiment in relation to the carriers of political power as huge as that of the president.

Coolidge advises us of the importance of seeming "natural." Roosevelt, far more intelligent than Coolidge as well as both visionary and ambitious about what is now generalised as "legacy," knew the importance to his popular constituency of seeming naturalness whatever it took. Whether or not any such naturalness is actually artificial is irrelevant: the attributes of celebrity are as they seem. Spontaneity, whether willed or unforced, is still spontaneity. (The theory of the emotions to which we are sticking insists that feelings both order and are ordered by thought in action.)

American "naturalness," however, assumes that easy resourcefulness of movement which is an American's inheritance.[20] Moreover, his namesake Theodore, his wife's uncle, had during *his* long presidency made (unnaturally) much of a boisterous, irrepressible, fat, and florid physicality, forever hunting, shooting, riding, and seeking military adventure. His bright colours dazzled his nation, and he was preparing to run for a third term in 1920 after circulating a rumour that he personally would lead a division of volunteers to France when the United States finally went to war in 1917.

Franklin Roosevelt would never emulate such a demagogue. Moreover, after the attack of polio in 1921 which paralysed him from the waist down, and in spite of years of therapy and arduous efforts to recover movement and sensation, he remained confined to a wheelchair for life. He had won the vice presidential nomination for the Democrats in 1920. The terrible illness demanded of him not withdrawal from public life—his ambition remained as invisibly incandescent as ever—but an unprecedented mode of self-presentation for a mighty leader and near-dictator.

That last is a tricky thing to call an American president. It affronts the self-congratulations of a nation regarding itself not unjustly as inventor and custodian of political liberty, as well as world promulgator of the blessings of democracy. Besides, there are substantial obstacles in any would-be dictator's way, including the Supreme Court and, on occasion, a hostile Congress. Yet many people have noted the advances made in the office across the twentieth century towards always greater autonomy of action in the White House and ever-enlarging opportunities for the exercise of tyranny.

No doubt the origins of such a tendency lie a long way back in the architecture of the Constitution. But their more recent burgeonings thrust outwards from the crisis of, first, depression and then world war, and the urgency of concentrating power in the hands of the one man on the spot capable of bringing things to a triumphant conclusion. The unlikelihood of such a man being a paraplegic ex-playboy, even one from the country's elite political dynasties, takes the measure of Roosevelt's genius and the continuing presence of his ghost in the shimmerings of presidential charisma.

He was always, for sure, exceptionally handsome and possessed of irresistible American charm, full of inoffensive raillery, delicate of perception and deception, both persuasive and adroitly flexible.[21] These are formidable attributes with which to get one's own way, and rather more lasting facets of charisma than the rages of a Hitler or the murderousness of a Stalin. Above all, they suited the American view of self-government, a mixture of local indifference, sentimental chauvinism, and the lively music of populist feeling.

So one has to credit Roosevelt as openly as possible with understanding how to combine affable intimacy with the sacredness of office. His hard years of slow, limited recovery became well-known; his famous appearances before nomination at his party's conventions, first on crutches, then on canes, became touchstones of his resilience; above all, he retained (what all celebrities seek) a vivid sense of his people's moral convictions and allegiances as they then were constituted by their hardworking lives, their inheritance of the pains of mass migration, their faith in the country. He could reach out and touch these things and, feeling them himself, was rewarded by the reciprocity of trust and affection. He had any number of enemies and people who hated him personally; he opposed the oncoming war in public and steered the United States into it, a little at a time, out of sight; knowing nothing about banking and currencies, he restored the nation's bank accounts; and he spoke to his people as to their souls.

He inaugurated, for this latter convention, a series of what came to be called his "Fireside Chats." These were talks broadcast to the nation, and more than anything else they were instrumental in building the mutual regard of nation and this single leader. They were not couched in Churchill's

highly wrought and rhetorical style ("We shall fight on the beaches …")
for that is not the way to talk at the fireside. Roosevelt explained carefully
and not without technicalities how he intended to repair the ruined economy in 1933. In his best-known aphorism, he told his people, again, as he
had at full pitch during his inaugural address, "We have nothing to fear
but fear itself" (not true either; there was plenty to fear by way of social
breakdown), but he also told them what they must do for themselves, and
he beside them: "You people must have faith; you must not be stampeded
by rumors or guesses. Let us unite in banishing fear. We have provided the
machinery to restore our financial system, and it is up to you to support
and make it work. It is your problem, my friends, your problem no less
than it is mine. Together we cannot fail."[22]

This is charisma in action, never more potent than where the passions of
the crowd, the words of the actor, and the form of the action coincide most
closely. In this case, the qualities it takes and the feelings these call out are
indeed "natural"—natural in the sense that these are the tones and words
which belong to firesides at which the family gathers, gravely and sensibly,
to discuss what to do in the face of great danger.

Roosevelt retained this natural authority and accessibility until his
death left his people stricken and parentless. After the late 1930s when he
summoned them to build "the great arsenal of democracy";[23] after Pearl
Harbor on December 7, 1941, "the day that will live in infamy," when
Roosevelt rose so steadfastly to the occasion; after the settlement at the
Big Powers meeting at Yalta in February 1945 just before he suddenly died
and when he was so comprehensively taken in by Stalin's impersonation
of a man to be trusted; after all these momentous occasions, Roosevelt
brought together the three great attributes of democratic charisma and the
sublimity of his office: quickness of apprehension and judgement; an open
and egalitarian sincerity of manner; an unshakeable sense of his rightness
in his position.

VI

It is a spacious house, the president's. It gives room to very different characters, few of whom can fill it, and some of whom look pitiful enough try-

ing to do so. It never, however, altogether loses its awfulness, and its sacred aura is even conferred on jeans and shirtsleeves as well as the innumerable tales of sexual transgression leaking out of every door and window in the White House.

This brief round-up of all that U.S. presidents have done to dramatise and embody our aspirations, and to do down the more horrible aspects of dictatorial greatness, can hardly conclude without recognising the difference made to the most powerful individual on earth by the advent of television. John Kennedy is our man at this juncture, very much because he intuited with such vivacity how to act and be the part in front of the television cameras as well as in front of telephoto newspaper lenses which, by 1960 and after the colossal success of the newspapermen and women in World War II, were everywhere on hand around the carriers of power and fame.

Kennedy, as everyone forgets, won the presidential election in 1960 by only a whisker of the popular vote. His redefinition of the office and its magic began at that date but quickened and expanded after his death. As is usual with presidents, plenty of people had known him well enough before he assumed his strange new aura, and they found him just another rich boy with a billionaire father trying to win his son the power and the glory he had missed himself. Joe Kennedy had been, among other things (all of them lucrative), a bootlegger and an intimate of the shady side of the Bostonian Irish. Having wangled his way, by services rendered to Roosevelt, into the U.S. ambassadorship in Britain, he put his foot in things first by getting out from under the bombs of the Luftwaffe as fast as he could, and then by announcing to the *New York Times* and without telling Roosevelt that British democracy was finished and the remainder of Europe Hitler's for the taking.

Sacked in consequence, he appointed, as tycoons will, his three sons to replace him. The first was killed in action; the second, after rather vague and inadequate political sallies, buckled down to winning the Democratic nomination and then the election. He was forty-three. He had married, at thirty-six, a wife ideally matched to his ambitions, apart from the trifling disqualification of their mutual Catholicism. She was an heiress, beautiful in the bony post-Monroe way fashionable in 1960, a stylish dresser, sufficiently knowledgeable about the arts and interior décor. Her cousin and

friend since childhood was the novelist Gore Vidal, himself almost as celebrated as she was, and his picture of her[24] does not so much close the gap
between the public and private faces of a person recognisable at the time
worldwide as make the gap impassable. In public, her beautiful smile, her
gracefulness and poise, her self-effacement and (successful) concealing of
rogue emotions; in private, with her cousin or her husband, careful, often
nervous, wounded by her husband's infidelities but never openly reproach-
ful, girlish in her uncertainties and political ignorance.

This gap marks the space where political celebrity certainly, and perhaps
all forms of this protean concept, is most tangible and elusive. This is the
gap into which the gossip columnists, the news journalists, the blasted
photographers—they make their first appearance as paparazzi in Fellini's
1960 classic film study of celebrity, *La Dolce Vita*—all pour and jostle,
fight and throng. Behind them, held back by the barricades and the police,
press the rest of us, some desperate to see and touch the famous, some
casual and curious—"she's just a woman," "he's just a man."

The Kennedys dramatised the gap between the public figure and the private person with unprecedented force. Much of the force which electrified
both figure and person was sexual. They were both young (enough, and as
compared with, say, General de Gaulle or Harold Macmillan), attractive,
rich, open in manner, sincere in appearance, beautifully dressed, athletic.
Nobody knew of John Kennedy's terrible back pains, the multiple opera-
tions, the near-death recoveries. But they knew about his sufficient bravery
when his torpedo boat PT 109 was sliced in half by a Japanese destroyer
in 1943, when Kennedy swam for hours towing one of his men, rallying
the others. Once, when asked how he became a hero, Kennedy replied, "It
was involuntary. They sank my boat."[25] The crowds knew of this laconic
modesty and doted on it. They liked his classy New England composure
in public and tried to shake him out of it as they pressed around him; they
liked him all the more when they could not, and Kennedy, ruffled but
grinning amiably, gently shouldered his way through the multitudes.

All political wives have to live by stretching themselves across the gap
between public and private life. Not until Mrs. Thatcher came to power
in Britain in 1979 did a woman bring off the trick of closing the gap and,
learning from the men, cast herself with an iron integrity a public personality indistinguishable from her private one. I write, I had better add,

as a bitter opponent of the destruction she wrought on certain absolute political allegiances; but she stands for the kind of late twentieth-century celebrity-with-power who has taken her lessons even-handedly from the Führer and from John Fitzgerald Kennedy and gloried in her success.

Kennedy carried off his inimitable manner precisely because he melded to perfection his public figuration and his actual character. This was his naturalness. There is a convention which I think one can see he established as such whereby the American politician, meeting his supporters in a crowd, will be expected to shake hands with as many people as possible, however tiny a proportion of the total. The charismatic touch in a handshake confirmed to the lucky palms the sacred passions for admiration, trustworthiness, and grace, whether sexual (unignorable in Kennedy's case) or numinous. Of course, during his thousand days, no one spoke of Kennedy's frequent and compulsive liaisons, what the beautiful actress Angie Dickinson referred to as "the most unforgettable fifteen seconds of my life." But watching the film of Marilyn Monroe, her gorgeous body stitched into a scanty, skintight evening dress, singing "Happy Birthday Mr. President," no one could have any doubt about them.

Kennedy, perfectly unembarrassed by her luscious display, turned the tribute into a men's room joke after dinner at the Harvard Spee club. The assurance with which he did this is of a piece with what Norman Mailer referred to in 1960 as his "existential quality," "the wisdom of a man who senses death within him and gambles that he can cure it by risking his life." Mailer, in his typical, rousing, and wild way, went on to wonder whether his nation "would be brave enough to enlist the romantic dream of itself and vote for the image of the mirror of its unconscious."[26] It is the kind of hot and reckless aphorism of which Mailer never reckoned up the consequences, but there is something true in it.

Kennedy, however limited his actual record over a very short reign, gave to his office a singular glow. If one says that he was a complete politician, it is not with the downward intonation the phrase often carries. His charm, physical beauty (physical agony notwithstanding), calm and steady will and demeanour, family loyalties, *and* raffish adventures fired "the hope that he could redeem American politics by releasing American life from its various bondages to orthodoxy."[27]

This is perhaps a trite way to put it. The celebrity he engendered mingled glad excitement with a delicious fearfulness. This was a new current of feeling, not yet established as a structure, coming through as all that the sixties were later to signify. Kennedy, out of his completeness as politician, his utter absorption in its day-to-day conversation, his needful cynicism, his rhetorical tropes, vacuous but rousing ("Ask not what your country can do for you—ask what you can do for your country"), brought all these qualities together and radiated them to his nation as a thrilling novelty, a transformative surge of new feeling and world-changing possibility.

It could not last. It had insufficient content. Only his appalling death gave longevity to the myths of Camelot. Celebrity itself, however—the concept and its value to the American people, to *all* people come to that— is still charged up by Kennedy's ghostly force. It reminds us how once upon a time sheer attractiveness, physical presence, calm resolution in manner, grace in conduct, and the signal good fortune of the Cuban Missile Crisis in 1962, combined to colour the old political machine with the brilliance and exhilaration of heroism.

VII

These effects are peculiar to their historical moment. In the case of presidents, they are also peculiar to America itself, to the extraordinary solitude and its companion power which the holy, unassailable Constitution so recklessly bestowed upon one man (man, so far). The founding fathers might themselves have been contriving the idea of celebrity as much as a tranquil polity, and given the uniformity of the earliest office-holders, no one could have foreseen how future presidents, sometimes pitifully inadequate, would be chosen for the match they made between the plausibility of their particular version of the American character and the popular sentiments of the day, swirling hither and yon, seeking incarnation in a leader.

The contrast, therefore, between Kennedy's youthful vitality and his next successor but four, Ronald Reagan, is useful as a measure of the change in such sentiment over sixteen years, as well as an index of the deceptions consciously and unconsciously fostered by the fame attached to supreme office. Reagan's memory is held in much the same affection as the man was in office between 1980 and 1988. Then as now he was esteemed as not perhaps the greatest intellect ever to occupy the White House, but stoutly principled according to widely cherished and all-American conservative values, homely domesticity, plain old-fashioned decency. But more than that, he was and is credited with devising the rearmament policies which ended the Soviet tyranny in Eastern Europe and finally proved Marxism as politics and as economics to be a failure and a sham.

Any such claim is hollow, no doubt. The sudden rush of events which terminated the Cold War and the Soviet Union together was, if at all due to the actions of a single individual, the result of Mikhail Gorbachev's refusal to use tanks to prevent imperial disobedience, his loosening of economic controls over the home market, his proposal to the seventy-five-year-old Reagan to scrap all nuclear weapons within ten years.[28]

Reagan's (and Gorbachev's, come to that) place in his nation's heart was symptom of the new importance of "character" of which Kennedy made, deliberately and involuntarily, so much. Kennedy had been, effectually, the first television president. He had spontaneously picked up the significance of Roosevelt's "Fireside Chats" on radio and presented his own version on national television.

On Monday October 22, 1962, Kennedy addressed the biggest television audience ever known up to that date in order to explain his course of action over the nuclear missiles suddenly installed by the Soviets in Cuba. Kennedy (and his speechwriters) duly found the trite and reassuring idiom in which to express the traits of character his country sought in him. To the young, athletic-seeming, and lighthearted charmer was added this grave, calm, and resolved individual, at once an obvious world leader, unrattled by the terrific demands of the role, and a plausible friend, fellow citizen certainly, recognisable as such in every one of the millions of homes in which his image seemed so at home.

This was the man just as reassuringly close and actual whom his nation saw smiling cheerfully as, on holiday on Cape Cod, he left Sunday Mass with his wife. This was the man whose assassination was brokenly announced on television within minutes by Walter Cronkite, the nation's trustworthy custodian of world news, himself publicly cherished as a character of irreproachable probity and sincerity.

These moments are gathered in a sort of unpublished national (and Anglophone) scrapbook of television memories. They testify by way of the chosen celebrity—in this case, celebrities central to the polity and its good order—to the virtues of character for which he or she may stand. After all, between Kennedy and Reagan, Richard Nixon badly damaged the image of presidential character, lying and (as they say) covering up an action in itself trivial and probably common. When we return to Reagan, therefore, we have shifted to a moment in which popular sentiment had sought out not a dashing young blade ("callow" and "callous" says his unforgiving cousin[29]), but a dependable, unrufflable, easygoing old cracker-barrel wiseacre. The comical discrepancies of this picture with Reagan himself vanished in the character the actor played to perfection. As Gore Vidal also remarked, "Outside political Washington I have never known a world so completely obsessed with itself as Hollywood, making the marriage between movies and politics inevitable."[30] Perhaps it is surprising that it took so long for Hollywood to find itself a presidential candidate.

When it did, Reagan, whatever his IQ, learned to play the political game hard and tough. The gap in his case was not between the private persona and the public role, it was between the genial, accessible, craggy character he played on and offstage and the hard, bold saloon bar player. As Paul Krugman writes of him:

> Latter-day hagiographers have portrayed Reagan as a paragon of high-minded conservative principles, but he was nothing of the sort. His early political successes were based on appeals to cultural and sexual anxieties, playing on the fear of communism, and, above all, tacit exploitation of white backlash against the civil rights movement and its consequences....
>
> ... Ronald Reagan began his 1980 campaign with a states' rights speech outside Philadelphia, Mississippi, the town where three civil rights workers were murdered .[31]

These sorts of thing come as no surprise, even to admirers, but they do not affect the popular version of the man. This is usual, I think, in all celebrity evaluations. There is a splitting of the self in question as he or she is imagined by other people. (This is *not* psychoanalysis.) Half is reserved, half disparaged. The disparaged half comes into and goes out of focus on the relevant tide of sentiment. History happened to give both Kennedy and Reagan a dramatic chance to play the best side of the part assigned to them. Kennedy got Cuba—and foreign policy was the part of the job which mattered to him; Reagan got Star Wars and the finally inconsequential melodrama at the Reykjavik summit. In both cases they were able to act impressively on behalf of a nation—a world, even—which therefore knew what to feel about actions the spectators largely endorsed.

VIII

These remarks on assorted presidents should not be thought of as a roll call. They simply follow as aspects of the construction of celebrity after the formidable lessons taught in the thirties by the leaders of fascism and communism, respectively.

The momentous and visible change, it is a commonplace to repeat, was the advent of television. As is the way with historians and their generalisation, when we remark on changes in public values and judgements effected by television, there are similarly large gestures to make over parallel changes in production, in technology, in the mobility and relations of labour. What this turns out to mean for our purposes is that, as I have already said in passing, *mass* occasions and movements thinned out. Mass meetings and demonstrations around the famous did not exactly disappear, but they turned into spectaculars for television reporting. The antiwar and nuclear disarmament marches of the past half-century gather their significance from the degree to which they were and are reported on television. The comic competition between supporters of the demonstration, talking totals up, and opponents (usually the state), talking down the numbers present, is a measure of this fact. The sea of faces, the paper hats and flags, the balloons at presidential conventions are not experiences but images to be broadcast nationwide.

This is not to say that these spectacles are simple mediations of action to audience.[32] They are *staged*; never more so than in the United States. When Roosevelt started his Fireside Chats, he was well aware that his mesmerising speaking voice, separated from his acute physical disability, would carry his charisma and its authority to millions of home hearths; it is not easy to imagine how that diabolic master of propaganda, Josef Goebbels, would have stage-managed similar chats by the Führer.

Roosevelt helped dissolve the huge close-up of the political celebrity on the newsreel into the homely presence, at once familiar and remote, of president and prime minister onscreen. It is a complex process, and some leaders—Kennedy and Reagan above all—are intuitive geniuses at carrying it off according to the dominant criteria of success in life as the public expression of privately exemplary character.

This is one of many points at which celebrity attracts scandal. A scandal, I suppose, is a tale told in which the permissible or admirable aspects of character are isolated by transgression.[33] Celebrity by definition attracts scandal. It does so, first, because fame invites envy, and envy denigration. This motion is nowadays become industrialised by the production and sale of celebrity television and magazines, let alone by advertising, the industry of propaganda. Second, however, scandal heats up the air breathed by the famous and makes their bodies glow in people's eyes because the political celebrity must embody the qualities comprehended and sanctioned by popular sentiment. There is, however, a powerful thrill to feel when those qualities are stained or vitiated by actions on the part of the powerful. When these actions split exactly those values the powerful celebrity is appointed to protect, as in Richard Nixon's concealment of law-breaking campaign operatives in the Watergate building, popular sentiment and moral outrage coincided. The president fell, and justice was done.

At the same time, when the Watergate tapes were played and it became apparent how routinely foul-mouthed the same president was in private, his language soiled beyond repair the image of dignity and propriety assigned to his great office. The chances are that no one human being could carry off those qualities to perfection—and the American people are quite tolerant, as we shall see, of trifling lapses. But Nixon, his signal achievements in China notwithstanding, had defiled the main principles of honesty, probity, good manners, and respect for the law. His office was removed from him, and despite a sort of cringing retention of ambivalent aura—he was a crook but he had after all been president—for many years after resignation he walked as celebrity's ghost.

Scandal, however, plays around celebrity of its nature. It fiddles with what count as the personal or private parts of the lives of the powerful, and never more so than with sex in those lives. This has been so for two centuries, as we saw. The sex lives of the British royal family, whose significance as heads of state is largely ceremonial, have flowed down the sewers of scandal ever since the Prince of Wales and future King George IV set up scandalous house for his mistress (who became, dash it all, his bigamous wife) in Brighton. Sex is what it is, no doubt, in our moral lives because intimacy is at its centre. To know intimately the intimacies of the powerful is to diminish the aura of power. It is to catch them with their trousers down, and thereby to make them quotidian, trivial, comical for sure, *exposed* (a painful fate for any of us, powerful or quite ordinary).

Over the years, sex has moved up and down in the visibility of fame. Roosevelt's mistress, Lucy Mercer (who remained very close to him after her marriage as Mrs. Winthrop Rutherford and for the rest of his life), was widely known as such but kept conspiratorially quiet. John Kennedy's much more frequent, at times daily, infidelities were well-known to his bodyguards and beyond but publicly ignored. Bill Clinton's, however, all but ejected him from office and brought about the unprecedented vote in Senate on December 19, 1998, to have him impeached for perjury and obstruction of justice.[34]

There were two forces at work in this. The first was the drastic and universal shift in attitudes towards and permission given for sex which moved across the world during the 1960s. The tide had its riptides, its ebbs and flows, but Clinton's self-indulgence was its commonplace flotsam. As Joan Didion wrote at the height of the scandal:

No one who ever passed through an American public high school could have watched William Jefferson Clinton running for office in 1992 and failed to recognise the familiar predatory sexuality of the provincial adolescent. The man was, Jesse Jackson said that year to another point, "nothing but an appetite." No one who followed his appearances on The Road to the White House on C-SPAN could have missed the reservoir of self-pity, the quickness to blame, the narrowing of the eyes, as in a wildlife documentary, when things did not go his way.... "I have acknowledged wrongdoing," he had told

America.... "I have acknowledged causing pain in my marriage. I think most Americans who are watching this tonight, they'll know what we're saying, they'll get it, and they'll feel that we have been more than candid."[35]

All the same, he remained on his feet. Nor can anyone doubt that he was victim, as his wife said, of "a rightwing conspiracy" to bay for his flesh and to harry him out of the White House. This little plot was, in turn, part of the new propaganda industry which fed off and fed the intercalations of power and scandal, ripest of all when scandal turned sexual.

Whatever Clinton's talents—and he was far and away the brightest president for a lot of years—he did not grasp or could not meet the demand that his office embody domestic propriety. Nor did he acknowledge that his amazing ease and charm, and his quickness of connection with huge crowds such that each individual felt personally recognised, could not transgress the common feeling that these gifts must constrain themselves in the name of the noumen of power, its seemly sanctity and mystery (nothing mysterious about sudden fellatio with a twenty-one-year-old as part of the day's work).

Yet the vast, unideological majority of the American people turned out to reckon that the pollution of sacred power by very ordinary desire for a girl with luscious black hair and a shapely bottom was, as you might say, unimpeachable. The president remained on his feet. He was in disgrace but not ineffectual.

Although the self-appointed custodians of outrage huffed and puffed at the reprehensible tardiness of most Americans to rise up and get the president, it would seem that the Clinton scandal yields a useful political moral. Walter Cronkite, surely the most accurate barometer of popular feeling that one could find, once referred to a rule of the press whereby "as long as his outside activities, alcoholic or sexual, did not interfere with or seriously endanger the discharge of his public duties, a man was entitled to his privacy."[36]

By the time of Clinton's case, the press had waived the rule. But the public had not. There is something here important about celebrity's value and meaning in politics. Surely it is that a people is well able to deploy, within the framework of its habitual feelings and the moral and sentimental allegiances those feelings shape, a scheme of practical judgement as to what really matters to them. Sex and lying about sex are too commonplace to matter much except to those people immediately wounded by faithlessness and the betrayal of intimacy. The details are choice and juicy things to know and smirk at, but Earth's foundations are unshaken by them. In the delirious and nauseating racket with which celebrity is now reported, these are reassuring thoughts.

Chapter 8

The Stars Look Down: The
Democratisation of Celebrity

The star system took shape as a series of careful plans some time after 1917 when Douglas Fairbanks senior and Mary Pickford began their famous affair. Studios, as everybody knows, hired actors like football clubs hired footballers. They were contracted to a fixed wage; they wore invisibly the company badge; they made as many films a year as the studio required.

For its part, the studio guaranteed them employment in a way which must have been very reassuring after the chanciness of theatre work, and it set up formal recruiting processes as well as hiring scouts to find likely lads and girls. Those they hired had to be good-looking, naturally, and if the producers were themselves any good—Zukor, Korda, Hitchcock, Lang, Chaplin—they could spot among the faultlessly regular features and shapely bodies those ambiguities and indirections, the awkward grace or recklessness of movement, which would make for distinctiveness and force of character onscreen and turn the individuals involved into something fixed as an image but infinitely elusive to their own selves.

The point was wittily made by Cary Grant when, as we heard, he said, "Everybody wants to be Cary Grant. Even *I* want to be Cary Grant." He was not, of course; he started out in Bristol, England, as Archie Leach, and like all the stars of Hollywood's and world cinema's greatest period—let us say, from 1935 to 1970—was modelled, polished, dressed, taught to turn and smile and kiss and speak according to a studied plan of contrivance. The result was then as perfect a fit as possible—and in the case of our chosen, world-famous, and world-historical examples, the fit *was* perfect—between the person they each discoverably were, the star the studio needed and would transform them into, and the feelings, desires, fantasies, and moral conduct of the audiences to whom they would be presented.

There was crudeness in this manufacture, as one would expect. The fashioned star was by and large kept away from wrongdoing in the action (except for those deliberately invented, like Jimmy Cagney, as gang-sters). The beautiful woman might hold out the promise of sexuality (Lil-ian Gish, Myrna Loy, Jean Harlow), but her passion must be sincere and her abandon offscreen. Grant, John Wayne, Errol Flynn were all strik-ingly handsome, manly, alluring, but their emotional fulfilment as part of the story was as firmly confined by decorum and propriety as was the president's.

If not well-known, these things are widely guessed at. But what is still underplayed, at least in academic histories of everyday life and its deepest feelings, was the promise of happiness held out by movies and the cinemas which housed them, and kept. Kept to the teeming multitudes who went every week. Plenty of people, twice or three times a week, spent out of what would often have been bleak poverty half a dollar or two shillings to melt away strain, pain, misery, and desperate tiredness in the delicious dark below the shining silver screen.

As the millions of strange shadows flickered ubiquitously across the globe and towards World War II, those magic faces came to transcend the contexts of this or that story and assume a life of their own lived in the lives of those who watched them with dreamy intentness. Thus stars were born. Richard Dyer observes that, for example (some example, too), Marilyn Monroe has "become before everything an emblematic figure, her sym-bolic meaning far outrunning what actually happens in her films."[1] But as he goes on to say, the star's symbolic meaning has enormous cash value. Her (and his) name, once the studio systems dissolved into the competi-tion of the corporate titans, attracted finance to new films, let alone con-sumers to the new products with the star's good-looking features attached to the advertisement.

Where celebrity is, there is always money. In the peculiar version of celebrity enacted, both wilfully and involuntarily, by film stars, there is a weird, ineffable interplay of forces making up the life—the life, that is, of the star's own daily labour and leisure, and the life of the star's image in the imagination of vast audiences. One of the most familiar spasms in a star's career is the moment (there are many such) at which she tries to break the decorated casing in which she is enclosed and strike out for a form of life she can call her own. Who would not? To be rendered a thing, a com-modity bought and sold for millions of dollars, is one hellish version of the incarcerations invented by capitalism as it tried to regulate consumers down to their last minute.

There is, however, no such regulation to be achieved, least of all in the production of movies. Their sole point, after all, is to be at the disposal of our leisure, that time we call free.[2] The prediction of success for any given film is impossible, and studio refrigerators are laden with turkeys no one would buy. The point of free time is, after all, that it is one's own, to pass (rather than to spend) exactly as one wishes, and to pass, moreover, without killing it. It follows that for a single film to be a success, however the filmmakers try to insure their colossal expenditures with the right stars, the right clichés and conventions, their monopoly of cinema distribution, success comes only by an unplannable coincidence between star and story; between subject and the surging tides of popular sentiment; perhaps most of all and most elusive, between the audience's sense of its freedom of action and the weight of political history at the moment the film is made.

These are big, unwieldy concepts with which to treat the variable careers of a handful of those stars who so decisively swelled the organs of celebrity sometime between 1935 and 1970.

These are the years, I claim—in the company of the social historians[3]— during which film stardom was of its purest, and when its heroes and heroines fitted most exactly the space in the social identity which the industry created for them. These are the years, more or less, before television sucked the experience of moviegoing largely into the living room, when the experience of going out to the pictures was treat of the week. They are the years, also, of the masses: mass movements, massed labour forces, mass leisure also (seasides, football stadiums, cinemas). In the 1930s, these are the years of mass unemployment, and from 1939 for much longer than the wartime years themselves, of mass conscription and the draft.

The stars, born, manufactured, self-made, of these years came to unrivalled national significance of a rather simple kind, peculiar, one would say, not only to that political era but also, as the potted history of presidents in the last chapter suggests, to that middling stage in the industrialisation of celebrity. In the 1930s, as we saw, gossip columnists were more respectful, the passion for celebrity less tainted by spite and envy (this is not an elegy for lost beneficence), social class membership stouter and more formative. Certainly, the film industry—as two dozen biographies testify—was rancid, vicious, and trivial-minded in its personal dealings and its public criminality. But it had to invent stars who, in the story of themselves which they lived onscreen, spoke to that best part of the national character narrative in which their audiences believed. That is also the duty of art, and the best of the stars found out a way of life not too far away from the national narrative. The anguish sometimes attendant on this effort, and her intolerable failure to keep the two lives in sufficient overlap, caused Marilyn Monroe to kill herself.

II

John Wayne was voted America's favourite star in a Harris poll taken in 1995, when he had been dead sixteen years.[4] Wayne's celebrity has proved durable in a way that stars tied more tightly to their eras have not. When Joan Didion wrote, as a star-struck young journalist, of meeting John Wayne as he made, at fifty-seven, his 165th movie, *The Sons of Katie Elder*, she thought of how this man, "riding through my childhood, and perhaps through yours ... determined forever the shape of certain of our dreams."

> It did not seem possible that such a man could fall ill, could carry within him that most inexplicable and ungovernable of diseases. The rumor struck some obscure anxiety, threw our very childhoods into question. In John Wayne's world, John Wayne was supposed to give the orders. "Let's ride," he said, and "Saddle up." "Forward *ho*," and "A man's gotta do what he's got to do." "Hello, there," he said when he first saw the girl, in a construction camp or on a train or just standing around on the front porch waiting for somebody to ride up through the tall grass. When John Wayne spoke, there was no mistaking his intentions; he had a sexual authority so strong that even a child could perceive it. And in a world we understood early to be characterized by venality and doubt and paralyzing ambiguities, he suggested another world, one which may or may not have existed ever but in any case existed no more: a place where a man could move free, could make his own code and live by it; a world in which, if a man did what he had to do, he could one day take the girl and go

riding through the draw and find himself home free, not in a hospital with something wrong inside, not in a high bed with the flowers and the drugs and the forced smiles, but there at the bend in the bright river, the cottonwoods shimmering in the early morning sun.[5]

Reaching for explanations of Wayne's durability, Garry Wills speaks of his "filling some need" in his audience, but this seems to me a bit thin. Wayne dramatised and embodied his compelling version of American patriotic manliness. Before anybody snatches at the cliché opportunity of calling the patriot, long after Dr. Johnson, a scoundrel, one must be quick to say how wonderfully Wayne cut his manly politics with disappointment, the lined features, the laconic orders and concessions, the flashes of temper, the calm resolution all muted by the expectation that things will turn out at best equivocally, that allegiance to duties is not merely the best, it is the only action, that the right feeling towards either victory or defeat is wryness, a dogged, even grim giving way to necessity.

He brings also to the screen a feeling of absolute assurance: like all the best American male stars, he was completely at ease in his body with its burly chest, huge hands, dainty feet and tread. The walk—well, everybody descants about his walk, and generations of little boys tried and failed to copy it. I cannot add anything new about his walk. But one can say that his was a way of moving with its own impregnable ethics. Someone who walked like that was not only in perfect possession of himself, he won instantaneous trust. Whatever passions compel such a man, and they may include sudden rage, bitter vengefulness (for example, against the Comanches in *The Searchers*), exasperated contempt for a man as good as himself (James Stewart in *The Man Who Shot Liberty Valance*), we can be sure they spring directly from a morality of cast-iron soundness.

Everyone knows that Wayne was born Marion Morrison in small-town Iowa; that he was a beautiful young man, a lovely mover, tall and solid with it, always in uniform, whether the cowboy's or the soldier's. Over the almost four decades of his moviemaking, he aged quite quickly into the rugged, lined, partly broken-down but always massive figure that we still instantly recognise. Frequently he ends the movie defeated; in nine of the greatest films he ends up dead. As Wills bleakly writes about the end of *Liberty Valance*, "Our own life is a burial place for our youth. The sad wisdom of going on, of making do—the quiet failures contained in any worldly success—all those things breathe through this wistful elegy."[6]

Wayne's definition of American manliness as he lived it on and off the screen is much more stoical, muffled, familiar with defeat, hard, and harsh than the parodies of manliness allow.

In living out these qualities, in becoming them outside any one particular story, Wayne not only reflected something back to America which all its menfolk and some of its women wanted to see mirrored and to understand. He also made that something stand up for itself, even though he only made it by pretending, as an actor, on the action.

He puts me much in mind of what D. H. Lawrence wrote, at just about the time Wayne began in movies, in his dazzling essay *Studies in Classic American Literature*. He is tackling "the myth of the essential white America." "[T]he other stuff, the love, the democracy, the floundering into lust, is a sort of by-play. The essential American soul is hard, isolate, stoic, and a killer. It has never yet melted."[7] Wayne embodied (taught, you might say, and to a very receptive audience, what is more) this hard stoic, killer if he had to be, solitary man against the sky.

I am selecting three men from the high-water period of stardom by way of suggesting just how strong and pervasive was the tutelage of their lives, the vastness with which they exceeded their roles and became popular aesthetic types, which is to say, ways of being men particularised in a gallery of films but enlarged to take in a broad swathe of social possibility.

John Wayne is the first, and purest. On the arc of masculine possibility in America, indeed (more mutedly) in the Anglophone world, he stands for and by the needfulness of physical action, the harshness of duty and renunciation, the painful loss of the trail, the rarity of gladness. From his place on the arc, Wayne looks out on a moral landscape in which all you have is what you are, and traversing which you can only hold on if you are ready to turn violent when you have to. "A man's gotta do …," etc. It will do as a worldview from that point of the arc because even when it leads you into a frightful mess, you will have a way of carrying on (Korea, Vietnam, Iraq).

This is to assign the film star celebrity far more effectiveness than presidents or press barons. Well, Ronald Reagan reckoned to model himself on

Wayne's demeanour,[8] and there is no doubting the sort-of-omnipotence of the image of John Wayne. But it is not, of course, enough. Plenty of people affect to detest it. My point is that his very durability, as well as the metaphysics of his presence, confirm the thesis that a star celebrity of his magnitude formed and still informs the life of a whole society in a way true of *no* other figures moving through its moral imagination.

Not alone. For adjacent to Wayne on the arc of imaginable masculinity as devised in our key period, and casting long shadows beyond it into the future, we find James Stewart, another Lincoln Republican and friend of Reagan, decorated war hero with a DFC (Wayne never made it to the front), sometime Boy Scout, small-town Pennsylvanian, married at forty to Gloria McLean and remaining so, shy, stammering, reticent, gangling.[9]

His place on the arc is certainly well along from that of Historic American. But Stewart no less incarnated and (as I am at pains to insist) *caused* to become livable a different, powerful version of celebrated maleness. It is the version seen at greatest complexity in *Liberty Valance*, where Stewart, running for senator, "believing," as he says, "in votes rather than guns," supposes himself, though a rotten shot, to have killed the horrible villain (played by the horrible Lee Marvin) and is thereby rendered a moral wreck, unable to move and act. Only when he learns the truth (marvellously re-played from a different angle by the producer John Ford) that Wayne is in fact the killer can he resume his vocation of bringing to the West, decorated with his unearned reputation of having killed its unelected regent, rule by the vote.

The two men, in two roles perfectly adjusted to the contradictions in one another, play off the irremediable opposition between the certainty of violence and the necessity of the law. That Wayne, by killing Valance, saves the life of the man who will take away the girl he loves only compounds the opposition between the two ideals: historic and domestic man.

Stewart was eternally boyish where Wayne was craggy, stammering not laconic (even in *Winchester 73*), married and parental, diffident: even, in *It's a Wonderful Life*, self-disgusted. Indeed, the programming of the latter movie as a Christmas Day postprandial sugars over its strong sense of horror as well as the rage, depression, and terror Stewart variously reveals during the action. The final, joyful return to and (too easy) reconciliation with his family releases its Christmas audience into happy relief; but the action has shown us that there is no escape from the existential panic attendant upon the most trivial insight into one's own dispensability, and therefore the dispensability of all those one loves.

To speak of an actor's range as limited is to be severe. Wayne was not so much limited as he was monumental, which is an appealing part for an admirer to aspire to. Stewart had enormous range. Think of the incomparable moment in *The Naked Spur* when, having finally killed the unspeakable bully, Robert Ryan, he breaks down in front of Janet Leigh and weeps at the knowledge that he does not have it in him to be a bounty hunter.

Stewart made a number of routine movies as part of the job—the awful *FBI Story*, for example. As our celebrities must, however, he always transcended the role and played himself. This was a wholly masculine self, while also being one shaped by very strong, not always controllable emotions. It is his Americanness to express and contain these.

He acts on their very edges, as it is the point of *Vertigo* to symbolise. After all, the hero of the movie is off his head, trying to magic the new love, Kim Novak, into the dead wife, lapsing into a complete and rigid depression in the mental hospital with only the frenzy and barely tolerable physical suspense and danger of the closing scene as convalescence. If this is the feelingful, domestic hero with lessons to exemplify of loving domesticity and manly emotionality, he is not very reassuring. In Stewart's own life, no doubt, he commemorates the statue of him outside the courthouse in his hometown. But the actor has surrounded the statue with the anguish of an exasperated, stricken spirit.

These contradictions are gathered up, by time and chance as well as his good sense, into something livable with and as. He can only be as lustful, nosy, godlike, omniscient, helplessly unhelpful because of his incapacity as he is in *Rear Window*. If he could do something, he would. The domestic feeling and awkward, anxious lovingness which are the typical attributes of his character are the best expression he can make of all those necessary passions which may run riot at any moment in the citadel of the self.

Standing on the further extreme of the arc of all-star celebrity is our third American, the Englishman Cary Grant. (There might be dozens more; for myself, I can hardly bear to omit Gregory Peck; these three give us some bearings; as for you, you will have your own.) Let us assign him that house in our imagination owned by the happy warrior. Thus far, history, home, happiness. The stars of the high peak of the picture-house era situated their audience in a history; taught them the homely virtues as assigned to men and women according to the divisions of labour; kept the promise of happiness, especially in rendezvous with Cary Grant.

> He was that most unexpected but attractive of contradictions: a democratic symbol of gentlemanly grace. No other man seemed so classless and self-assured, as happy with the world of music-hall as with the *haute monde*, as adept at polite restraint as at acrobatic pratfalls. No other man was equally at ease with the romantic and with the comic. No other man seemed sufficiently secure in himself and his abilities to toy with his own dignity without ever losing it. No other man aged so well and with such fine style. No other man, in short, played the part so well: Cary Grant made men seem like a good idea. As one of the women in his movies said to him: "Do you know what's wrong with you? *Nothing!*."[10]

Everybody agreed about this. If John Wayne was The Man, Grant was—well—my man, your man, man about the house, the only male actor in the world who could appear in a fur-edged ladies' negligée and *still* be the symbol of gentlemanly grace. Moreover, like the two other heroes of this section, he was as he seemed. No one could doubt that the character he plays in the great Hollywood comedies of remarriage[11]—*It Happened One Night, Bringing Up Baby, His Girl Friday*—might falter in his poise, might doubt himself, might move nearer to the sinister opacity of the murderous husband he plays in *Suspicion*. Indeed and in truth, his confidence in himself and in life wavered at times towards depression; his five marriages each represented his ardent and sincere search for married fulfilment. The failures of the first four (his wives mostly left him), for which afterwards he always took the blame—"It was not the fault of Hollywood, but of my own inconstancies"[12]—left him wracked and anguished.

At the same time, however, Grant was as he acted he was onscreen. He loved women, one at a time, and they loved him. In *His Girl Friday* playing a newsman, he has driven his wife away by his nonstop, crazy pursuit of

good stories, and his tearing high spirits, his cheerful, charming indifference to and ruthlessness about what happens to other people, including
wives and comrades, as he does so.

The moral point, however, is not aimed at the amoral journalist. It is
that some people simply are like that, and there is quite enough of a moral
kind to say in approval of such people. In any case, without them there
simply would not be any news journalism around, and we need journalism
not because modernity makes us want news but rather because in modern
society we have got to have enough information to stop things getting even
more out of hand, to hang on to something frameable as sanity.

Rosalind Russell understands enough of all that and has been herself
a very successful journalist and wife beside Cary Grant, doing the same
work, called to the same vocation. Something in her, timid and wrong
or sound and sensible, has made her mad at Cary Grant's madness. She
has divorced him before the beginning of the film. At its start, she arrives
at the office with her new affianced, a pleasant, incurable rube played to
perfection by Ralph Bellamy. From the start Cary Grant simply will not
countenance either that she will give up being a journalist or that she will
marry Ralph Bellamy. What she will do is come back to him, without his
having to be any less mad than the madness which drove her off in the first
place. His needs and wants are inseparable: he needs her intimately; he
needs her as a journalist.

The big story on hand is found in the Criminal Courts Building, where
most of the action takes place. In a jammed press office, the city newspapermen wait for the execution of a self-confessed murderer, a pitiful
defective creature hardly responsible, barely guilty, desperately poor. The
wretch, however, is victim (and agent) in *comédie noire*, never darker than
at the moment when he escapes, having retrieved his gun, and is hidden by
Rosalind Russell with Cary Grant's delighted complicity in a rolltop desk
in the press room.

Her purpose, naturally, is to protect her story. The awful politician,
mayor-running-for-Congress, is to have the murderer electrocuted to
boost his giddy popularity. A pardon arrives. He tries, with the sheriff's
help, to conceal it.

By then Rosalind Russell is, in spite of her other self, utterly caught up
in the job once more. Many of the relentless twists of the tale turn, like

the *Goon Show*, on crowds of people (newspapermen) tumbling into the empty press room, seizing a telephone from the black forest of them on a huge central table, and tumbling out again, leaving the room eerily empty once more—except, at a later stage, for the hapless and incompetent killer sealed in the rolltop desk. Russell and Grant have their most vital conversations—their true *connections*—on the telephone, and at the marvellous moment when, to one's quick thrill of sympathy, she chucks off her hat and coat, grabs a phone, and asks for Walter (Cary Grant), we know that Bellamy's poor rube has had it.

As Stanley Cavell puts it, with an insouciance which would lose him his job in the marriage counselling bureau, "They simply appreciate one another more than either of them appreciates anyone else, and they would rather be appreciated by one another than by anyone else ... whether or not they can live together under the same roof."[13]

Cary Grant's comedies of the thirties are love stories, all right, but love turns out to be a quantity inseparable from high spirits, hectic excitement, sudden switches of mood, perhaps from devotion to exasperation but mood as merely that, and not something to stain or split the lived action which is love, married love, itself.

No one could call it a comfortable doctrine, and no doubt it is one a durable marriage would need to qualify as the years tolled and told. But Cary Grant carried it off in his movies until well into his fifties, and even at the high points of high physical adventure—cat-burgling on the roofs of the Riviera in *To Catch a Thief*, hanging by his fingertips onto Mount Rushmore in *North by Northwest*, he remained undisfigured by sweatmarks and perfectly clad for the occasion.

The beautiful suits, the even tan, the knife-sharp parting in his hair were the invariant signs of his presence, whether inside or outside the movie. So, too, were the white teeth, the wonderful smile, the kindliness of his gaze even as he moved towards seduction. Not that his directors allowed him any easy lays: think how Grace Kelly keeps him on the nervous *qui vive* at the picnic in *To Catch a Thief*. She offers him cold chicken, calmly asking, "Do you want a leg or a breast?"

No one can write about Cary Grant without invoking that mysterious essence (if that is what it is, appearance maybe), charm. Grant had charm in bucketfuls, but charm has its weaknesses. It is, Evelyn Waugh made one of his characters say, "simple, creamy, ... the great English blight.... It spots and kills anything it touches. It kills love. It kills art."[14] One knows what he means, that dreadful, cold cordiality of the quondam English ruling classes. But Grant's charm cast its spell by its tender attentiveness, the softening of his beautiful features as he bent towards his leading lady, the wry, easygoing way he had of admitting himself not just in the wrong, but looking an ass (all the time in *I Was a Male War Bride*, not that it mattered, but it mattered that it did not matter). The leading ladies themselves— Leslie Caron, Eve Marie Saint—testified to that tenderness, that attentive care for others, the attribute not so much of the perfect gentleman as of the perfect American democrat with the perfect Anglo-American accent ("Nobody talks like that," Jack Lemmon tells Tony Curtis in *Some Like it Hot*, as he accurately mimics a Cary Grant millionaire).

I suppose the quality he most exhibits, especially in the films of the 1950s but even in the most knockabout comedies, is his courtesy, where that used-up term best translates into grace—grace as in gracefulness, he could and did (in *Indiscreet*) dance a highland reel with scrupulous footwork—but grace in its more sanctified sense, grace as a courteous offering of one's best self to another person who, in accepting the offer, will herself become the best person that, for the moment, she can be.

That is what made his countless admirers (still going strong, me too, as is obvious) so happy. What made them so happy was the sweetness of fit between, first, time and the narrative; second, between Cary Grant, the hero, and the attention of his audience, always anxious, always reassured; third, between the rich and fluid longings he aroused and the fulfilment the manners of his storytelling permitted and permit. That all this could be brought off only by somebody so good-looking, so grown-up, so undetached and living and acting so fully at the front of his features, his body and being, cannot go without saying. Caught up in a Cary Grant movie, one's rapt attention opens at its centre and gives birth to a happiness instantly recognisable as your own.[15]

The three stars we have looked up to persuade us by the metaphysics of their presence that our own lives could attain the same proportions as those of the best-loved of their movies.

Indiscreet (1958), Ingrid Bergman and Cary Grant. Warner Bros / The Kobal Collection

III

The great film stars, in their best films, make us happy. This achievement is partly a work of art and partly a matter of luck. All stars grow old, or die young, and the happiness they create is fashioned out of the feelings they express which match feelings in their audience of a more swirling, undefined sort, brought into order and given their object by the star and her performance. Such feelings have their suitable venue and their moment. Structures of feeling, as I have insisted, have their era.

So to turn now to a woman film star, and that woman Marilyn Monroe, perhaps the most world-recognisable film star ever, takes a lot of nerve. The feelings she once commanded have been reshaped by time and chance, although, goodness knows, she still summons and commands enough.

There is a sequence of photographs of Marilyn which illustrates that perfect, historically determined balance of feeling between the star's expressiveness and the people's desire. Shortly after the ceasefire in Korea in 1953, she set off to Japan with her husband, Joe DiMaggio, a sometime baseball star and businessman who remained her devoted confidant and effortful protector ("Be sure none of these damned Kennedys come near the funeral"[16]). The couple is mobbed in Honolulu, forced to take an eight-mile motorcade in Tokyo. This was the most famous woman in the world.

Feted by American generals at a party in Tokyo, someone suggests she make a quick visit to Korea to entertain the frontline troops, a convention established during the Second Wold War. She goes to the marines (who else?), a little way behind the lines, and is flown in by helicopter. As she approaches the massed and waiting soldiers, all in a state of boisterous expectancy, she has two airmen hold her by the feet and, leaning far out from the door, waves and blows kisses to her cheering fans while telling the pilot to make repeated passes low over their heads.[17]

The troops are, understandably, extremely excited. They are also very decorous, grinning happily at the enchanting star from not too close, entertaining her at quickly improvised receptions in the tented battalion messes. She plays the part which is her best self, somehow balancing the promise of guiltless sex against the wonderful safety of domestic devotion, nervous and stammering and sincere as James Stewart, historic and

GI Monroe. Hulton Archive, Getty Images

American as John Wayne; she wrapped up these comparisons and trumped them with her bewildering innocence, flashing quickness of appeal, her irresistible erotic presence. There has never been anyone quite like her, we say helplessly, and it is true.

When she sings to the troops, in her tiny, sweet, little-girl's voice (remember "Happy birthday, Mr. President"?), she dresses "in a clinging gown of plum-coloured sequins, cut so low it exposed much of her breasts to the frigid winds." These were Korean winter winds and well below freezing. Decked in rhinestones, she sings "Diamonds are a girl's best friend," pretend-cynical, meaning none of the words, meaning all of the meaning. Suddenly she stops. She steps over to the edge of the platform and bends her amazing body down towards a soldier. She snaps the cover off his camera lenses, murmuring, "Honey, you forgot to take it off." A long, laughing, loving roar rises from the crowd. Asked afterwards about the cold, she said, "I swear I didn't feel a thing, except good." She is the centre of every man's well-mannered desire, as close and as impossible as fulfilment itself. Also, she is happy, and therefore she makes the men happy. This shines out from the news photographs with all the truth of black-and-white wartime pictures. She gathers into her strong, unreliable body the X-rays of longing, desire, admiration, envy which thousands of eyes have poured into her. She is like a top that has been whipped and whipped. She is ready to explode with the forces of attention she has absorbed. She must smile all the time. Marilyn's smiles are part of the legend; they were invented for her by Scott Fitzgerald on the Riviera.

When she leaves Korea she is running a temperature of 104 degrees Fahrenheit. It subsides only as the charges of desire leave her body.

This is stardom at the extreme, and Marilyn Monroe lived it in extremis. It is a truism repeated even by her most famous husband, celebrated in his own turn, Arthur Miller, that living like that, intelligent and aware of the radiation damage caused by all that adulation, she would have to die young, as she did, at thirty-six.

Of course she did not have to. There is something repellent in Miller's complaisance, when he heard the news, "It had to happen. I didn't know when or how, but it was inevitable."[18] Still more inexcusable was his self-exculpation in his autobiographical, mesmerising play about the marriage, *After the Fall*. But in these leftover scraps and the tides of prurience, worship, sound affection, straight gossip, and awful psychobabble which have washed over her grave since 1962, we may certainly find plenty of moral lessons about the manufacture and the uses of celebrity.

She had enough damage done to her from early on to make for tragedy. Norma Jean was born to Gladys Baker and an absentee father on the edge of Hollywood. She would claim, with passionate sincerity, that her psychotic grandmother tried to stifle her, her mother went screaming mad; she is fostered, in an orphanage, neglected and cared for by a succession of poorish households, she is set up for a marriage at sixteen, weds a poor sap of a working-class lad, Jim Dougherty, who goes to war and they drift apart. She suffers terribly and all her adult life from endometriosis, a condition in which the uteral membrane spreads into the abdomen, causing the fearful period pains which would sometimes drive her to crouch in agony on the floor and moan in pain, and which almost certainly prevented her having the baby she so badly wanted.

It was a hard American upbringing; there have been many harder. During it, she learns that complete mastery of makeup with which she brought her fresh, clean, and lively beauty to such a tremulous and enticing fullness and variety of expression. The makeup made her magical. It gave her, in the fashion of the day, a cherry-red and cupid's-bow mouth, and this, below her ash-blonde bleached hair, her serious gaze tilted upwards, made her unforgettable face above her soft, strong body, its beautiful bosoms and big bottom, into the ideal of womanliness for an epoch. T. S. Eliot's lovely line from his poem *Marina*, lost daughter found, "The awakened, lips parted, the hope, the new ships," could have been written for her.

So much has been written about her that any fresh attempt sounds immediately corny. But as is obvious for our purposes, not only can she hit the heights of *Some Like It Hot* (and half a dozen others nearly as good), a movie which never breaks the promise of happiness, but she also so lived the terrible drama of stardom that it exacted—no one knows for sure how—her death. In *Some Like It Hot*, as Sugar Cane, she fills exactly with her splendid body and sweet innocence a space which any other actress could only have brought off as pastiche. Her star genius is to be in fictional actuality that impossible American woman, maternal schoolgirl, sex-object-with-a-subject, nesciently virtuous, guiltlessly available. Only Monroe could have done it; one easily dismisses Tony Curtis's nastiness about kissing her as being just what Killer Yankees, upstaged by a good woman, will do to get their own back.

Interwoven with virtuous sexuality and girlish trust was Monroe's struggle to find the character she never had and which the institutionalised cruelty of Hollywood was bound to deny her. She fought for it with brightly lit courage, never more so than in marrying Arthur Miller.

She was unique, and the constellations of stardom would have been much dimmer if she had not invented herself out of emotional obscurity and a fleshly certainty as complete as Michelangelo's *David*. She was also, as Mailer says, "one of the toughest blondes ever to come down the pike (there in the concentrated center of her misty blonde helplessness)."[19] Miller was a celebrity also, celebrated as artist, intellectual, and for the principled way he spat in the eye of the House Un-American Activities Committee and then wrote his masterpiece, *The Crucible*. So the combination was unprecedented, and no wonder Miller could not see past her dazing physicality—she was funny, too—to the domestic disorder, the heedlessness of normal working routine (always late on set, sometimes just absent), insomniac, rattling with the pills of a dozen prescriptions and patent medicines, tearful, unable to make out who to be. At the time of her marriage, she announced she was converting to Miller's low-key Unitarian kind of Judaism and would cook him kosher menus.

If Miller were dazzled, well he might be. But years afterwards, he wrote unwittingly in his autobiography of just how ignorant of himself and her he remained. It is no surprise that it was plain, dogged old DiMaggio who saw her off to the grave.

> [T]here were a dozen people in the departure lounge, and almost all were watching her. She was in a beige skirt and a white satin blouse, and her hair hung down to her shoulders, parted on the right side, and the sight of her was something like pain, and I knew that I must flee or walk into a doom beyond all knowing. With all her radiance she was surrounded by a darkness that perplexed me. I could not yet imagine that in my very shyness she saw some safety, release from the detached and centerless and invaded life she had been given; instead, I hated my lifelong timidity, but there was no changing it now. When we parted I kissed her cheek and she sucked in a surprised breath. I started to laugh at her overacting until the solemnity of feeling in her eyes shocked me into remorse, and I hurried backwards toward the plane. It was not duty alone that called me; I had to escape her childish voracity, something like my own unruly appetite for self-gratification, which had both created what art I had managed to make and disgusted me with its stain of irresponsibility. A retreat to the safety of morals, to be sure, but not necessarily to truthfulness.[20]

If Miller was not up to her—and he was not—then no one could have been. Until Jackie Kennedy took the stage in the last year of her husband's life and the first few weeks of her widowhood, Marilyn Monroe was at the centre of the national imagination and kept there by a million flashbulbs in a way no other woman had been or would be in American history. This is something a social critic like Richard Dyer, concerned to psychoanalyse her appeal and earnestly dismayed at Monroe's failure to presage feminism, cannot grasp.[21] She entranced people, even the people. The self she was able to act made people happy. Certainly she served as sex object (to use the damned cliché) and therefore, to tens of thousands of helpless wankers, as the magazine cover they kept handily to hand. But in the daily life of the culture, she walked in certainty of admiration and curiosity but untouched by the malice or even the envy of her audiences.

Yet she concentrated into her short life all the punishment the good celebrity will take and must not be broken by. The trouble is that if, like Marilyn Monroe, you are as open and tenderhearted as she was, then success, fame, the people's gaze, the studio's coarseness, your (male) fellow actors' ordinary irritation and impatience with you, will quite probably kill you. When you add to that burden the attention of the politically mighty and cannot resist a love affair, clandestine except for the police bodyguards, with the president's brother the attorney general, then the nation's sweetheart is set for tragedy.

> She had no common sense, but what she did have was something holier, a long-reaching vision of which she herself was only fitfully aware: humans were all need, all wound. What she wanted most was not to judge but to win recognition from a sentimentally cruel profession, and from men blinded to her humanity by her perfect beauty. She was part queen, part waif, sometimes on her knees before her own body and sometimes despairing because of it.[22]

If celebrity, like any other social value and the concept which captures it, is compounded out of a succession of the relevant human actions, the actions of Marilyn Monroe lent the concept new radiance and plaintive civility. She still lurks in its power to enact either modern comedy or its darker mask.

IV

The quartet of stars—three men and one woman—who have danced us to this point in our historical argument were not only larger than the life they represented on screen. They were also somehow representative of their

nation, available to all who watched them as picturing the impossible version of the best selves audiences could hardly be in everyday life. The three
men, as men mostly do, got away with this more easily than the woman.
They got away with their lives. But even in the squalid confusion of her
death (did she mean to kill herself with Nembutal? How did she swallow
all those pills without water?), Marilyn Monroe remained spotless.

This singularity is emphasised if we glance at the career of the woman
who seemed, in Europe at least, to match her for irresistible gaiety and candid sexuality. Brigitte Bardot may have been put down, in a spasm of typical *Normalien* snobbery by Simone de Beauvoir, doyenne of feminism, as
being "seductive as a chambermaid,"[23] but she fairly flared out as a symbol
of happy sex for a whole adolescent generation after *Et Dieu Créa la Femme*
in 1957. The fame the movie brought the wretched girl the bombarding
cameras, the cover stories and strip pics, the throngs of gaping sightseers
where the sight was one very pretty girl, sent that girl, as her looks faded
and normal domestic life proved unlivable, off the edge of due balance
and self-awareness, perhaps of sanity itself. It left her in pitiful age, solitary
except for her money and a hundred cats.

Bardot, poor thing, missed the match between popular sentiment and
fresh young beauty. The frame of feeling had moved, for better and worse,
not only towards new freedoms for sex, but also towards a new coarseness
and cynicism in the presence of fame.

The point is most firmly made if we compare the stars of British cinema,
at that stage still independent enough of Hollywood, as they worked to
represent the British people to the British people a little time after their
moment of enforced and unusual unity during World War II. What happened then was not analogous to the cheerful star-making of 1930s Hollywood. The situation was as grave as could be; the movies must not falsify
the gravity but must nonetheless make it endurable and, so far as movies
may, help overcome it.

In addressing myself to the English and their Englishness I intend no
offence, these neurotically offendable days, to either Scots, Welsh, or Irish
still ambivalently gathered under the heading "British" (and still formally
recognising the Union Jack as their national flag), still less to the 5 percent
of the population whose parents left the old empire some time between

1950 and 1970 or so for the promise of life, liberty, and the pursuit of happiness as held out in Birmingham, Bradford, Liverpool, East London, and elsewhere. Yet in part, indeed, I *am* addressing that smallish diaspora, since they came to what was thought of, not inaccurately, as the parent-nation in expectation of what parents should give, and that parent in particular: comfort, support, shelter, justice, authority, steadiness, love, trustworthiness. These were qualities which, it was alleged, the British at large and the English as dominant had contrived into the practices of a culture and the formations of a state. Those practices and formations were no doubt spotted and disfigured also by the usual bloody cold of the English as well as their mildish racism, but they would nonetheless pass liberal muster in most historical reviews. Englishness had for a season an honourable moral content and a place to which it belonged. That place was home, a term as absent from the indexes of the official classics of political science as it is central to the political values each of us instinctively invokes if we want to talk about politics in everyday life.

In offering a detectable solidity in the relations of history and more-or-less historical films, there is implied a no-nonsense theory of representation in which a flat screen, black-and-white photography, a family parade of extremely familiar and gloriously indistinguishable theatrical heroes and stars playing unknown warrior-heroes, and the direct gaze of unself-consciously English directors combine to tell true enough stories about real enough events.

Such a task can be brought off, of course, only at those few historically privileged moments since the invention of film at which popular sentiment, technological recording systems, and the forced march of quotidian eventuality can be made to fit together with comparatively little interpretative play or slippage. These conditions held pretty tightly in the 1950s. War itself had provided a comprehensive account of eventuality, not only one in which the mere facts of life could be rendered immediately intelligible by surrounding them with strategic explanations, but also one in which conduct itself, whether admirable or not, rarely provided a moral puzzle. The deadly sins and the cardinal virtues assumed significance in terms dictated by the plot of the anti-Fascist war and its compulsory conception of duty.

Finally, in this happy coincidence of camera, fact, and feeling, that elusive historical necessity, popular sentiment, was keenly actualised in the forms of contemporary narrative in the 1950s. Men and women in their thirties and forties (and more: the period is also striking for the common lack of distinction in the dominant structure of feeling as between the generations) looked back on their shared experience of wartime as it began to come into an always provisional and evaluative balance. That is to say, they were in a position to judge the films for truthfulness as picturing a people's experience of what Angus Calder called in his book of that title *The People's War*. For the first time in cultural history a huge and historic sequence of events was narrated and represented not on behalf of a powerful elite and as redounding to its credit, but on behalf of a whole population, permitting them to judge for themselves whether they came out of it well or badly. Our family of directors, writers, and performers contrived a common, popular aesthetic within whose polished, intensely organised styles the criteria of plainness and accessibility, of trust in the truths of feeling, domestic beauty, and the reassuring factuality of *things*, came together in a noble declaration of unironic faith in some great romantic simples: love, solidarity, character, home.

Sixty-odd subsequent years have corroded this innocence. Consumer capitalism and the absence of war have together worked to underfeed "solidarity" until it has become so thin we can see through it, and placed the values of radical individualism (identity, fulfilment, self-discovery and so forth) at the centre of the board. But I will nonetheless represent the war films of the 1950s here, in the face of supreme unction on the part of all-knowing postmodernism, as themselves representing pretty faithfully the feelings of a full generation as its members looked back ten or fifteen years to a time in which they belonged to an inclusive and acknowledged narrative, a time during which this generation could be said to have had the chance to live well, as well as watching others die, on the whole, to the point and with credit.

These remarks provide a brief footnote to my history of the feelings. The representation of those feelings in the great British war movies of the 1950s, made at just about the right distance from the events to permit immediacy and detachment, had to be (and were) more or less faithful to the facts as lived and vividly recollected by their audiences. The directors who made these movies—Michael Powell, David Lean, Anthony Asquith—were at one with the ideals and emotions of their audiences. Those same ideals, modestly egalitarian, mildly socialist (more Morris than Marx), internationalist-minded, generous-hearted, and courteous, were what brought into being by way of the postwar Labour government such grand achievements of the British polity as the National Health Service, the Welfare State, and comprehensive education.

The stars they appointed to embody the vision and its feasibility are much smaller than such giants as Cary Grant and Marilyn Monroe. But that is exactly the point. John Mills, Michael Redgrave, Jack Hawkins, David Niven; Dinah Sheridan, Muriel Pavlow, Celia Johnson, Kathleen Byron vanish into the parts they played. The women made much smaller stars than the men, for this was Britain and with an English ruling class. But all these names, for all their being picked out in bright lights, are barely distinguishable from the roles they filled with such accuracy. *They* were hardly recognised in the street, but their dramas were held close to the heart of the nation for quite a while.

I make no effort to suppress an idealising note in these remarks. But the matter is, so to say, theoretic for all that. Certain stars melt into role and narrative, but only when the films concerned are absorbed completely by the sensibilities and moral imagination of a mass audience. Two films must serve to illustrate my contention.

Powell and Pressburger's wonderful inauguration of this small cinematic epoch of war films is, of course, *A Matter of Life and Death* (1946). It anticipated the 1950s by four years and starts its action in May 1945, only a day or two before Germany surrendered. It opens with a young poet (David Niven) commanding a doomed Lancaster, frantically quoting Andrew Marvell and Walter Raleigh to the young American woman checking the bombers home from a coastline control tower. Niven jumps out into the night with no parachute rather than be burned to death, misses his guardian angel in the dark, hits the sea, survives to meet and fall in love with the American. He is then tried in heaven for his life with the defence that because he has fallen in love *after* the official moment of his death, heavenly bureaucracy is at fault and his death revocable.

His prosecutor, ally and friend of Paul Revere, keeps up his nation's old enmity against the English. The jury, appealed against, as being as all of

them victims and judges of empire—Irish, Indian, Chinese, and so on—
is promptly replaced by exactly the same people as all-American citizens.
God is, naturally, a (Jewish) Englishman, but more important, he is the
surgeon who repairs the lesions in the hero's brain, restoring him to poetry
and to a long and happy marriage with the American. The vision of an all-
powerful, just world order whose finally reconciled citizens are apotheo-
sised in the benignity of a hospitable United States was simple, rousing,
and, as the Marshall Plan opened its coffers the following year, plausible
as well. Michael Powell's vision of fair play as shared by Anglo-Americans,
and domestic love and happiness as cherished by everybody, retains the
right kind of big sentimentality, the kind politics now needs.

This noble film is an overture to the epoch. Thereafter, what one finds
in the remarkable succession of honestly made, well-built, and tightly told
war films is not at all a threnody to empire or an aesthetics of decline, but
rather a winning story about the necessity of duty, its visible fulfilment in
modestly efficacious action, and the confirmation of its significance in the
bonds of trust.

The Cruel Sea (1952) stands as one eponymous masterpiece at the head
of all these films. What is striking about the film is the deliberately prosaic
nature of its epic poetry. As the two senior officers on the little ship, so
unobtrusively played by Jack Hawkins and Donald Sinden, close in friendship and shared hardship, held apart by rank, say at the end, there were
only two enemy vessels sunk. Five years are concentrated into less than
two hours, but such are the demands of the form; that form must hold in
the tension of art the large frame (or structure) of feeling within which the
English told themselves, not untruthfully, the story of the war.

In form and feeling, *The Cruel Sea* looks at first blush like a remake of *In
Which We Serve* (1942). Made, of course, as pretty well a piece of straight
propaganda, Noel Coward's film is in any case based on the unmistakably heroic but redolently regal early wartime caveats of the Lord Louis
Mountbatten and his ship HMS *Kelly*. One can therefore scrape off its
surface a slight but sugary glutinousness permissible in the circumstances
but quite absent in the successor film. Jack Hawkins aboard *Compass Rose*
is given no domestic life at all; Donald Sinden takes up, in a series of
mere glimpses, with the formidably intelligent as well as beautiful Virginia
McKenna, but it is the tacit and taciturn friendship with his captain that

counts. Friendship, for sure—Sinden turns down a command in order to stay as Hawkins's Number One—but friendship defined as the faithful discharge of mutual obligations to the crew, to the service, and—though no one would ever have put it like that—to the country and the necessity to defeat fascism.

Much more, however, is made of saving lives and losing them than of cutting down or up the enemy. *Compass Rose* rescues sailors (including Scandinavian merchantmen), their lungs clotted with machine oil; in pursuit of a U-boat which they fail to catch, they run down their own shipwrecked comrades struggling in the water; when the second of the two ships in the story comes finally home in 1945, the last word of the film is the bare order: "Shut down main engines." Meiosis is its stylistic trope, and that seems to square with the record. The chance of a second marriage for the plump, wholesome, and widowed sister of one petty officer with another of his mess-mates goes down without a comment and with the ship. The beautiful Wren is not waiting on the quayside. One trivially unpleasant officer (Stanley Baker) malingers his way to a cowardly shore job; another, unimportantly courageous and dryly ironic volunteer officer, previously a barrister (Denholm Elliot), is first cuckolded and then drowned. It is the surprisingly domestic story of duty confirmed by significant action and set off by an upright courtesy towards death. The action is held within a polyphony of the sentiments still active in English society and, it may be, still giving a bit of spine and substance to Englishness.

Such movies make no intentional stand against stardom. They simply fill a chapter in the starstruck history in which feeling and form coincided, and the actors dramatising both were, for once, identifiable as the comrades of their rapt audiences. It would be silly to say that I would rather have John Mills than John Wayne as popular hero. What I mean is that when the stars look down, some of them are smaller and nearer and less amazing to behold than others.

V

As I hinted a few pages ago, this coincidence of history and private life was much emphasised by the advent of both the newsreel and its corol-

lary, the news presenter. Newspapers had proved themselves, in their er-
ratic way, absolutely necessary as a means of understanding the modern
world. Human beings take what they can from those they know, from
the places they live in, from the experiences we privilege as "direct." The
mass daily press which began to shift such prodigious loads of paper once
the new press barons—Pulitzer, Hearst, Northcliffe, and company—had
got the idea of the broadsheet daily did so by way of the near and the
recent.

It was then merely natural to interpret the incomprehensibility of the
world and its bewildering cities in terms of visible and powerful individuals. The gossip-columnists, as we saw, gave their sweet-and-sour savour to
this process, placing the rich, the politically powerful, and the different
orders of stardom in the single category of celebrity, a new sort of social
role with a new kind of self to fill it. That self was less a character than a
"personality," a usage which, OED tells us, becomes common only well
into the twentieth century.

Such figures, a docile population quickly learned, were there, as far as
the citizens were concerned, just to be looked at. The custom of gathering
to see the famous was quickly assembled, sometimes with high audience
participation, as at Nuremburg or at tickertape welcomes in Manhattan,
sometimes simply in a dense crush outside a hotel or official building. On
these latter occasions, as we all know, people throng to the barriers just to
watch him or her arrive, smile, wave, and vanish. Whatever is happening
inside is privy to the powerful, the stars, the rich, who court or endure this
exposure as the price of their distinction.

Occasionally, as in the case of the gossip-columnists, some of the common people are admitted in the guise of our representatives. They emerge
to tell us, balefully or gushingly, what they were told and what they saw.

This is an elaborate ceremony of more than a century's standing. It was
deepened and elaborated by the coming of the newsreel, and then radi-
calised and levelled by wartime. The newsreel mediated the experience of
the crowd outside the hotel. In the news theatre, all those not on the spot
could still see the famous faces and catch them waving. I do not think this
practice should be condescended to. We go to see the celebrities and the
powerful not so much in adulation, though that may be part of it, as in

keen curiosity. What are they really like? Is she *really* (that all-enveloping adverb) as beautiful as her pictures? Does he really walk in that swaggering way? How ill does the king seem? Will the president look as worried as he surely is?

These questions and two dozen more bring people to see what they can see. Then the newsreel and its ancillary, the news photo, arrived to extend the audience's desire to know, and also to pervade quotidian life with the imagery of importance elsewhere. This distantiation, and its consequent belittling of the local and heartfelt, still holds. But it was abruptly closed for a season by war, and the beneficent consequences of that closure are still with us, alongside the transient glimpse of her and him caught for a split second between the dodging heads in front, blocking your gaze.

For what wartime brought with its newsreels was the candid recognition that everyone was in this together. As I noted, the stars in black-and-white war movies were in the same uniforms and similar predicaments to all those who watched them. Moreover, the newsmen and a few newswomen (none finer than Martha Gellhorn, sometime Mrs. Ernest Hemingway) went to see the action and tell us about it. When they did, they found for themselves a new kind of stardom, but only as telling those at home about what was happening to their mothers, husbands, cousins, fathers, friends, and sweethearts ... and happening to those they did not know. Martha Gellhorn hitched a lift in May 1945 to Dachau and talked to a doctor there.

She likes the doctor and he has plenty to tell her. He had been a prisoner in Dachau for five years. In her report at least, he shares Martha Gellhorn's gift for controlled understatement. It may be that she filled his style with hers, for hers—bare, plain, "objective" if that means telling a story with few adornments, scarcely any descriptive detours, few adjectives, fewer adverbs, simple vocabulary—is as quick and vivid and clear to see as scenes in great literature should always be.

The doctor spoke with great detachment about the things he had watched in this hospital. He had watched them and there was nothing he could do to stop them. The prisoners talked in the same

way—quietly, with a strange little smile as if they apologised for talking of such loathsome things to someone who lived in a real world
and could hardly be expected to understand Dachau.

"The Germans made here some unusual experiments," the doctor said.
"They wished to see how long an aviator could go without oxygen, how
high in the sky he could go. So they had a closed car from which they
pumped the oxygen. It is a quick death," he said. "It does not take more
than fifteen minutes, but it is a hard death. They killed not so many people, only eight hundred in that experiment. It was found that no-one can
live above thirty-six thousand feet altitude without oxygen. [24]
    She listens to more from her doctor about a similar experiment in which
six hundred people died while the Germans placed them in vats of ice-cold
water, varying the temperature in order to establish the compelling statistic
that a human being will live for two and a half hours in water temperatures
of minus eight degrees Fahrenheit.
    "Didn't they scream or cry out?" He smiled at that question. "There was
no use in this place for a man to scream or cry out. It was no use for any
man ever."
    In tiny ways Gellhorn shapes the prose so that it tells. Maybe the doctor
really did repeat "scream or cry out" and "it was no use," but however it
was, the dual assonance of the phrase is chillingly effective.
    When she has given them their say, she finally bursts out with hers. It is
of course honest and eloquent, hard to better as the response of those our
people sent to tell them what they found in the heartlands of the hideous
enemy as that enemy reached the end of his tether.

We have all seen a great deal now; we have seen too many wars and
too much violent dying; we have seen hospitals, bloody and messy
as butcher shops; we have seen the dead like bundles lying on all the
roads of half the earth. But nowhere was there anything like this.
Nothing about war was ever as insanely wicked as these starved and
outraged, naked, nameless dead. Behind one pile of dead lay the
clothed healthy bodies of the German soldiers who had been found
in this camp. They were shot at once when the American Army en-

tered. And for the first time anywhere one could look at a dead man with gladness.[25]

The newsreels confirmed what she said. That is what newsreels did, and do on television: they confirm what the reporter says; we can see for ourselves (again) that she was telling the plain truth. As a consequence, a new kind of celebrity was fashioned for very necessity and out of the interplay of news photography, the diaspora of a generation fighting world war, and the mutual craving for a safe return home.

Ed Murrow stands as paramount in this continuing interlude. He serves to actualise that now ubiquitous figure, the news presenter, who speaks those stories we tell ourselves about ourselves. Murrow himself makes a pretty sufficient hero. Starting on radio, he and his ally, William Shirer, devised the forms of modern political news broadcasting: on-the-spot live commentary ("being there"); interviews with leading actors in the drama (generals and corporals, prime ministers and bombed-out citizens); round-the-continent reports, a voice in every capital or key location, so that the listeners can build in imagination a usable map of events and take their bearings as citizens of the Allied nations. Then the voices led back to London, where Murrow stayed and worked an eighteen-hour day, broadcasting live to the United States in the middle of the night, as the bombs exploded all around him, and he gave his crisp, incisive summary, closing always with his famous signature line, "good-night and good luck."[26]

Ed Murrow, we can say, established the radio-and-television news presenter as celebrity. He belongs in the galaxy of the stars first of all in his own right; the part he invented and played brought certain key qualities into public play, just as the best film stars did. He was trustworthy, blunt, brave, intelligent, and an Anglophile American. He called out those qualities and the feelings which shaped them first from millions of listeners, and then from millions more watchers.

But he matters also in this rough chronology of stardom as creating a new source of social authority, analogous to that of the film stars. He gave his audiences a credible and a realisable way of thinking and feeling about the world. The anchorman and -woman, as television accelerated to its present imperial and oppressive scope, became guides to the conduct of one's bearing in the world and how to feel about it.

It is, as we will see in chapter 10, an enormous genealogy. It has of course long lost the high seriousness and stern grandeur of a Murrow, the principled ease and familiarity of a Walter Cronkite (can anyone forget his reporting, in honest tears, of John Kennedy's assassination?). But Murrow's descendants—Fox News excepted—make a decent fist of truthful story-telling, and the best, as we shall see, do sufficient honour to the vocation of stardom, to which few are called but far too many are chosen.

Chapter 9

From Each According to His Ability: Sport, Rock, Fashion, and the Self

Our narrative begins to close upon the present. Naturally enough, people live in the here and now, there being nowhere else to do so. It has been my method, however, such as it is, to insist on our historicality, and discussion of the present, for all its zest and keenness, is bound to point out just how historical is the contemporary. Amiable old fogies (me, too) look at the capers of the celebrities of the present day and with varying degrees of distaste tut and wag their heads and see it all as the end of civilisation. But even the most nauseating manifestations of our leading men and women, and even the most repellent of the magazines, the TV chat, and phoney quiz shows, were all shaped and prepared for in the close and distant past. While this extraordinary bundling of the facts and fictions has taken place, the oceans of mass emotion have swept with the tides in and out, mingling, as oceans do, innumerable crosscurrents in the harsh suck and recoil of the waves pounding the beaches people live on.

Tides have always been metaphors of time. They serve good purpose in doing so. For our feelings move as with many conflicting surges, and these have their origins in a dozen different sources in the past. The game of condescension in the 1780s, the "civil affections" of Hume's middle station, the tempests of Romantic love celebrated by Verdi, the raptures of wealth in Newport, Rhode Island, the abandoned yearnings of fascism, the blissful solace offered by the stars, the blankness of inaction and the insoluble puzzle of individuality: all these strong currents of feeling, now hot, now cold, now thick, now thin, pour past and through us like the sea, the sea. Small wonder people do not know what to feel and turn to those graceful figures which are the cynosure of all eyes in order to find out.

The solutions are, this being modernity, more a matter of regimentation and routine than one might expect. For a hundred years and more, critics have been telling us about the slow dissolution of human freedoms, the nothingness attendant upon the radical individualisation of experience, the loss of principles of continuity and culture, the destruction of nature herself, all the dire effects of consumer capitalism run riot.

You cannot say they are wrong, only that that is not all there is to say. Indeed, I have deployed several of such reach-me-down explanatory slogans earlier in the book. We cannot do without them if we are to understand anything about the world, but they are not much help. In any case, what better world impends? The dreams of state socialism finally sank with the end of Cold War, the great rush of people hurrying to get out of the sometime socialist republics and to join the happy shoppers on the other side of the iron curtain. Of course there is, whatever the longings of old leftists for the virtuous state and common ownership of the means of production, so much to be said for the great happiness of shopping, for the physical ease of mass consumption, the comfort of its furniture and cars and pharmacology, the packed and gleaming supermarkets. All this for four-fifths of every rich nation! Who wants the earnest tedium of membership instead, the dreary duties of the citizen, the endless meetings?

Some such argument is audible at the back of all the inevitable discontents of contemporary life. In societies without lively participation or keen political debate, television serves up the official conversation of the culture, and those who speak or act on it are the dominant figures in the collective imagination.

Naturally, they include politicians, and even in a European climate in which politicians are routinely decried, they undoubtedly embody a hierarchy of real power and are greeted as celebrities of a peculiar kind accordingly. Things are different in the United States, where political passions, at least for those with jobs and houses and a franchise they intend to use, run a good deal higher than in the European Union. There, the American Constitution retains a religious force and lends politics its numinous glow, even to shopworn old senators and Supreme Court judges long past their best.

All the same, politicians are sure still to count for something on either side of the Atlantic, and they do so count in virtue of the raw commodity, power. That marks off their celebrity from other kinds. Theirs is the fame of efficacity, and if they prove to be ineffective, fame becomes infamy. The world of celebrity without power is marked strictly off from politics even though politicians delight in the company of the powerlessly famous, which brings them, according to choice, warm little benisons of association—with this star's niceness or beauty, with a rock musician's deafening appeal, with a sportsman's athletic grace or world-beating victories.

These vibrations are released in the images of grand parties in the capital, where the stars' fame glows around the men and women of power. Then the stars can return to commonplace stardom, enhanced by trailing little clouds of glory.

These rituals may be watched weekly. It is important to note, nonetheless, just how rigid is the barrier between political power and mere celebrity. This goes deep in social structure. Only in times of social breakdown does the division fail, and rock or film or even academic stars climb on the podium and wield their fame to rouse the people. The philosopher Leszek Kolakowski did this in Poland in 1968 and was exiled for his pains; the folksinger Victor Jura did the same in Chile in 1973 and was executed. Only the playwright Vaclev Havel is the exception to my rule, and he won office in Czechoslovakia's "velvet revolution" in 1989.[1] Ronald Reagan and Arnold Schwarzenegger had to do extensive basic training as jobbing politicians before winning America and California, respectively.

II

The high charge fame gives out, in other words, is contained within the special zone reserved for it in social identity. Even the crazy hysteria of football is confined to the stadiums, the match, and the centre of the big city where drunken supporters go to work up and work off the peculiar rage the game is assigned to create. By the same token, all those thousands who attend, in happy squalor, Britain's mammoth rock festival held in muddy fields close to the country's small headquarters of barmy folk-magic in Glastonbury find in the occasion what is assigned to it. They cheer and sway and sing and dance and in modest quantities trip and screw while their appointed poets multiply the show of excessive and clamorous feeling with the music on stage. Then everyone goes peaceably home.

Sport and rock have become, not only in the rich nations but worldwide, the two forms of social leisure which are sure to draw hundreds of thousands away from television and into the ambit of action. Everyone agrees that you cannot get the true feel of a football match or a rock concert without being there, even though the numbers watching such events on television far exceed those present. Nonetheless, to see the live match and hear the live music is the true experience, and the value set on it by such participants—mostly men and women who still count as youngsters, under forty, let us say—is much higher than the value placed on attendance by TV in the living room, and much higher still than turning out in the wet to watch a political cavalcade speed by or to get a glimpse of the stars arriving for their own awards at the Oscar or BAFTA orgies of self-congratulation.

There is a reassuring continuity in this. People prefer to see and hear celebrities doing what they are good at. The connection between achievement and renown holds up. In the case of sport and its huge spectator following, this goes a long way back. Like all serious human characteristics (and "serious" may, indeed must, take in what is comic), sport has its metaphysical meanings. The official histories always try to find its origins in medieval larkings-about, but sport only transpires in a recognisable shape as the industrial revolution begins to roll, and working men begin to struggle for a bit of the leisure released by the machine and already so noticeably enjoyed by their masters. The metaphysical point of sport is that it presages and embodies the active, expressive, and beautiful life of men and women contained within a benign and munificent nature.

Games are at root nonproductive expressions of joyful, playful, competitive cooperation. You try to beat the other fellow for fun and afterwards, win or lose, are united with him in happy exhaustion and the restoration provided by plentiful food and drink. These are the lovely lineaments of sport, though it may sound slightly high-pitched to say so.

Games were first shaped by industrial capitalism in its hemispheric imperium in Britain after 1770 (when the Hambledon cricket club was founded), gradually spreading to Europe and North America. From the first the football fields, and only a little later the baseball stadiums, were built in the heart of heavy industry: the huge stands *looked* like factories; the huge, civic crowds were identical with the men pouring through the factory gates; the numbers produced by the game—goals, batting averages, points, numbers of spectators—were analysed like industrial statistics. The industrial architecture enclosed the little sacred plot of the field, the only patch of green grass for miles; the uniform the players wore—that unexpected mixture of the nursery and the vacation (those shorts, those bright shirts, those knickerbockers!)—was a deliberate negation of working clothes.

So too, in England, the great cricket grounds enclosed the green turf like a holy grove. They were much roomier than football fields, and they often included a few trees as befitted a summer game. The terraces were more gradually raked so that summer sun could warm the joints stiffened and made knobby by hard labour. The players wore the leisure clothes of the leisure class which codified the game—long white trousers, well-ironed white shirts, knitted woollen sweaters with coloured piping—and the key building, the pavilion, was as unlike the giant girders and corrugated iron of the football stadium as could be. Instead, the pavilion was a seaside Queen Anne affair,[2] with neat little wooden balustrades and fretted bargeboarding along its eaves and gables. Their reference, whether in Scarborough or Tonbridge, Manchester or Leeds, was to holiday resorts and country house weekends.

Finally, the last of the first mass spectator sports systematically invented in the nineteenth century was horse-racing, and that too took a very substantial strip of green real estate on the outskirts of some of the biggest industrial cities in England (it was only transplanted to Celtic Ireland, not Wales, nor—or not properly—Scotland). But its real coordinates were at Epsom and Ascot, two points of a calculus whose ellipse was the revealingly named Home Counties, and its grandstands, enclosures, gambling industry, and display were tokens of a sport unusually dominated by the emblematic summits of the old ruling class. The monarchy shook hands with cricketers and gave cups to footballers, but it *owned* bloodstock. In racing, the cooperation of the classes was assured by the presence of status and old corruption. In football and cricket and such endearing siblings as bowls, tennis, hockey, and even mountaineering or golf, first British and then world-class and -race divisions and oppositions were transcended in the celebration of a natural enclave in which all that was produced was beauty, happiness, and victory.

To talk about happiness I need a hand from that unhappy man, Walter Benjamin, once again. If each epoch dreams its utopia, a good society in which the best form of a prehistoric past is perfected upon the unknowable form of the future, and if this *is* popular culture, then sport dreams of a garden in which the free, productive effort of equal men and women issues in efficacious action and the happiness of victory unresented by the losers. In this utopia, the struggle of the game represents that labour of love and love of labour in which nature gives us her motherly sustenance without herself being depleted. We win, and neither she nor you minds. We embrace, afterwards, as equals. To be a good sport is to be virtuous.

Sport, I shall say, was conceived, against the dreadful privations of the new industries, as a dream of coming home and being happy. Walter Benjamin wrote of fairy stories that "their liberating magic" points to "the complicity of nature with liberated man."[3] In the fairy tale, nature, whether as tree, wind, rain, or helpful creature (deer, nightingale, hound), lends a loving hand or obtrudes a warning obstacle. Thus also in works of art grown out of fairy tales, such as *The Magic Flute* and *The Caucasian Chalk Circle.* Thus also in the sports which have made us happiest and been recollected as folk and individual memories, the particular occasions in which great deeds were done by great heroes, even, in a diminuendo, done by oneself, were then gathered into the collectivity of family or national storytelling.

It is the proper childishness *and* childlikeness in sport which restore us to nature and, we feel, to our true nature; as Dickens remarked in a similar context, it exacts that close and accurate observation of life which is remarkable in those people who typically "retain a certain freshness, and gentleness, and capacity of being pleased, which are also an inheritance they have preserved from childhood."[4] One of the happiest consequences of a love of sport is precisely that close observation of the life-in-action which sport *is*, and which (we may hope) is a form of attentiveness learned at play and subsequently brought to bear upon the game of art.

It is the combination of aesthetic power, emotional familiarity, physical expenditure, and topographical beauty which makes sport matter as it does. If one of these fails, because of age or accident, the sport fails for us. If all work together, the sport tells a tale, like the fairy story, of the comity of a free woman, man, or child with nature.

It may seem a bit shy-making to speak like this. I am anxious to declare why it still seems to me right to take sport seriously and with a gladsome heart. What is afoot when thousands of young men, always European and mostly English, break out into horrible excesses of drunkenness, vomit, brutal fighting, and loathsome racist chants is worth pausing over in a chapter on sport and fame. The answer may be most readily brought out by our preferred method, a couple of brief biographies.

Stanley Matthews is an eponym of English football, but although unmistakably a star who has retained a distinctive place in the folk memory, he is a figure inextricable from his home and culture in a way not true of the stars of Hollywood nor of the sporting stars of later generations. He was born in Stoke-on-Trent in 1915, at a time when his hometown was capital of the "Pottery" towns, European centre of the huge china, plate-, and pot-making industry, an indistinguishable conurbation speckled with the towering chimneys of the trade, threaded by the earliest black industrial canals, and thriving below a permanent, heavy black cloud of smoke from the never-extinguished kilns, the town dominated from the green hills beyond by the stately home and long-established dynasty of the Wedgwoods.

He was a spare, wiry man, astonishingly quick off the mark and possessed of extraordinary lightness and grace while controlling a football. Matthews's father was a professional boxer, and Stanley became a professional footballer in 1932, having been spotted by one of the talent scouts in those days forever patrolling the touchlines of junior matches. Two years later he was picked for England.

In those days, the tactics of play dictated that the ball be passed out to those on the wings of the team, out beside the touchlines. The winger's task was to retain the ball close to his feet ("dribbling"), to swerve around opponents, and then to cross kick the ball to a point in front of the goal from which the inside forwards might win a chance to shoot at goal or, better still, to head the ball into the net.

Matthews, on the right wing, proved incomparably quick, deft, and inventive at these tasks. The balls were in those days absorbent leather, the wintry weather wet, the badly drained pitches muddy, but he made the ball, the grass, the heavy lace-up boot of the footballer all seem equivalently light and airy, the placing of his kicks across of supernatural accuracy and swiftness.

My heartfelt reminiscence—I saw him play when I was barely thirteen in the early fifties—attempts to weigh up just how good he was at a time when the conditions of play so often worked against the beauty of the game. But the game had another beauty, in its provenance, its geography, in the affecting mutuality of the player and his people. Throughout Matthews's career, professional footballers of whatever talent were, if they played league football, all paid the same wage, just like the working men from whom they were recruited. The players' trade union negotiated wage rises for the trade, just as the multiple potters' unions did in Stoke on Trent for the men who made the plates and teapots. In 1950 that wage was £14 per week.

There was therefore no huge discrepancy between the money paid to the celebrity player and the wages of those who watched him. They met their man in the street, they knew him as Stan, there was no call to crowd outside his home to get a glimpse of him getting out of a chauffeur-driven car to disappear into a mansion. His house looked like theirs, and when he turned out in the town's (Stoke City FC) red-and-white striped shirt, a collarless shirt much like those in which thirty thousand male spectators went to work, they cheered him on as their hero, for sure, and as their own man.

It is impossible to exclude an idealising note from this little fable, and I do not try. Matthews's kind of sporting celebrity is one best part of the making of the very idea and remains as such in the strands of its value as they are twisted together over time. He was, moreover, an irreproachable sportsman, never once booked by the referee, played his last first-class match at the age of fifty-one, and was admitted by the queen to the national pantheon as a knight in 1965.

In 1947 he had changed clubs to Blackpool, the potteries' pet seaside resort, ninety or so miles away on the coast of Lancashire, and when at last he retired, his spare frame and thin, lined face etched with the lines of thirty-five years of work just like all the other members of his class, he bought a hotel in Blackpool and kept it until his death in 2000.

Sport thrives and holds its meanings in the space between the civic polity (such as it is) and private life, strictly so called. This is the realm of leisure, as well as the neighbouring but not always assimilable area of hard-won and hard paid-for "free time." It is also the realm of life in which profit is specifically *not* at stake, the transactions of which are as free as possible from the ignoble taint of a *reward* and in which the pleasures of free creativity and production have no cash value at all. The sporting ideal gathers into one place and a single action the residual values of play, its artlike good-for-nothing-elseness, its joyful spontaneity, its healthy restoration of adults to childishness, its glowing image of happy harmony between the human being and the natural world.

Well, this realm is in the grip of the hellhounds. You might say, if you were feeling psychoanalytic, that the rage and hate apparent at the edges of most big occasions in football are expressions of a thwarted desire amongst the hooligans for the loss of simple playfulness and manly manners in games which modern football can no longer express. However that may be, the harmless, sometimes beautiful game now has to bear far too much.

It was the great English sport lover and journalist John Arlott who, in 1978, predicted that money would destroy the best parts of football.[5] The contemporary career of David Beckham makes his point. Not that Beckham lacks genuine achievement. He is a splendid athlete and a man of striking good looks as well as some grace and strength of character (a strength celebrities must find, if they are not to be smashed up by fame). He has kept pretty steady under the lights and in front of the cameras and once or twice has transformed a match with single strikes of stunning un-expectedness and beauty.

Yet these matters are less well-known and esteemed than his immense wealth, the purported tensions of his marriage to a pop star of no great ability but, as sometime member of a pert little group of girlie singers called the Spice Girls, celebrated enough in her own right, his own range of branded products, his variable haircuts, his plentiful tattoos. My kind of elderly social commentator praises him for putting his fortune into a football academy while looking doubtfully at the little boys who are drawn to football less by its human artfulness and more by the hateful corruption of the calls to highly improbable fame.

Capital and its engineer technology, forever seeking and saturating new markets, moved massively into leisure time sometime after Stanley Matthews went to Blackpool. On the way it scooped up the realms of play, art, and sociable freedoms (shopping, drinking, flirting, idling) and trans-muted them into a highly differentiated but regulated management system (football has its work-rates, taste and fashion their turnover).

These are dark as well as blank strictures. Open-air games have proved resilient; they are not immortal. Like most parts of expressive culture, they depend for their success in value-formation upon happy accident and local improvisation. Cricket, golf, tennis, squash all illustrate this. But for all the crowds who follow them, capital-driven technology has smoothed away the sheer difficulties (and therefore artistry) of, say, car-racing, sailing, mountaineering. It is money poured into research technology and the industrialisation of celebrity which holds these games in their positions of social prominence.

III

Once again, a couple of biographies may suffice to illustrate the argument. The folklore of golf tells us that the game began on the links of the Scottish coast, and the happy accident of their whin-and-sand-and-cliffside-turf variousness. The historical reach from St. Andrew's to the shaved greens, cavernous bunkers, and noble stands of carefully arranged oaks and beeches of the American country club courses is not much more than 150 years in length. The distance is more accurately measured in dollars, and men's lives.

In 1930 Bobby Jones, in the journalist Alistair Cooke's memorable words, "the easy, debonair, modest Southerner with the virile good looks," won the golfing Grand Slam—the British and American amateur championships and the two Open championships, so-called because open to both professionals and amateurs, at that time kept strictly separate by a compound of class snobbery and that strong feeling I have mentioned that sport should not be played for money, a feeling you can only really cherish if you have enough money for sporting leisure in the first place.

Jones had exquisite style and the supple, easy grace of the born athlete. His gifts and his prizewinning as an amateur golfer who did not play in the winter[6] made him instantly the companion of other newcomers to the category of celebrity. He played golf regularly with Douglas Fairbanks and with the mighty baseball star Ty Cobb. The Harvard degree and family law business gave him the time and money to play whenever he pleased, and as Cooke (who knew him well) adds, "I doubt there was a man, woman or child in America or Britain who did not know about Bobby Jones." He ends his valediction: "Well, the word gentleman is by now very much an

Bobby Jones, cover of *Time* magazine, c. 1930s. Source: Age Fotostock

anachronism. It got worn out by covering too often what William Emp-
son once called "utter grossness of soul tempered by a desire to behave
nicely." But in an older and better sense, that of a man who unfailingly
combines goodness and grace, it fitted Bobby Jones like no other man I
have known."[7]

Jones commanded this regard nationwide. Rich and leisured as well as
dedicated as he was, he resembles Stanley Matthews in the tears of pleasure
he brought to the eyes of those who watched and admired him, and in
the easy, cordial accessibility of a famous man one could nonetheless greet
across the street or the fairway. His unrivalled accomplishments, that is,
were not such as to be separated from his presence and his human qualities. He was not only defined by golf.

This makes him recede into the mist of time. It is no longer possible
to be that kind of golfing celebrity (the kind who retired from the international scene after his amazing quartet of victories, at the age of twenty-
eight). The unstoppable torque of new golf technology, the differently
sprung clubs, the novel aeronautics for the ball, lighter shoes with a better
grip, even the greener, smoother turf brought by the latest fertiliser, have
done what comparable developments have done everywhere: deepened the
specialisation of labour.

Stars of golf nowadays look like Tiger Woods. Or rather, they aim to.
For there can be no doubting that Woods's convincing composition of qui-
etness, modesty, perfect play, and resolute character matched up to Bobby
Jones's great example until his marital disgrace in 2009.

Whatever Woods's own calm inhabiting of a highly disciplined self, and
whatever his failure at making his public and private character fit together,
it is only his colossal financial success which commands such universal attention. While there is no doubt that, like Bobby Jones, millions of people
know his name, what they mostly know about, without knowing the exact
sum, is the heap of his winnings. The sporting journalists no doubt report
on the amazing certainty of his various passages to victory, but their columns, like the internet biographies, count success as defined by dollars.

For all the differences between golf and most other spectator sports—its
sheer spaciousness and the special beauty of its artificial landscape, the
extreme leisureliness of its rhythms, the demands on concentration, the
brevity of its key actions, let alone their fierce intensities of gracefulness,

accuracy, timing, trigonometry—all those differences shrink beside the indices of money and fame, the two poles of success.

Tiger Woods's response to his position has been, when playing golf or when otherwise on view, to turn himself into an expressionless automaton. Once, after over a decade of uninterrupted victories which began in 1996 at the age of twenty-one, he was asked to explain an unlooked-for failure in a major championship. He replied laconically, "I wasn't hitting my irons as close as I needed to."

At the time I write, he is only thirty-four. The astounding record of his victories since he began to win everything in 1996 was recently broken off by a damaged left knee which had been operated on three times. With notable courage and frequently in pain, in the summer of 2008 he overcame the injury to win the U.S. Open championships again.

His fans and his journalists loved it, as well they might. One cannot doubt that the destructive demands of modern sport—too many competitions, too much travelling worldwide, the ruination of the game's joyful irresponsibility by capital about which I have already descanted—have cut short his competitive career. This does not matter as far as his earnings and fame go, though it might diminish his happiness. His fortune is already a matter of legend. In spite of myself, I adduce a few details exactly because this is what, by contrast with Bobby Jones's day, constitutes contemporary celebrity.

In the eleven years after his first sweeping victories in 1996, Woods won prizes totalling $770 million.[8] He has contracts with assorted firms making golfing equipment and with half a dozen using his name in irrelevant toiletries which, the newspapers say, have brought him $100 million and more. He and his wife, Elin Nordegren, whom he met while she was working as an au pair for a Swedish golfer, own six homes, one a $39 million mansion on Jupiter Island, Florida. When Woods began, he won his first U.S. Masters title by twelve strokes. He was a child prodigy whose late father (his coach and career adviser) reported that at the age of five Woods went around a nine-hole course in forty-eight strokes.

This is the stuff of sporting celebrity, all given weight and shine by the fact of Woods's black skin and mixed racial birth. This is unignorable, like the inevitability with which chatshow presenters used to invoke him as a "role model" for black kids and an egalitarian force in an "elitist" sport. In point of fact, plenty of the best American golfers before and after Jones arrived from the working class, and Woods himself was from a comfortably off home, first appeared on television at age five, and graduated from Stanford. But he has been readily fitted into the celebrity cliché accommodation, comprising singular talent, beautiful wife (and two children), stupendous wealth, multiple homes...and flavorsome scandal.

It proved too damned hard even for so steady-seeming a man as Tiger Woods to keep his balance between the hard work of disciplined practice at his game, the living of something like a domestic life amid the extravagance and pointless luxury demanded of and provided by great fame (who needs six homes?), the comporting of himself with due sincerity and in the public gaze as artist, genius at the game (for he certainly is that), modest victor, good loser, dutiful husband ... it is a frightful list of requirements, and deadly is the public vengeance wrought by conspicuous failure under that last heading. Or rather, deadly and loathsome are the buckets of spit and spite emptied over an offending celebrity by the official organs of celebrity notoriety. What readers and viewers really think and feel, as we learned from the Nixon and Clinton scandals, comes through more slowly and, at times, judiciously.

IV

What is happening to us in the rich nations dominated by television (but this is true also of, say, Malaysia, New Zealand, Venezuela) is that experience is being everywhere transformed into spectacle. This is not the opening of a hymn of hate against television; television is our first instrument with which, cognitively and emotionally, to grasp the world beyond the front door, and its mutations. No one could live without it and count themselves not just citizens and democrats but even half-educated. Understanding the world as spectacle, however, cuts us off, as I have already suggested, from significant action. Democracy, one could say in passing, either is out of the question or has been *put* out of it as unfeasible by old power; the best we can hope for is *responsible* government.[9] People watch and learn (there is a deep contradiction here) about what is going on. But they cannot act. The only political action they can take, apart from a largely symbolic four-year vote, is to turn up at the electoral conventions or out on the street in a demonstration of their own helplessness. The protest march protests against unitary powerlessness in the name of private lives; the moment it goes public and a window is broken or a razor wire fence cut, the police move in.

In the spectacular society, the star has been appointed to perform our significant actions for us. The star is the crux of that institutionalisation of envy which we call glamour. The emergent meaning of sport in the larger redefinition of the culture is glamour. Sport has, with popular music (as we shall see), become the vehicle of glamour, and sporting stars the essential bearers of the imagery whose dazzling silhouettes are represented as the irresistible enviability of the ads. This is painfully evident in the narcissistic fatuity of the stars' very own self-expression. *Their* individual feelings, poor wretches, are bent by routine towards the tiny range of mass gesture: punching the air, sinking to the knees, or that frenzied crazy running with outstretched arms of the goal scorer—each of them an utterly fake, dreadfully sincere acting out of the role of the star even unto crocodile tears.

This is the social problem—with a downward intonation—of all popular culture in general, as well as sport in particular. Sport is required to contain and express too much. Significant action being difficult, membership gone and democracy nonexistent, sport remains a human arena—for all that it is a vehicle for fantasy, it *does* actually take place—for connecting a tumult of personal feeling to public endeavour. The trouble is that personal feeling and personal experience are at present incommensurate. Too much of the first and not enough of the second. This is true of both star and spectator, especially where the star is detached from any geographical loyalty or tradition of class by stardom itself. Hence the fan at fever pitch, queer as a clockwork orange and ready to kill for West Ham even though he comes from Bradford.

This is an outline of a new psychology of jingoism, grounded not in any army and a distant war, but in a football team, a beautiful German or Argentinian tennis player, a gigantic black baseball pitcher or Indian fast bowler.

Stardom distantiates and magnifies the dominant images of liberal capitalism, so that they appear both hugely familiar and quite untouchable. In the star personality itself this is certain to produce an ultimate version of the narcissism so general in the culture. The star understands herself as the object of other people's gaze. Typically, there must be a displacement in her identity to correspond with this: there is herself-as-watched-by-the-spectators and herself-as-capable-of-autonomy.[10] The two will coincide as fulfilment when her desires and the spectators' desires converge to fuse in a single action. She makes the winning serve on the Centre Court; she scores maximum points for her pirouette on the Olympic ice rink.

The lens which focuses and holds steady this tension of distance and familiarity is television and its partner, the long-distance telephoto news camera. That tension provides the form for the apotheosis of the spectacle. The spectacle of sport, whether live or screened (an increasingly difficult distinction to make), betokens a society unable to tell the difference between close attention and mere continuity, between lust and boredom. The playback and the sports video anthology take the depth out of history and the treasure from memory. The star, having no place to rest his or her head, breaks the link between game and home. The spectacle replaces lived experience with the imagery of glamour. Its power is the contemporary version of the timeless attribute of all power to actualise itself in public show. Its present-day version emphasises our distance from it and our mutual irresponsibility. We cannot affect it; it has no affection for us.

V

On the bare and barren landscape of political ideas and civic ideals, certain celebrities take on an emblematic representativeness. It is a peculiar fact about our topic that few sportspeople do this, more film stars make the effort, but a surprising number of rock musicians mark out such a space in public feeling.

Sporting heroes, especially those watched by tens of thousands in the big city stadium, by now remind us keenly that the industry of sport is, like all other industries, globalised. You might never think so, going by the glazed-eyed devotion of some fans who give their chosen team (which may well be located a couple hundred miles from where the fan lives) their reckless loyalty. But then the team itself, if it is one of the international superleaguers, is sure to be studded with stars from cities the other side of Europe or from the coast of Brazil. There is a comic anecdote about a Brazilian superman called Robinho being bought from Real Madrid for £32 million (a ludicrous sum, a substantial proportion of which is, by contractual law in football, paid to the player) by Manchester City, and his saying on his arrival how pleased he was to be at Chelsea. What is more, the owners of the biggest football clubs in Britain are mostly the new world billionaires, and Americans, Russians, or Saudis flaunt their acquisitions as fabulous accessories to their show of global power.

It has so happened that the hole in social identity this loss of representatives has left has been filled by the rock musicians.[11] Here we need a slightly glib piece of social history. For the rock musicians emerge quite suddenly at the beginning of the 1960s as an identifiable social presence, and that brief historical moment is apt to turn the brains of social historians and cultural commentators quite addled, to thicken their prose with cliché and their blood with sugar.

For 1963 is the moment at which, by common assent, a new generation broke decisively from the control of their seniors, discovered new independence with the new forms of employment brought by the postwar boom on both sides of the Atlantic, and, no longer tied to the exhausting rhythms of working-class labour and forced apprenticeship to lathe, coal face, or early motherhood, created overnight the new leisure culture and its rapturous music for which the Beatles are the best-known name.

Nothing now can be added to the copious literature which commemorates the Beatles' fame. It is still worth underlining their Liverpudlian origins: their undoubted musical talents[12] and the accident of their coming together at the club depended for its peculiar good fortune upon local traditions of song-making, of harsh scouse humour and the male friendships it expressed, of the recent advent of the guitar as the cheap, accessible toy of young men improvising for any occasion a new readiness to copy the whirling, thrilling dances imported from and by the American soldiers who had been visible everywhere since 1944.

It is never too much to utter a short elegy over that moment. The jobs were there, the money was there; young Americans, young Britishers, and as the ruined cities were so swiftly rebuilt across the European continents, young Germans, Italians, French, and Dutch joined spontaneously in a hemispheric rock-and-roll. Starting it all was put down to the credit of a tubby, cowlicked, sort-of-country-and-western bandleader called Bill Haley around about 1956, but it was the Beatles, neatly dark-suited, girlishly coiffed, breezy, gifted, lissom and *young*, who, against any odds, gave its best feelings to a cheerful generation.

Their music and its manners brought together a spirit of lighthearted protest and the public feasibility of change; they put into their music the hopes of young love, of course they did, but they added to that the joy of the dance, the promise of a fulfilment in which youthfulness and optimism would win out by virtue of their intrinsic admirableness, and the stiff and elderly would step back into the shadows.

It was a lot for a band to stand for. When the music stopped and the new generation asked, what shall we do to be saved, there was not much on offer except the century-old action of marching and booing and breaking things and being a bit bashed about by the cops. Nonetheless, rock established itself with inconceivable rapidity as a capitalised industry, for sure, but also as a meeting point of strong, undefined passions and their individual expression, exactly tuned to an epoch, by the Beatles themselves, by the Rolling Stones, the Doors, Jimi Hendrix, Eric Clapton, Freddie Mercury, Bob Geldof, and the wandering journeyman-genius, Bob Dylan.

As these epic figures, all of them men—the women turn up later, give or take a folksinger or two like Joan Baez—established a degree of durability as well as emulability (millions of fourteen-year-olds were given guitars and shouted in their bedrooms till the ceiling cracked), they gravitated naturally towards the condition of bohemians.

The Beatles, that is, put away their charcoal-grey suits and polished black lace-ups, grew out their neat bobs into shaggy locks, and assumed knee-high soft leather boots, sprigged hussar coats, and kaftans of many colours, and adorned their fingers and wrists with old silver and agates the size of eyeballs. The Rolling Stones, dominated then as now nearly fifty years later by the piratical Mick Jagger, turned themselves contrastingly but just as historically into *poetes maudits*, stoned Stones in grubby old shirts and holed sweaters, lank and unwashed hair, torn jeans, all in the service of terrific energy, raucous, rousing rhythm and to-hell-with-them lyrics. The Beatles followed Wilde and Beardsley, the Stones followed Baudelaire and Courbet.

Those same origins go back, as Robert Darnton tells us, to the revolution in France.[13] Puccini's *La Bohème*, the sentimental story of the penniless artist and his beautiful, deathly singer-mistress was first performed in 1896, but bohemians, acquiring a nickname from the Romany gypsies of Bohemia and Romania, were cultural drifters living on their wits, their songs, stories, and poems, somewhere well the other side of respectability. The leading bands of the sixties made huge sums of money, were eventually decorated by the queen and entertained by presidents and prime ministers, but battled to keep themselves unrespectable and genteelly debauched, not-quite-law-abiding, scandalising received opinion, living off their earnings all right, but those earnings as made outside the usual means of production, made from culture not capital.

Rock musicians moved into this wide margin of society, where they remained in rich ambiguity and, for the successful, amid straightforward riches as well. For capital, as of its nature it must, followed them to soak up this new spring of money. The rock musicians battled in turn to live like the bohemians their public needed them to be, and to harbour the profits at the same time.

Thus they confected their special version of the celebrity, slightly different from any other version, whether the politician's, the financier's, the virtuoso's, the film star's, or the sporting hero's. The great diva or the great painter still wears celebrity with a touch of raffishness; each has transcended her or his bohemian beginnings but alludes to them affectionately. The rock musician, even at sixty-odd, must keep faith with that connection in order to keep faith with the generations which are the audience. By now those generations span half a century, and the audience must delude itself about its very own bloodstream: the still-passionate admirers of Freddie Mercury and Eric Clapton have to square the old feeling for dissent and rebellious optimism with tiredness, disbelief, and simple settlement.

There are dozens of biographies with which to chronicle this sequence in our history. As befits the bohemians, they are characterised by the savoury legends of excess in offstage life—drunkenness, drugs, dress, sex, suicide—to match the excess of expressiveness and emotion in performance. The rock stars took to intoxicating extremes the enacting of emotion first given its dramatic conventions by the virtuosi of the concert hall in the mid-nineteenth century. The best of them also lived in a margin of ordinary domestic life where ceaseless travel, tumultuous adulation from delirious audiences—audiences which turned up precisely in search of delirium and adulation—staccato love affairs and marriages, and fragments, scraps, bits, and relics of intellectual life and reading came together with intense, patternless significance, given shape and inwardness with the creamy hit of heroin.

Eric Clapton was one of the most celebrated as well as most talented of the travelling players who have come to apotheosise this latest platoon of the avant-garde. What is now striking about him and his most eminent coevals—these musical wanderers are all men—is that although they were once emblems of and for the subcultures of youth (as they say), they are many of them—Clapton, Paul McCartney, Bob Dylan, Bob Geldof—still going strong in their sixties. Longevity in the public eye has mellowed some perhaps, but more accurately it has given the palimpsest of their lives the coherence, patina, ruggedness, and texture (the qualities of a good painting) which the concept of celebrity usually works to flatten and abbreviate.

VI

Take Eric Clapton's complicated, far from admirable life.[14] Remove the electronic technology and it belongs beside Bernhardt and Baudelaire, let alone Byron, and his life is as well-known as theirs.

Clapton was born to unnamed parents in 1945, his father a serviceman who pushed off promptly to Canada after his son's birth. The child was brought up by his grandparents, long supposing, as was the way of things in those days, that his mother was his elder sister. He failed his eleven-plus (the then universal examination which admitted or refused children to a grammar school education) and at thirteen was given his first guitar.

There was no doubting his musical genius from an early age, nor the moodiness, darkness of disposition, difficulty with ever discovering the transient happiness of childhood, which he saw in and for himself, and which so colours his music. He fits the pattern set by the Romantic poets, painters, and musicians: very gifted, dedicated to his art, passionately living in spurts—now concerts, now love affairs—striving to hold the world of immediacy at impossible levels of excitement, and keeping it there by way of heroin, alcohol, sex, and the power of rock, endlessly rehearsed, played just right.

Describing such lives in a paragraph or two draws heavily, as you see, on cliché. Better to stick to the facts in order to show how close allied are the lives of Byron, Paganini, Sarah Bernhardt, Ava Gardner, Clapton, and Freddie Mercury. Their dramatisation of celebrity is inseparable from their peculiar genius, but renown, desire, the thrilling sound, and the crazy schedules of the work and its unceasing mobility ejected the rock heroes from any chance of a domestic life and appointed them to the cast-iron role of glamorous and successful bohemian.

What this meant for Eric Clapton was life lived in bright flashes, the only unbroken thread between which was the music. The bands he joined or formed—Roosters, Yardbirds (which first brought him fame), Cream (in 1966), Blind Faith (in 1969)—were of their nature fissiparous. The music itself, like early jazz, was always changeful, the styles evolving and colliding and whizzing away like so many photons, the musicians competitive, egotistical, hot, quick, driven men, the glamour glossed from outside, the inside without rest or peace or quiet.

Clapton invented a quite new way of "picking" the closely laid twelve strings of his guitar, and this method gave his music its extraordinary alternation of heavy plangency throbbing out of the amplifier and the drifting, fading melody of strings plucked much more lightly and distantly. It is a signature as unmistakable as Stravinsky's, and heard to most powerful effect in the soundtrack he created for the incomparable BBC political thriller, *Edge of Darkness*, in 1985.

This latter was Clapton's kind of story and made, I would say, one of the greatest works of television art ever broadcast—a nuclear melodrama, a police thriller, a father-daughter love story, a bitter satire on the delusions of political and capitalist weapons-gambling, a plea for the planet.

The music matched the high seriousness and poetic force of the five-hour movie. It brought out the best of the man who meanwhile married Pattie Boyd while fathering a child with Yvonne Kelly and then another, Conor, with Lori Del Santo. Clapton loved children and fatherhood—unlike Byron, he paid up for and tended his children—and when Conor was killed at the age of four, hurtling to his death fifty-three floors below the window of a New York apartment, was as agonised and inconsolable as the Argonaut Jason, another bereft father.

Finally, at fifty-four, he married Melia McEnery, twenty-odd years his junior, proudly fathered three new daughters, was awarded an official honour (the CBE) in 2004, and assumed the role of mature celebrity, calm of mind, all passion spent, which in these days of extended longevity awaits the elderly celebrity still with creative energy to spare and money to be charitably dispersed. Hardly remembered now is Clapton's disagreeable endorsement of the crude racism promulgated by the British politician Enoch Powell forty years ago. Now he is invited to play in North Korea, of all places and pays, perhaps as conscience money, for a multicultural charity called the Crossroad Centre in the West Indies.

Throughout this packed and convoluted tale it is easy enough to trace the modern morphologies of glamour and fame, art and unhappiness. As required of a rock musician, Clapton performed each life ingredient in public—one of the best-selling songs of "Slowhand," as his nickname once was, is entitled "Cocaine"—and brought each, in his sixties, to a close.

The contrast with perhaps the most flaring and colourful of the musicians of the age of rock, Freddie Mercury, is marked because of the latter's early death at the age of forty-five of AIDS. He was born Farrokh Bulsara of Muslim parents in Zanzibar in 1946, a thin, *chétif* young man who was much later to take pride enough in his successful bodybuilding to perform stripped to the waist in the group's world-famous Wembley concert in 1985.[15]

The group, Queen, was formed in 1970, and Mercury is now the best-known name in the legend because of his emblematic end. In 1991 the AIDS epidemic was at its height and at that date unmitigated by much in the way of treatment by retrovirus, and Freddie Mercury made a public statement of his illness just before he died. The group, which had always performed without a lead and on equal terms, gave a concert by its remaining three members in commemoration of their dead comrade which raised a million pounds for the Terence Higgins (AIDS) Trust, packed out the stadium, and was watched on TV, it is said, by a billion people.

Queen was probably the best-known rock band in the world in the seventies and eighties. Their music was far less brutally bashed out than that of the well-named heavy metal bands, and such of their big hits as "Bohemian Rhapsody" in 1975 and "A Day at the Races" (the friendly, jokey title of a main album) in 1976 were much more melodious and, so to speak, orchestral than the deafening din and dizzy strobe lighting with which later bands concealed their lack of talent. Nonetheless, Queen pulled in vast crowds, 130,000 in Sao Paulo and Rio, and their greatest triumph, though not their biggest audience, a decade later at Wembley.

The manners of such a band defined their particular brand of celebrity. Freddie Mercury himself was much given to light white-and-scarlet ensembles sartorially placed somewhere between a matador, a hussar, and a trapeze acrobat. He was a pretty, girlish man with protruding teeth which he sometimes concealed with a strong moustache, making himself up on occasions with mascara, eyeliner, and shiny coiffure. The band was the first exponent of what was much later called Glamrock, a smart and typical coinage which now sorts well with their stylish turnout, Brian May the only one who kept to the conventional rocker's shaggy locks, all of them positively clean and shining in contrast to the studied squalor and (in the patois) grunge kit of their punk predecessors.

The music was, well, glamorous also. It swelled big with feeling, whether erotic ("Get Down, Make Love"), raging ("Tie Your Mother Down"), sweetly valedictory ("Sail Away Sweet Sister"), or meltingly plaintive ("Teo Torriatte"). It spoke worldwide, to millions of fans in Japan and millions more in Brazil. Their most devoted admirers reckon the band went off a bit after *The Game* in 1980, but they stuck with them all the same.

Queen played its music according to the usual stage conventions: Freddie Mercury threw himself acrobatically about the stage, holding only the hand microphone, while the other three combined, in the way of their trade, sonorous fingerwork, drumming, and the expressive abandon of the virtuoso, heads gyrating till you think they will come off, legs widespread, the guitars flagrantly used to mimic the phallus, the whole effect a crazy, stamping corroboree, wild, throbbing, and stylised as Noh drama. Freddie Mercury would play the crowd as all stars must do to a huge turnout, whether footballers, musicians, evangelists, or dictators. It is the moment the tens of thousands come for, the participation television cannot provide. The star gives them the versicle, the crowd returns the response, then again, and again, until the crowd breaks into a roar of approval, and the band goes into its next song.

The tiny figures under the huge lights surrounded by the vast and darkened auditorium packed with perspiring thousands of all ages (for rock,
once the defining cultural property of the young, has now collected two,
even three generations, on the crest of its rolling tide—rock fans are a
faithful bunch) are the single most compelling image of celebrity of our
time. It is what it is, and it needs no earnest reading-of-the-meaning beyond itself. The pleasure of the music, its heavy rhythms, the communion
of souls, the direct connection between performer and listener as well as
the stirring membership of a crowd in passive action, all these ingredients
come together in the communal work of art a rock concert certainly is and
permit a union of feeling and loss of one's little self all too rare in our kind
of society.

VII

There is never a simple speech to make about the deturpations of culture as
found in the book of rock. It has its scatological and repellent harlequins
like Alice Cooper and its tough, indestructible pirates like Madonna. Then
it has its gallant knights—Bob Geldof and Live Aid, Mick Jagger's patient
and unobtrusive backing of the British film industry, and a long, long
history of musicians celebrating and defending history's losers and rebels
and their own social class: Johnny Cash, Woody Guthrie, Joan Baez, the
Chieftains, Bob Dylan, celebrities all, for sure, but of that particular kind
who find a way of speaking and playing directly to and for a human constituency which urgently needs and wants the music but cannot make it
for itself. Bob Dylan provides our coda to this eulogy.

There is first, however, a minor academic argument to refute as prelimi-
nary. Critical discussion of popular culture in general and rock music in
particular has tended to claim for all forms of pop these past thirty years
a political validity somehow transcending its expressive significance. In a
commendable effort to overcome the crude opposition of the lofty tradi-
tionalist between popular and high culture, this line of criticism finds in
popular culture some of "the weapons of the weak" (to take the title of a famous book advancing the argument[16]), whereby (in another such slogan[17])

certain "rituals of resistance" are played out on behalf of the oppressed and in opposition to their rulers. By this standard, working-class boys break windows not because it is fun breaking windows but to declare guerrilla war on the class enemy.

This theory of motives not only overlooks the fact that by and large the poor steal from the poor, but is hardly usable in connection with the huge phenomenon of rock concerts and their multigenerational and multiclass (let alone multicultural) composition. Nonetheless, Bob Dylan himself testifies to the complexity of the folksinging, sometimes rebellious tradition which he confected for himself, and although he is gingerly about picking up the badge of "protest" music, he says himself:

> Topical songs weren't protest songs. The term "protest singer" didn't exist any more than the term "singer-songwriter." You were a performer or you weren't, that was about it—a folksinger or not one. "Songs of dissent" was a term people used but even that was rare. I tried to explain later that I didn't think I was a protest singer, that there'd been a screwup. I didn't think I was protesting anything any more than I thought that Woody Guthrie songs were protesting anything. I didn't think of Woody as a protest singer. If he is one, then so is Sleepy John Estes and Jelly Roll Morton. What I was hearing pretty regularly, though, were rebellion songs and those really moved me. The Clancy Brothers—Tom, Paddy and Liam—and their buddy Tommy Makem sang them all the time.[18]

Woody Guthrie, as everybody knows, was formative in the life and the music of Bob Dylan, and Dylan would visit him often as the prince of American folksingers declined into dementia, speechlessness, and motor collapse in an asylum in New Jersey. But Dylan discovered and assembled as a function of his genius a medley of migrant musical traditions which he turned into his poetics. Like T. S. Eliot forging that extraordinary Pentecost of tongues, *The Waste Land*, Dylan blended into his own distinctive idiom the songs of Woody Guthrie, the plangent richness of blues and root music, the haunting plaints of his friend Pete Seeger, something of the cowboys' catchy laments, something also of the thin, wailing, incantatory prayers his Lithuanian forebears had brought to America in the previous century.

If one tries to enumerate these chorded echoes in Dylan's music, one ends up with a list, not a body of artwork. There are many compulsions blent in his enchanting airs. If "Blowing in the Wind" is his single most famous song, it will not do to take to heart its rather vacuous rhetoric. One has to take in the whole performance—the scraggy, rabbity lad playing his comical one-man-band, the mournful eyes, the trademark cap, the wandering demeanour, the long, piercing chords, the simple, unforgettable melody, its sadness and its desolation.

Then one turns to study the calendar of his renown. At the back of Bob Spitz's zestful biography of Dylan, the author's collaborator lists all Dylan's concerts and his concert recording sessions between 1961 (when he was twenty) and 1988.[19] There are over one thousand entries. This was a dedicated artist. He composed copiously, unstoppably, and the music he wrote, and wrote to play, became as much a comprehensive biography of American emotion as *Leaves of Grass*.

Like all great poets, Dylan did not merely play back to his people the feelings they felt, he showed and shaped for them the feelings they might and should have. There he is, in a photograph of a concert in a football stadium, alone and tiny with his guitar and harmonica frame in front of him, and two hundred thousand Australians filling the pitch, the stands, everything. He begins with two or three lesser-known or less esteemed songs, and the crowd waits, knowingly. Then "The Times They Are A-Changing," and a great, slow roar of acclaim and recognition unrolls towards and over the small singer, rolls back and leaves him with his song, not alone but with two hundred thousand little souls waiting to be bathed in the sweet, strange, familiar sounds.

This is the friendliness of fame. The members of the crowd have no need to "meet" Dylan. They meet him in the expressive community of the song. There, in that transport of delight, they feel as best they can (some will be better at feeling than others) what the song and its poem tells them to feel. (A good poem turns us into poets.) Dylan once said of his own song in an interview: "I'm the first person who'll put it to you and the last person who'll explain it to you."[20] The listener, like the reader, finds and sees what he or she can, in song or poem; the more they see, maybe, the better they like it.

He turns the crowd intimate—not something a politician could do. In his astonishing study of Dylan's songs just cited, Christopher Ricks takes us through (with boisterous delicacy) the tricks and feelings of that marvellous song, "Lay, Lady, Lay":

Lay, lady, lay, lay across my big brass bed
Stay, lady, stay, stay with your man awhile
Until the break of day, let me see you make him smile . . .

Ricks adds, "With "day," something should dawn upon us."[21] Is she, is he, a good lay? His voice catches: "His clothes are dirty but his—his hands are clean." He thinks about a dirty joke, but no call, no call. His voice catches, with desire no doubt, but there is no catch in it (Ricks thinks). She is a good catch, though.

The crowd sways in approbation, seeing the jokes, feeling the feelings, liking the story and the people in it. This is more than just celebrity in action; it is performance at its best, and Dylan is the best at the job, at the art, in his particular world.

It is a much maligned world, as well as one which draws to itself such adulation, such messy living, such mountains of money. The figure I have placed at its centre is, as the songs betoken, complex, learned, elusive, solitary. He was also loving and lovable, maddening, ambiguous, laconic, and very bright. He looks for love, for the right woman and for *any* woman, he is stoic, glum, but restlessly on the move, going, gotta go. This is not the awful upper-class Englishman's muffled and evasive, "Well, I must be off"; it is the American's mobility, unillusioned but on the road, looking forward, filled with hope, looking out, lips parted, for the new ships.

From the crossroads of my doorway
My eyes they start to fade
As I turn my head back to the room
Where my love and I have laid
An' I gaze back to the street

The sidewalk and the sign
And I'm one too many mornings
An' a thousand miles behind.[22]

Dying well, you could say, is to discern the form of loss, and yet to be sure that those you love, dying with a little patience, still have lots to lose.

The social phenomenon of rock, let alone that of sport, has so much in it as naturally to make any decent person look away in disgust that it seems odd to end this chapter by praising this handful of famous men. Yet that same phenomenon—think how many other rock or sporting celebrities I could have celebrated—seems to me one of the best parts of the culture of the past fifty years. Its best musicians, its best players—and their admirers knew them clearly for the best—brought such direct happiness to millions, brought home to millions of them the shaping spirit of memory, brought them together in selfless tribute to the beauty of the music, the action, and the moment, made them, for a season, better people.

Good art does these things, making history as it does so. The fame art brings is inseparable from its beneficence.

VIII

Sport and music touch all our hearts and contribute their great riches to the sum of things. No one would contest the commonplace that life would be much poorer, have less lovely colours and lightness of heart, without the beauties brought to it by the momentary splendour of a football game or the heights of the best rock concerts. But fashion? Haute couture? It may be all very well to swap stories about the mannish, exotic, black-and-white Coco Chanel on the Riviera in the 1920s, and it would be a crying shame not to have seen those two all-too-affectionate satires on the fashion industry, *Prêt-à-Porter* and *The Devil Wears Prada*, there to have admired Meryl Streep's devilish queening of it over her hapless employees, as well as to be entranced by Sophia Loren's almost-strip. But every old curmudgeon has a speech ready about clothes-crazed young girls thronging the shopping malls with nothing on their tiny minds but magic dust makeup, thongs, and glitter jeans.

Such not very bright young things do not, however, herald the end of civilisation, etc. Or if they do, things have been going to the dogs for the whole two-and-a-half centuries chronicled in this book. The fashion trade got under way before Reynolds arrived in London, was put on an industrial footing before Paris had finished with its several urban insurrections after 1830, was fuelled colossally on Fifth Avenue and the corner of 33rd Street once the fortunes poured into Wall Street when civil war was over. Present preoccupations with what to wear are only now so very noticeable because for the past half-century the sometime poor and the slightly less hard-working class has been able to buy clothes rather than mend the ragged remnants of their elder brothers' and sisters' wardrobes. That their taste is now so awful and so at the dictation of a handful of preposterously vain and mannered designers, paid millions to be copied and cheapened by the mass rag trade, is something merely to be grinned at and borne up against as well as one can manage.

It is then no more than a tiresome moral detail that the poor bloody models make such a splash in the world of celebrities that one is bound to feel the drops falling on one's head. Fashion models force upon one the recognition that celebrity balances on a fulcrum between action and appearance. Athletes or rock musicians have to be some good at what they do. Their actions turn into their accomplishments, and, cruelly enough, when their actions become ineffective, they vanish.

Fashion models, on the other hand, are all appearance. They are all women (the male models being little more than robots, and remain nameless); all they have to be is beautiful in the fashionable way of their day, and able to walk with that curious long swaying stride, the feet pointing exactly straight, the features almost expressionless, almost insolent—that "who-the-hell-are-you-staring-at?" stare ahead. Small wonder that their public personas are so much the same, compounded of a wonderful smile, a habitual narcissism, and a nasty temper.

Having no accomplishments to display, no action to render as artistry, pitifully lacking such personal resources as reflective intelligence and meaningful experience, they are quick to take offence, and, living between public adulation on the catwalk and in the restaurant, and the hot, endless tedium of the dressing room, it cannot be a surprise how many turn to the deathly, uncreative recreations of passing sex and playful cocaine.

I do not doubt that there is something collectively crazy about the prominence of fashion in the conversation of the culture, and it is hardly surprising that something of this madness is deposited in the veins of the undead who wear clothes only to be photographed in them. The celebrities of fashion are the most transient examples of our phenomenon, their *only* meaning to look just so, and to be envied, desired, admired, and despised accordingly.

They play the plaintive diminuendo of this chapter. The name of artist is often given to the exotic zombies of design in fashion—Armani, Versace, Gucci—but as this book is at pains to make clear, an activity so completely defined by moneymaking cannot do the job of art. A love of nature and a love of art now must do the work of religion, religion itself being over. If mere money can be held at bay, sport and rock can do their bit for our highest hopes and our immortal longings. Clothes, on the other hand, can make you happy all right; on a good day, they surely do plenty for one's feeling good. But they cannot (do I have to say this?) do anything for the meaning of life. Maybe that is why the celebrities of fashion are such empty creatures, the thinnest and most translucent of our characters.

Chapter 10

Stories We Tell Ourselves
about Ourselves

These pages are full of references to culture, a notoriously elastic concept. A concept (to say so again) is not necessarily a single word. It may be a phrase, a set of terms, or something more obscure, but in whatever form it serves to pick out certain features of experience and isolate them as an object of thought. If, however, such a term becomes too elastic and is required to enclose too many features at once, the object of thought becomes vague and impossible to think about. At this point the concept is vacuous.

All the same, the philosopher Wittgenstein reassured us by asking, "Isn't a blurred concept sometimes exactly what we need?" and to be sure culture is one such.[1] In these pages, it is first of all to be distinguished from politics (the realm of power and law) as well as being kept well away from psychology as explicator of human conduct. Culture, we shall say (following the great Clifford Geertz), is the ensemble of stories we tell ourselves about ourselves.[2]

With this reach-me-down definition at hand, there is one class of celebrity to which, caught in a televisual and powerless mixture of oligopoly and intermittent democracy, we naturally turn to hear the stories about ourselves which will help us grasp the commonplace weirdness and banality of ordinary life.

This group of people may be thought of as involuntary celebrities in the sense that we select them rather unpredictably from a range of the television candidates on show. There is of course always a throng of applicants for such positions, and we pick our favourites by way of a mixture of accident and availability. Long service and good conduct have their place—no one can remember the blankly pretty faces of the Fox News presenters, and they therefore fail to be appointed friends and celebrities. Certain long-lasting, friendly, and authoritative figures, telling us mostly political stories at six, seven, and ten o'clock in the evening, take on (and merit) a trust, a familiarity, a genial representativeness (they are on our side, they speak for us) something like that of our earliest and best schoolteachers, those who remain in our memories as having been personally interested in us, as having taught us things we understood and retained, as having recognised us afterwards, as having been consistent, likeable, intelligent but not too much so, intelligible also, interesting, ours.

These are abruptly more demanding criteria of admiration and affection than would ever be applied to athletes, to film stars, even to politicians. Presidents and prime ministers have their *noumen*, as we saw, and must at the same time bear their burden of obloquy, some of it extreme and foulmouthed. News anchors are rarely targets for abuse, though they are indeed subjects and objects of arbitrary affection or dislike. Their only action, however, is to report; they cannot "do" anything except tell us what to think and how we might interpret the world.

In this guise, they have become the *safest* celebrities we have around, and even amongst those paranoids who make a Pyrronhist principle of scepticism, the newscaster, familiar in our mouths and living rooms as a household word, is an emblem of trustworthiness, likeability, ordinariness. Out at the extremes of the more virulent and lunatic radio chat show different conventions apply, but the functions of such airwaves are quite another matter and do not concern us here.

Besides, this is not a functionalist bit of analysis. The function of the mainline news presenters on CBS, NBC, PBS, BBC, RTF, all those impregnable initials, is to read aloud the news without stuttering and from the teleprompter. No one could have planned or foreseen how, first, those voices and, later, those faces, hands, and torsos would become sources of reassurance, of nerve-steadying clear-sightedness when things were very bad (Ed Murrow), of courageous normality as bombs burst around and on Broadcasting House (Cedric Belfrage), of spontaneous tears of distress on his own behalf and the nation's (Walter Cronkite).

These people and their successors became a special kind of celebrity, perhaps even the most important kind. As the richest economies stretched to breaking point the old ties of neighbourhood and community, as the comradely, dangerous connections of the old heavy industries (steel, coal, railroad, shipbuilding, docks) dislimned and reappeared in the Far East, television stories of news and soap were raided by the people in order to fill the empty spaces in their crowded, lonely streets.

The "knowable community"[3] of TV newscasters and the known, even if fictional, community of soap opera provide many cultures with much-needed nutrition. The news, of course, must be factual, and the news presenters responsible, dependable, at once detached *and* humanly involved. Theirs is the fame belonging to the great events which they report on our behalf, representing us as the news tumbles in from other newspeople, not so well-known, whom they gently interrogate for their and our edification.

Over the past several decades, a new division of labour became normal as between the newscaster and a specialist colleague who told the newscaster and the audience how more particularly to comprehend the latest stories. Cronkite was probably the first such figure to become world famous after Ed Murrow, and he combined both roles at will. But then Cronkite had been a heroic journalist of the old school, crash-landing in a glider during the airborne landings of Operation Market Garden in 1944, his apartment searched and smashed up by the KGB during a spell in Moscow.[4] In the days before the teleprompter, he memorised the key names and a list of topics and spoke impromptu as "to that single individual in front of his set in the intimacy of his own home."[5]

It makes one look down a bit disdainfully on the teleprompter. Cronkite's devising of the role across the early years of such work during the 1950s makes beautifully clear just how experience turns into style, how man and manner are blended into something well called integrity. Cronkite's quickness and calm, his readiness to turn the unexpected into a small news paragraph, his pleasure in human comicality and his strong, unexamined principles of individual sanctity and self-reliance, of unassuming liberty and presumptive politeness, all fuse in the excitement of the new job he pretty well invented, thereby creating a new kind of publicly celebrated character whom his successors would have to live up to. By the time he finished as anchorman, aged sixty-five in 1981, Barbara Walters with many of the same talents and qualities had built a rival pedestal for an anchorwoman, and the national anchor, as the metaphor requires, was an instrument on whom the people built an absolute trust.

The connection between the private and public characters of a very well-known public figure is shifting but simple (the public-private dichotomy being nothing like as fixed as is supposed, and there being, come to that, nothing intrinsically sacred about privacy[6]). The public character is a magnified version of the private one, with those attributes and accomplishments which constitute the grounds of fame detached, enlarged, and projected onto the public screen without any of the blur, inconsistency, and weight of those other details which taken together make another person mysterious and unassimilable to us.

Cronkite's success does credit to the necessity of celebrity. He brought off the contrivance of his public character with a truthfulness and integrity amounting to genius. This was partly a consequence of sheer longevity, which as we have learned is needful if a celebrity is to count for something and as somebody in our scheme of values, and not merely become, in the useful, revolting phrase, a bucket of warm spit. But crucial to Cronkite's achievement—one with definitive properties for all those who followed in similar positions—Dan Rather, Peter Jennings, Barbara Walters, David Dimbleby, Anna Ford, Huw Edwards—was that he was nearly enough *really like that*. His audiences recognised and knew that fact. So when he turned on his own principles and made a public stand on television against the Americans' remaining in Vietnam after the 1968 Tet offensive by the Vietcong, it was no slight matter. The nation heeded him; the president himself, Lyndon Johnson, turned from the set and said simply, "If I've lost Cronkite, I've lost middle America." Two months later, Johnson announced he would not stand for reelection.

Cronkite could matter so much only because he was the kind of celebrity he was, known and honoured as such. When he quit the job, he uttered a malediction over the insanely high salaries paid to anchors when their juniors could be laid off in droves, and he pointed out, just as trenchantly, that his generation of journalists was part of the common people with whom they ate, drank, shopped, queued, and died. They did not come cruising into crises and take the microphone smoothly from youngsters when the politics was lit in bright enough lights. Hard to keep that sort of critique away from inaccurate reminiscences of the good old days—hard only until you look at the sums paid to presenters to hold commonplace conversations on studio sofas with powerful or well-known people.

This objection is more than a fragment of the curse to be spoken by all honest egalitarians over the fact that, in 2005, the top thousand CEOs in the United States were paid salaries (and share options and all that) 473 times larger than the average wage of their employees.[7] For the presences on the sofas and your friendly political commentator telling you what to think about the goings-on in Congress or Parliament are symbols of success as much as useful sources of information or temporary distractions from housework.

Cheerfulness must keep breaking in, however. The older, better way—journalists living and dying alongside everybody else—is by no means vanished. It was only the day before yesterday that, in 1992, John Cole completed eleven years as political editor of the BBC, rising to that position by way not of Oxford or Cambridge but a correspondence degree at the University of London, eleven previous years on the *Belfast Telegraph* before taking his pronounced Belfast brogue to (where else?) the *Manchester Guardian* (as it still was), the *Observer*, and Broadcasting House.

Cole's job at the BBC was not to be an anchor like Cronkite, but to improvise news-with-editorial comment on camera. He did so with his exceptional and principled good humour and likeableness. It is a hell of an occupation and, so short a time ago, not rewarded by crazily inflated levels of remuneration. BBC news tells a nation about its political condition, not about an individual class, still less a ruling elite. The political editor must have ready access to that elite, must not favour any political party, must speak a formal, simple language about often very intricate matters, must love the political life, and must be prepared, to a degree found otherwise only in the lives of war-zone correspondents, to take the phone calls wherever he or she may be, disrupt vacations, go sleepless, quit hospital early (Cole suffered a burst duodenum, a heart attack, and *still* resumed work[8]).

In doing all this, seriously but not solemnly, humanly living an inhumane schedule, Cole became, so to speak, the well-loved author of a long-running comedy of manners-in-politics. It was his duty, and that of his successors (who have not made it seem as easeful and intelligible as he did), to tell a story of the lived drama of political events within which his audience could make themselves at home, but to do so without mitigating the dangers and disasters blowing daily in the winds outside the door. Naturally, Cole told the stories in terms of the individuals observed, for that is not only how people make political history make sense, it is how it happens. But he never lost his lively sense of the historical connections of those individuals to institutions larger than themselves—party, trade union, department of state, nation, or neighbourhood.

To pay my tribute in these terms, to note the general esteem and affection in which he was held by a huge national news-watching class (millions of them in those predigital days), is to fix him and his brethren in a special niche of a country's public understanding of itself. No one was in any doubt as to who he was and what he did, and the recognition of his undoubted celebrity is confirmed by the national joke of the elegant but ageing grey herringbone topcoat which he invariably wore for outside broadcasting. The coat became his badge of office, and the office itself was to be political homemaker to the nation, to tell it a bedtime story (there is no belittling in this designation, I write with candid admiration) of wars and rumours of war, to make sense of them, to encourage nonetheless a quiet night's sleep.

II

This is what television does for us, though in the competitive welter of commercial channels, coherent stories become drowned by the tumultuous variety. The tradition of political storytellers embodied there by Cronkite and his fellows in the United States, John Cole in Britain, was founded in essence by the BBC (which so powerfully influenced Ed Murrow) and CBS and invented a style in response to world crisis and world war.

These circumstances gave the dominant narratives, as I have indicated, dramatic form and domestic relevance. They were, that is, easy and gripping tales of common significance. Meanwhile, as television accelerated past radio and provided the narrative stock of whole peoples, it brought to birth an amazing variety of life stories, most of them fictional but even these, as I have indicated, possessing an immediacy and familiarity which made their characters almost as actual to the audience as the slowly loosening and dissolving communities in which they lived.

Needless therefore to enumerate those actors from the soaps who, in this diminished way, took on a significant life in the terms of their fictional character but somehow transcending it, photographed for the tabloids and the new, repellent rush of fan magazines not as themselves but as the part they assume onscreen. At the same time as this weird distortion, the domestic life of the actual original is pursued and harried for the usual flaws and catastrophes: drink, drugs, adultery, bankruptcy, miscarriage, etc.

What on earth is going on here? For the same ravening pursuit is in evidence across show business, the same pitiless pursuit of the celebrated in the keen hope that they may be exposed in wretchedness or betrayal or mortal illness.

A thin answer is to be found in our short history of the feelings. The virtuosi teach us the form of the passions. The actors in the soaps and in the cop and hospital series display the strength of their feelings for emulation. "The great emotional crises of modern life are fought out in silence," said W. B. Yeats in the 1930s, but it is truer to say that they are now fought out in clichés. The actors show the audiences their fictional feelings, and the celebrities are reported to readers in the same melodramatic terms. Those who watch and read about them are invited to a twofold orgy: in the first they recover the pleasurable abandon of infant tantrums and greed. On their behalf, the actor and, according to the journalists, the other celebrities all release themselves in a fine frenzy of unself-aware emotion. "They kick and bite and scream all right," as the old song goes, and thus inventing feelings to have, escape the dreadful blankness of unfeeling.

The parallel orgy is one of sanctimonious fascination and distaste. "If that is success, I'll have none of it." "If this is fame and fortune, better not to win the prize." The encouragement of spite, envy, and malice needs very little by way of context; the present treatment of celebrity is a kind of saturnalia, which is to say, a ritualised occasion for the display and indulgence of antisocial feeling, thus keeping such misconduct in a marked-off zone of permission.

I am not wholly persuaded by this social psychological explanation, not least because these excesses are given such a general run well outside the boundaries of saturnalia. There is a widespread expression of such social poison as spite and envy, and much is clearly the product of an industry working up those feelings for profit. There is a consumer fascism as well as a militarist fascism, and both depend on the irrational working up of sourceless passions at the expense of victims, for the benefit, on the one hand, of a Führer or, on the other, of the sales.

The celebrity magazine is the most revolting as well as most visible manifestation of this renewed mass movement of the emotions. It is the work of a moment to dispatch them as so much nauseating scum on the surface of the deep waters of popular sentiment. There again, they sell in huge numbers, and their editors and producers laugh away criticisms on the way to the bank. Indeed, a system of minor prosthetic officialdom has invented itself in order that a celebrity may limp out of sight by hiring a spokesman to brief the mags. A Mephistopheles in Britain called Max Clifford has amassed a fortune by such judicious and slimy interventions, speckled with insincerities about "deep concern," "vulnerability," and the emetic jargon of amateur counselling—"I don't personally believe she's in a very good place," "She loves [errant husband] to bits," "I think we all know that she's got an addictive personality."[9]

The journals are unvarying in content and presentation; it would be gratuitous to conduct a protracted analysis. They undulate from interviews such as the one with Max Clifford to a succession of close-ups of negligible stars while purporting to detect assorted varieties of cosmetic correction, whether face-lifts, liposuction, or botox enhancement. The interviews mingle sycophancy with suggestive malice ("But you're so thin—you must see why people are interested"), always hunting for weakness, "revelation," deceit according to the techniques of the early gossip-columnists but here brought to a pointed unpleasantness and a readiness to press suggestion as far as mendacity (after all, litigation is good for circulation, and the awards are rarely punitive).

The articles are interspersed with advertisements indistinguishable from the rest of the copy, tirelessly emphasising the narcissism of the whole mad business. Cosmetics and clothes alternate with the repetitive diet of celebrity stroking-and-stabbing. In a famous polemic, Christopher Lasch identified the shallow narcissism which directs the helpless and exasperated spirit in the search for fulfilling emotions in the rich modern city.[10]

Such language is everywhere to be read in *Heat, OK!, Sunday Sport, FHM, GQ, National Inquirer* (along with the much crazier stuff about Elvis's resurrection). Perhaps, however, there is a more encouraging lesson to be read in readers' expressions as they peruse this sugar-and-carbohydrate literature. You can see the stuff being read on any big-city train or bus, mostly by young women mostly dressed and made up in more modest as well as more tawdry versions of the girls in the ads on the inside pages. What is striking is the expressionless and casual speed with which they scan the pages. The readers are close kin to the waiting, worried individuals in Philip Larkin's hospital, forty years ago:

> There are paperbacks, and tea at so much a cup,
> Like an airport lounge, but those who tamely sit
> On rows of steel chairs turning the ripped mags
> Haven't come far. More like a local bus,
> These outdoor clothes and half-filled shopping bags
> And faces restless and resigned ...[11]

Our young women are better dressed and with better teeth than in 1972, but they sit tamely enough, their faces restless and resigned, and it is hard to suppose that this awful fast-food-for-thoughtlessness is going to be very bad for them. *Heat* and *OK!* are symptoms, not causes. Insofar as narcissism, which is to say a psychotic cycle of self-referentiality and exhibitionism, is a modern condition—and it is—the business of celebrity may be both remedy and narcotic.

Most people, I would guess, read the magazines in much the same way. That is, they leaf casually through each identical issue, idly scanning the lowering stories of infidelity, weight loss or fat gained, cosmetic transformation, and the drearily repetitive round of hedonism on the part of the rich and famous on Caribbean beaches and Colorado ski slopes. I very much doubt that these readers are racked with longing and envy; they con this stuff as they might eat popcorn.

This is to put a lot of faith in Wordsworth's great phrase, "certain inherent and indestructible qualities of the human mind." Most people, I contend, have no difficulty judging trivial rubbish for what it is. A little commotion was worked up in Britain recently by the returns in some social survey or other indicating that all that ten-year-olds want to be when they grow up is a celebrity-on-television. Fifty years ago on this side of the Atlantic they would have wanted to be Bobby Charlton or Frankie Lane; and across the pond, who? Doris Day, Pancho Gonzales, Wesley Santee, or the most remarkable athlete ever to come out of the United States, Muhammad Ali? Celebrities figure in our children's imagination precisely because they are so visible. As the long roll call of names invoked in these pages bears out, the celebrated individuals are a pretty mixed bunch, and a sufficiency of them not without strengths and nobility those same children would find little harm in emulating.

Something, nonetheless, surely has changed from the days when little girls sang "che sera, sera" and little boys believed in the actuality of Roy Hobbs, "the Natural," with his magic baseball bat "wonderboy," cut from the heart of a willow he loved, with which he lofted three consecutive pitches twenty rows up into right, left, and centre field stands.[12] Show business and sporting industry were as corrupt and seedy then as now. The glamour was as real as the smell of crime was everywhere. The mannered chivalry of Hollywood on its best behaviour and of sportsmen who stuck to the official ideals of sportsmanlike and gentlemanly principle were what people saw and loved onstage and front-of-house. Round the back was the old, filthy hoo-ha, the bribes, the lying, the crooked dealing, and the grim facts of loss and age, drink and deadly illness.

What has changed in the manufacture of celebrity is first, as I have so much repeated here, the sheer quantities of money thrown about, and second, the opening of universal access to the platforms of fame. I have spoken of the tameness and tranquillity with which (mostly younger) people read the ghastly magazines, and it is a commonplace observation to see with what stolidity, even stupefaction, many people can sit through hours of ghastly quiz shows, celebrity interviews, talent spotting, and what was named a few years ago by an adman's horrible inventiveness, reality TV. At the same time, however, the sheer mass of these programmes as well as their changing constituency, has made it all the more possible for thousands more to be glimpsed onscreen by the many millions who are not.

III

There is a much-quoted dictum made by the pop artist Andy Warhol three decades ago to the effect that everybody will have their fifteen minutes of celebrity. Not everybody (he must have meant), but many hundreds more than was once the case. In the beginning and with so many fewer TV channels, access was difficult until you were hired, onscreen, and familiar. Then you were on for good, and audiences cherished faces and manners, quirks and quiddities they recognised and liked. This is still a strong feature of television appearance and, as I shall suggest, one of the most restorative aspects of celebrity.

Over the years, in addition to the mechanism whereby the faces we know revolve and return, there has been a kind of demotic opening up of access. I doubt that this has ever been a conscious policy, more a common change in sensibility. But messy as it is, one cannot regret a slow disenchantment of what it is to appear on television. What is then gained is not only a much greater variety of human performance, but also a much thicker mingling of the inevitable creativeness of ordinary everyday life[13] with the making of civic culture.

To talk with such uplift of the unfailing awfulness of the *Big Brother* and *American Idol* programmes is enough to make the cat laugh. What is on display in such programmes is the contemporary human inability to know what to feel, and this is the inevitable consequence of there being no true action capable of directing feelings. The only point is to see in what order people are voted (voted! as if voting were just a spasm of liking or disliking) out of the house. Finally, the whole dismal charade boils down to a cheque for the hapless, happy victor, along with the hope that there might be more TV employment to come.

When one turns to the actuality of the human exchanges in, for instance, *Celebrity Big Brother*, one goes weak at the knees at the sight of such pitiful passions and mutilated speech. Writing in 1945 about sex-and-violence thrillers, George Orwell braced himself for the novels of James Hadley Chase by saying, "Now for a header into the cesspool."[14] Well, now for it. This was a notorious exchange between three young women on one such British programme in 2005:

X: Do you get stubble?
Y: She wants to be white.... She makes me feel sick. She makes my skin crawl.
X: She's a dog.
X: They eat with their hands in India. Or is that China?... You don't know where those hands have been.
X: [We] are really good friends—you're just the cook.

X: [Z] is a dog.

Y: It's not the only fucking thing you ordered, you liar.... You're
     not some princess in fucking Neverland.... Go back to the
     slums and find out what real life is about, lady.... You fucking
     fake. You're so far up your own arse you can smell your own
     shit.

Z: Oh please learn some manners. You need elocution lessons.

X: I think she should fuck off home.[15]

The squalid penury of language and feeling here stops your heart. But then
everybody thought so. Millions watched the show, but it became the most
complained-about programme in British television history.

What else could one expect? The stiff, unnatural conditions set for the
participant and invited volunteers ensured the certainty of horrible behaviour and trivial human loathsomeness. This stuff tells us nothing about
the meanings of celebrity except that a new category has been admitted of
those talentless few whose foul mouths and ugly judgements (each deliberately worked up and on for show in the show) make them, very transiently,
topics of public gossip and easy condemnation.

Nothing to build on there. Nothing much worth pondering either. This
is so much scum on the sewage of popular prurience, and prurience itself is
a concept bringing together human smelliness, uncontrollable itching, and
sex. It is a mixture human beings may be counted upon to sniff out and
up with zeal. Mass TV programmes aimed at irritating the itch will not tell
us anything about the meanings of celebrity; they will only confirm that
culture includes rotten remains and stuffed black bags worth examining
for quite different purposes.

Those purposes will out, however. It is the unrehearsed but cooked
up nature of *American Idol* and *Celebrity Big Brother* which makes them
reek. They remind me to use Chekhov's exhortation to his people in
nineteenth-century Russia, "You live badly, my friends. It is shameful to
live like that." But notoriety will do for those who cannot win fame well.
The *Jerry Springer Program* catches one's eye and ear as deliberately opening
the black plastic bags of culture and shaking out the contents on the floor.

Springer sets himself, his blond hair well brushed, his good blue suit
well cut, only to shake out the bag. He refuses, as they say, judgemental-

ism; he only frames the tide of accusation and recrimination within the allotted time and often brings in his dingy craft with a timely flourish. There is a kind of artistry in him, exercised not on beauty or imaginative power (as I hardly need to say) but on feeling and unfeeling, on directionless anger and blame, and on inescapable misery. Just occasionally he shapes things towards certain to be short-lived reconciliation; then he glows with a faint beatitude. But his show is indicative and hugely popular because it reenacts to its vast public those helpless uncertainties of domestic feeling and impossible action which thwart and distort the lives of the urban poor.

Jerry Springer's only method is that of the therapist: a vague, authoritative presence conducing to mutual candour and controlling open rage. He is the programme's only celebrity; all those who take centre-stage in Aeschylean torment are forgotten by the following week. But Springer himself is now the subject of a successful opera, and the very emblem of the confessional celebrity with nothing to confess about himself.

The study and analysis of feeling for its own sake is what I mean by "confessionality." This is the mode of emotivism, or the doctrine that one's feelings are the guide to one's conduct. I have argued in these pages that so they are, but only those best feelings of which one is capable in the circumstances, and these in any case adjusted and reordered by moral thought, thinking in and with the grain of experience. Confessionality, by contrast, supposes to itself that by pouring out of one's heart one's bitter resentments and disappointments, one will be cleansed of life's poison and feel better.

This is the predominant moral assumption of everyday, and the industry of counselling makes for its productivity. It is not only sentimental and delusive. The cry of the soul pleading to be heard is a terrible thing, and much good has come from the newish machinery now available to process the crying. The trouble, as I contended in chapter 2, is that, insofar as the process refuses as a function of its good-hearted liberalism to tell people what to do, once they have purged feeling for a while by recounting it, they can only be baffled not only as to what to feel next, but also as to what action will move life along.

This is almost the only dramatic content to the soaps, whether picturing old-fashioned family rows in the working class, as in Britain's *EastEnders*, or making comedy out of the universal predicament of emotional stasis and blankness, as in *Friends* or *Sex in the City*. Everyone loves, of course, the familiarity of these scenes; knowing the TV characters better than their real friends—or rather, vigorously entertaining the fantasy that they do—they anatomise motives and theorise emotions with the keen pleasure and the sympathetic self-pity that the virtuous narcissist most enjoys.

Well, that is where we are. The dismal mediocrities who pass for the famous in the yellow press and the preposterous weeklies and monthlies are abjured, belittled, and sneered at according to the ethics of emotivism. (The philosopher's jargon has the merit, entirely lacking in confessional therapists, of a critical grip.) Yet the doctrine cannot simply be dismissed. It is too widespread for that, and it has its poignant force, hence its omnipresence.

The most famous television chat show in the world is Oprah Winfrey's, and after presidents Obama and Mandela she is the most celebrated black person alive. Her show is a case in point because she fully understands and applies the ethics of emotivism to all those who appear with her, and she in herself clearly endorses and lives them in her own life. Her unaffected tears of joy onscreen the night of Barack Obama's great victory went well with a direct and sincere personality (directness and sincerity being key values in emotivism, and quite right too). They were also token of her moral consistency as evinced on her long-running chat show.

There she regularly proves herself a wise woman, whose celebrity is inseparable from her authority. She is politely scornful of the phoney (memorably so in the case of the film star Tom Cruise, who played the fool foolishly jumping about like a big baby on her studio sofa and was icily received) and, always responsive to spontaneous feeling, is at pains to distinguish it from "working off on yourself feelings you haven't really got."

Oprah Winfrey would briskly condemn working off feelings you do not have, while standing up for *her* definition of sentimentality, which would be (I claim; I have not asked her), the open expression of strong, good emotion, as prescribed by the therapeutic handbooks, but also as prescribed by the great Romantic poets and musicians of the nineteenth century.

She is never at a loss, even when lost for words. At such a moment, she lets speechlessness speak for itself. She turns private lives into public spectacles—that is the point of her programmes and her fame—but her touch and tact are such as either to leave what is private inviolate or, in rendering it public, join it to the privacies of her audience's feelings, thereby making privacy communal, whereby the painfulness of self-exposure is melted into a shared reassurance.

These are not my ethics; the danger of a lapse into mere narcissism is always present. But there can be no doubt that she lives and works near the centre of popular sentiment, that her enormous fame is due to the sanity of her teaching and the delicacy of her responsiveness. If people actually use her and her moral examples as curiosities, then that is the price of a celebrity who does much for those thinned-out values of modern life—trust, compassion, solidarity. The story in which the doctrines of confessionality, the concupiscence of celebrity, and the old monstrosity of social class come together most tellingly is in the short happy life of Diana, Princess of Wales.

IV

No need to rehearse any more than briefly that brief life: the gawky, pretty-ish, rather blurred nineteen-year-old with no education but an upper-class family attached to an awkward, throttled heir to the throne, fifteen years her senior and long in thrall to serious adultery with the wife of an old friend.

The duckling becomes a ravishing beauty and queen of fashion, bears the sons and future kings she was conscripted to bear, recoils from the lies at the heart of the marriage, takes refuge in forced vomiting and slicing her arms and legs with ladies' razors, is distantly consoled by the old stager Prince Philip ("Dear Pa"). The marriage splits asunder, the princess goes on television to Tell All, does so, turns into the most photographed woman in the world, takes lovers of very uneven character—an honest Indian doctor, a playboy son of an Arab millionaire close, it is alleged, to the terrain of criminality, dies in a ghastly car smash in Paris, pursued by the hellish hordes of (as we have all learned to say) the *paparazzi*, Italian for mosquitoes.

The TV interview is one climax of this glutinous as well as tragic tale. Tragedy? Yes, the destruction of loved and admired beauty by malignant forces, the beauty herself being also a painful parody of confessional poetics. She appeared gaunt, dark shadows on her drawn face, and out for the vengeance to be won simply by telling the truth. The Prince of Wales himself had done something similar, but without blaming anybody, including himself. Princess Diana said bluntly: "there were three of us in this marriage, so it was a bit crowded ... people were—when I say people I mean friends, on my husband's side—were indicating that I was again unstable, sick and should be put in a home of some sort to get better."[16]

The emphasis shifts in the interview to the princess's treatment at the hands not only of the press but of those on "my husband's side" who, in the jargon, briefed against her. Her tone was toneless but her resentment bitter, as well it might be. She also saw clearly that her beauty communicated so beautifully to the crowds who came to admire her by way of her naturally exquisite manners—helplessness, hysterical rage, broken tears, and willed vomiting were kept for the royal family—and these carried her far higher in public esteem than her wooden consort. "When I go abroad we've got 60 to 90 photographers just from this country, coming with me, so let's use it in a productive way, to help this country."

She adopted the readiest device and defence of the beautiful celebrity and young mother in order to break the enemy's grip: she became a heroine of world peace and a gentle virgin to "people rejected by society ... drug addicts, alcoholism, battered this, battered that."[17] She was photographed walking a cleared path through a civil war minefield as a gesture against antipersonnel and weaponry industries. She was not insincere, just trite and ineffectual.

The sensational point of the TV interview, however, especially for this book, was that here a very peculiar kind of celebrity, one whose position combined old condescension with new confessionality, class privilege, and centrefold sexuality, gambled everything on a throw for revenge, certainly, but also on winning an independent future for herself.

She made her appeal to the whole country, that is to say, and in open court, to the ethics of confession; and won. She spoke throughout of "being loved" by strangers, that "I'd like to be a queen of people's hearts," and thereby wrote herself a role ready-made by the canons of celebrity. She became, with every justification, victim of a frame of gone feeling, one in which public duty and the clenched withdrawal of spontaneous feeling permitted personal jealousy and cruelty an open licence.

When she won her bet, she paid the price of shifting into the social margin occupied by bohemians, the more self-revealing kinds of film star, and the reckless, raffish ranks of the rootless and international rich. (Jackie Kennedy made something of the same move when she married the Greek shipping tycoon Aristotle Onassis.) Involuntarily or not, she invited the continued attention of the merciless hordes of photographers who followed and, in the end, as it cannot be doubted, killed her.

In the posthumous papers of the eminent *Guardian* columnist Hugo Young, there is a brief, relevant note about a conversation he had with the princess.

> She realises she will never be free of fame—thank God, I"m sure she feels. She will also never be free of the palace, "because of my sons." She was, all in all, better value than I had expected. Within her limited field of interest, she has thought quite a bit. She was surrounded by politesse, but quickly established that it was possible to be reasonably daring in one's attitudes and questions. She liked the cut and thrust, turning on the charm and girlish giggling when appropriate. I don't really think she suffers all that much, though the snappers are a great nuisance. I think she actually likes most of the attention she gets.
>
> It was interesting how many people in the *Guardian* building were straining to see her, waiting by the windows to see her leave. She took a tour with Alan, and many shook her hand.[18]

Young never missed much and was a shrewd and lively judge of people. He saw the ordinary pleasure celebrity brought the girl, as well as the vestiges of old deference. The "snappers" remained, of course, villainous.

A word is in place about these murderous felons, the image-makers and -breakers of celebrity. I have already mentioned Fellini's masterpiece, *La Dolce Vita*, which understood as long ago as 1960 their predatory necessity in the industry of publicity. For make no mistake. If what we cherish and draw strength from in famous lives is inseparable from a culture's innate vindictiveness and groundless hate, then either way we—the force of "we" is irresistible in this context—demand pictures, innumerable pictures, from outside but as near to inside as we can get, of those bodies and faces whose fame is such a spur to our living and feeling.

The life story of Ron Galella, though he did not catch Princess Di on camera, illustrates the illustrations.[19] He remains the most successful, the most hard-boiled, and the most indifferent to human frailty of the hordes of the paparazzi, but he also remains the most gifted photographer of the wolfpack. There are half a dozen of his collections in print, from *Jacqueline* in 1974, whose main subject was the most famous widow in the world and who finally won a court order to keep him at least twenty-five feet away from her, to his latest, *No Pictures*, in 2008.

He was irrepressible in a loathsome way, but by God he could take a picture. Marlon Brando punched him in the mouth and knocked five teeth out, so Galella wore a crash helmet in his subsequent pursuits of Brando. Brigitte Bardot's escort at the time hosed him down. He was unstoppable. "I"m very quick, that was the technique, fast shoot. And you nail the picture like that, you get the surprise expression. Beauty that radiates from within." And he did. He staked everything on the stakeout, digging through Doris Day's hedge to catch her sunbathing so the poor woman moved house. "Deep down, everybody wants to be famous," and when the celebrities get angry with him, Galella puts it down to "hypocrisy."

Paparazzi are fairly despised and are fairly despicable. But, as Galella points out, we feed eagerly on the photos. When the wolves took off in pursuit of Princess Diana and her driver, slightly drunk, took up the challenge, raced away in the huge black Mercedes, and crashed into the underpass concrete to kill himself, her, and her temporary suitor, the Arab princeling and playboy Dodi Fayed, the gross and deadly photographs fetched a fortune. Not many people looked away.

The desperate tale of Princess Diana and the photographers brings out with nuclear force the present pass of celebrity. She was a beautiful girl with a small, wounded ego, few intellectual resources, sporadic feelings of any kind, and a helpless desire to be loved, all served well and enhanced by her beauty and the manner she had naturally assumed with strangers. The photographers then transformed her into a giant image of the person she wanted and was compelled to be. Do as you would be done by? She was done in, on one hand, by the person she was trying to become, and on the other by the becoming person they, the photographers, and we, their customers, wanted her to be.

V

Happiness, on this showing, is when the two divisions of one person meld as one celebrity. No doubt, especially at this moment in history, that happy consequence may well be unlikeable, may even be horrible, but is damned hard to refuse. There are a couple of novels which may serve to illuminate these contradictions, and indeed to suggest how the predicament may, with courage, intelligence, and a lot of good luck, be refused. But that is the point. The woe and wonder of all the stories about celebrity is in smaller part how enviable it all is, the money, the luxury, the being clapped and recognised; in much larger part the stories tell how its peculiar kind of success poisons and corrupts and breaks lives in half. True success is then to cast off celebrity, to grow beyond it, or to live quietly in the middle station without it.

So when, in 1966, Jim Hunter published his admirable novel *The Flame*, the public hero is morally secondary to his brother, the private one, struggling low down in the middle station to make ends meet.[20] But he is happy in his small struggle, a Londoner married to a black American, blessed with a baby they can barely afford, keeping a little photographic business going. Martin Cameron is no Italian mosquito; his photography is local, portraits, weddings, school groups. He records the daily variousness of things and loves them for being ordinary.

His brother Douglas is the famous one. Tall, handsome, with a shock of ash-blond, near-white hair, charismatic by nature, by class upbringing (Martin missed both), and by virtue of the calm, serene, invincible self-righteousness which he brings to his vocation. His calling is to him simple. It is to show to his country, for which he feels such an unaffected patriotism, how to redeem itself from its godless materialism and empty pursuit of its consumerist decadence, and to rediscover truth and true happiness in bearing witness to Christ.

He starts an affirmative Christian movement. It catches fire (the flame is its lapel badge of membership). It is called, in Hunter's marvellous trope, New Vigour. Thousands flock to its standard, Douglas Cameron appoints organisers, local chapters, calls and is called to huge meetings to affirm spiritual rebirth, becomes the Lion of a new revivalism, is feted nationally for his mesmerising charm and persuasiveness, his good looks and tossing locks, for his simple pieties and old-fashioned poetics, for his unself-regarding incorruptibility, for his certitude, his goodness. This following moment catches something central in the magic of transformation from citizen to celebrity:

> House-lights suddenly darken out; the band leaps into view and stands erect for another of the great moments, the Messenger fanfare of Stephen Styles, known to everyone by now as the "Cameron" fanfare. It's a moment Douglas himself disapproves, but now in the passageway he hears the first violent notes and nods with relief to Johnny. He has been waiting five minutes for the band to arrive at this point; now in sixty-five seconds time he will again have the audience at his mercy. During forty seconds of frustrating cross-rhythms and abortive climaxes he braces himself, studies the palms of his hands, fingers his tie like an ordinary man; then in the last, vulgar, tearing bars, steps suddenly through and on to the white-lit rostrum, at the central point of a great sphere of sound.[21]

They plan "The Night of the Fires"—a nationwide show of bonfires bearing witness on St. George of England's day to the flame of faith. It is a huge success. It makes visible the sheer numbers who support New Vigour. This is a beautiful touch: the only mass politics is the politics of gesture. Numbers demonstrate—what? The numbers of private lives whose only political action is to walk peaceably in hosts through London or to turn out around evening bonfires.

The new movement catches the attention of old politics nonetheless. A tough old politician of the right is drawn into things, starts making nationalist speeches with barely a nod to religion, explicitly sets old white working-class Britain against the new black immigrants, earths a long-dormant charge of racism in Douglas Cameron's packed multitudes.

This figure, Russell Blenkiron, strong, demagogic, sincere, cynical, speaks in the accents of John Enoch Powell before Powell himself summoned the dockers to expel Britain's black interlopers. Blenkiron calls New Vigour to go political. Cameron opposes him publicly. Some hate-filled brute lets off a bomb at the gates of a mixed-race primary school, killing three children (this is only a year or two after the black church school was bombed in Birmingham, Alabama). The action ends, first with a glimpse of Douglas's now deranged wife, then with the great leader battling to keep command of his movement in the name of his sacred purpose. At the close Hunter leaves us beside Martin, as his wife waits to go to hospital for their second child, and "his anxious happiness; and of all that was well."

It is a homely moral, still fresh as a fragrance after forty-odd years: that charisma is not to be too much trusted; that mass politics, indeed mass feeling, is as dangerous and appetising as any other drunkenness; that blazing certitude and the utter goodness of one man may turn just as rank and smell just as bad as horrible old fascism or the nastier incarnations of any old nationalism.

Celebrity poisons, the story goes. So it does still, says Andrew O'Hagan.[22] This time, a child comes to show business, a star is born, then almost dies in the appalling exertion of the will we diagnose as anorexia, as she battles to fight off maturity and keep her body in the state of childish fleshlessness which was the condition of her success.

> Nobody ever heard a little girl sing like that before. The sound came from somewhere else. She gripped the microphone and swayed into every note; she bent her knees and clambered up for the feeling in the words; her eyes grew wide and then suddenly narrow: she couldn't be without the song. She spread out her fingers and beamed and her eyes filled up with tears. She pulled back the wire of the microphone, throwing her head back, hugging herself, raising herself, stopping dead.[23]

If one were to compress this novel into a fortune cookie—and thereby to violate its subtlety as well as its great generosity of heart—it would be something to the effect that children should not be admitted too soon to adult, or even adolescent, practices. This admonition is never more pungent (and quite right too) than when children (mostly girls) are dressed up, made up, sexed up to take part in talent shows (as they say) or fashion shows on the way, as their crazed parents hope, to lifelong success and fame in the evanescence of showbiz. Mrs. Temple used to say to her daughter,

Shirley, first in the line of child stars which now stretches out to the crack of doom, "sparkle, Shirley, sparkle," and this novel dramatises the creative and destructive effort which goes into infantile sparkling.

It does so with wonderful vividness, draining into the action a throng of figures from the actuality of show business. O'Hagan brings onstage Hughie Green, the real-life (the phrase is unavoidable) presenter of *Opportunity Knocks*; Les Dawson, the much-loved working-class comedian; and by suppressed allusion throughout, the very original from whom O'Hagan takes his story, Lena Zavaroni, daughter of Italian immigrants living, of all places, on the Isle of Bute off the west coast of Scotland, who was a child star on British television and died of anorexia in 1999.

It is a postmodern tale all right, fact and fiction interchangeable, switching from direct dramatisation to inner monologue to imaginary newspaper reports to the epistolary form to the never-written autobiography of Hughie Green. But the author holds firm to a plain conviction that to impose on children the dreadfully sincere insincerity, the great washes of musical sentimentality, the emetic glitter of clothes and cosmetics all inseparable from the murderous competition for infantile celebrity, is to twist them out of their natural shape and turn the children into either phantoms or monsters.

O'Hagan's Maria is a wraith. Nor is our conviction of the awfulness of her fate affected by her own passionate commitment to her career, her fame, and her fans. As she labours on towards the end of the novel, strung like a bowstring with the effort to eat "inches of toast, slices of banana," she is walking with her loyal lover, Michael, through a London underground station when a scruffy, grubby man "with a wet smile on his lips" asks for her autograph; he is brusquely rebuffed by Michael:

> and later, after they had laughed about other things and Michael had kissed her in the ticket hall, Maria felt glamorous. Going down the escalator, the sound of a saxophone at the bottom, the moving steps conveying her at speed past faces and coloured posters, and Michael somewhere behind her, she filled up with a sense of soaring strings and advancing audience. The audience that loved and needed her. The audience that lifted her over the chaos of things. She opened

her eyes wide as the escalator took her down the long staircase; she smiled and heard applause, the orchestra swelling with pride, the world waiting.[24]

Unlike Lena Zavaroni, Maria survives, loved back to weight and presence by Michael and his patient teaching, above all his teaching of sexual tenderness and all sex will do for surpassing the childhood fame she has fought to retain by starving herself into littleness and lightness.

Her last of the hallucinations anorexia brings is that she is chosen to be the subject of the British TV show *This Is Your Life*, in which a celebrity's past is assembled by bringing all the people associated with her to a sentimental reunion. (O'Hagan's ear for the diction of this occasion is flawless.)

The hallucination fades. Maria is cured. She has grown up. Celebrity has done its worst and is defeated.

Cherishing Citizens

The power of celebrity is, its critics claim and, goodness knows, can show, intoxicating, deadly to individuals, lethal to our sense of ourselves, our membership one of another. Is that it?

The point of this book has been to show that that is indeed it, but not all of it. The system and production of celebrity is intrinsic to the prosperous nations, probably to the whole world. As birth and lineage diminished in advantage (though never to vanishing point), as the idea of success became dominated by money, as elites became internationally visible, and as they played out their self-entrancement worldwide, so the stars of the celebrity galaxy have come to provide answers to some of the great life-questions: What are we worth to ourselves? Is not the value of success more than just a matter of money? What does it mean, in terms of well-lived lives, to want to be recognised in the street and to be seen on television? Have the big, blunt, old words lost all authority: modesty, humility, virtue, fortitude, temperance, justice? Those still holding to religion still pray using these words, but the religious and the secular alike can hardly keep apart from the worship of money nor turn their faces away from fame. But then when celebrities are mentioned or flash onto the TV, everyone in the cultivated classes is ready with their dose of denigration, while everyone else watches with more or less of envy, admiration, or malice.

Of course, part of the undertaking of this shortish history has been to show that these ambivalences have a life going back two and a half centuries. Garrick kneeling to the jeering audience, the Prince of Wales (the Regency one) having his coach pelted, Byron on the run from cuckolded husbands, Courbet feted for his revolutionary probity in the narrow streets of the Latin Quarter, John Jacob Astor mincing down Fifth Avenue in his spats and skimmer—these figures and their mixture of the tawdry and the glamorous have been making history for a long time. Indeed, you might say that our present ambivalence, nasty spite mixed with judicious evaluation, takes the right measure. People are learning to weigh up the worth of celebrity pretty well. The best of the bunch merit the regard they are granted; the worst of them vanish down the drain where they belong, into the pages of *FHM* and *GQ*.

That sounds like common sense. But it is far too summary. One intellectual crux is that the one-word concept "celebrity" conceals the variety of its application. There are many different kinds of celebrity and, if one thinks of society as a machine more or less rattling along as different parts perform different functions, then different kinds of celebrity work at different functions and keep the machine on the road. If, on the other hand and as this book has much protested, one thinks of society as "a constellation of enshrined ideas,"[1] a drama to be interpreted and a text to be read, then the fresco of celebrities tells us many different stories about ourselves, some unsettling, some bracing, some beautiful, some ugly.

To try to sort amongst them is then the duty of the historian and of the citizen. I shall do so by elaborating a brief list of social roles-and-meanings borrowed from a philosopher puzzling out the nowadays much-vexed meaning of identity. Amelie Rorty flips swiftly through a list of the terms we use to think about human beings in ordinary conversation: "Characters," "Figures," "Persons," "Souls," "Selves," "Individuals," "Presences."[2] Each has its application in picking out particular ways of seeing and interpreting human conduct. She too is of the view that our powers of self-knowledge are at present stalled by an incapacity to turn feeling into action, to know without undue hesitation what we are truly feeling, and what to do about it. Our self-absorption deprives us of the powers of decision.

> When we have a sensibility in quest of a rightful definition, a character whose scope of action is simply to establish the uniqueness of its own perception, when the point of consciousness becomes a light rather than a power, then action is no longer agency, and the order of perceptions become arbitrary ... wholly unique individuals become obsessed with the horrors of choice: they come to see themselves as the inventors of their own principles, inventors without purpose, direction or form.[3]

This is her bleak vision of the nihilism to which absolute individualisation leads. As far as literature is concerned, this is the passage from Henry

James to Samuel Beckett. As far as celebrity is concerned, the same passage moves us from the jolly concupiscence of Edward VII before he finally clambered onto the throne to the mad old age of Brigitte Bardot.

Things are not quite so bad as that, and our celebrities can hold out a kind of redemption. We still aspire, as a matter of moral habituation, to fashion ourselves a character we can call our own. In our ethics, our pedagogy, our politics, to have a character of some durability and fixity remains a mark of success in a life freed from the bitch-goddess. To have made oneself into such a character is, at this late date, to have followed the precepts of Aristotle's ethics,[4] and to have found and nurtured in one's life those virtues in one's disposition which come to us naturally enough and may be counted our own.

A celebrity of good character has to be lucky. The character he or she just *is* will fit only some aspect of society and not others. Let us pick an example. Let us try out Paul Newman's character for this fit.

He comes on undiminishably big. The fabulous good looks, the amazing blue eyes, the smile as wide, dazzling, and open as the American Dream itself, all serve to justify his fame and fire it into your heart. So does the laugh; think of the wonderful spontaneous laugh with which, playing the outlaw Butch Cassidy, he greets his partner's, the Sundance Kid's, confession, that, trapped on a high cliff by the marshals of the law with the only escape a deathly leap into the river at the bottom of the ravine, he cannot swim. "Can't swim? Why, the fall will probably kill you."

The style is the man. Newman found his action offscreen as a more-than-capable racing driver—car racing being a manly form of action, vividly individual, dashingly attired, wholly dependent on a selfless team of sure-fingered craftsmen. He made a huge fortune from the Newman's Own brand of salad dressing with a garishly inaccurate picture of himself on the label (handsome is as handsome does; he was quite without vanity) and gave it all, all of it (a third of a billion dollars) away.

He went on acting into his late seventies and exhibited a moral variety and unpredictability which make him not just the rival but the victor over John Wayne and James Stewart, a garland he wins exactly because he is more morally ambiguous than they were (*The Colour of Money*), less American and heroic (*Cool Hand Luke, The Verdict*), yet fitted the times and looked lively in them. He took an active part in politics, gave half a

Portrait of American film actor and director Paul Newman dressed in a sponsor logo-covered racing jacket at Moroso Motorsports Park, Jupiter, Florida, mid-1980s. Photo by John Pineda/Getty Images, photographer: John Pineda/Contributor. Hulton Archive, Getty Images

million dollars to the leftist journal *The Nation*, was a delegate to Democratic presidential conventions, was married to that great, perhaps better, actress Joanne Woodward for fifty years. "Integrity" was rightly invoked by admirers at his death.[5] This is the key value for a "character." A character has no inside-outside; he or she is given. It has a gritty feel, the word integrity; Newman allied it to charm and to astonishing physical beauty. That renders him entitled to his celebrity and us right to bestow it.

"Figures," even "figureheads," come close, Amelie Rorty tells us, to their prototypes in myth or sacred script. The anthropologist Claude Levi-Strauss says that the contemporary origin of myth is politics,[6] and it is inevitable that we look to politics for figureheads, complicated as any such search is in Europe, where present individualism holds politicians in such disesteem.

For all that, Nelson Mandela remains a global figurehead. So does, in the name of evenhandedness, Margaret Thatcher. Mandela brought off a more or less pacific revolution by *being*. He bore privation and humiliation during his twenty-five years on Robben Island with meekness and resilience. He left prison in serenity, smiling all the way. He forgave his enemies and thereby made reconciliation imaginable, and all this without invoking religious sanctions in a South Africa split by violently different versions of Christianity.

He lasted only long enough to effect the transition from white to black power. For he was an inadequate economist and an ineffective policy-maker. But he became, as figurehead celebrities must, allegorical. His benign smile, his Hawaiian shirts, his informal readiness to cut a caper, take a turn on the drums, drink tea in the townships and entertain any and every passing dignitary come to pay homage, each aspect of the man captured and made real the celebrity peacemaker, gregarious and good-humoured.

Praising Margaret Thatcher is too much for the gorge of herbivorous old Labour Party members like this author. And yet no one could withhold the status of celebrity from her, nor deny the affection and admiration she aroused in many bosoms. The certain fact that she desecrated many of the most venerable shrines in left-wing politics—trade union solidarity, the welfare state, the industrial North—and brandished the Union Jack when imperialism had become a stain on the socialist conscience is not to reduce her significance. She was a celebrity politician, and in being so brought the exercise of visible, publicly explicable power into a balance with its acceptability. People understood her actions and endorsed her ruthlessness. She made herself visible and her reasons transparent. This struck a strong chord in her nation's preference (in its cherished self-image) for plain speaking, and her reward was to be appointed celebrity by a right-wing press, and have this appointment popularly ratified.

She played the part of figurehead to the full, overplayed it maybe (as, for instance, President George W. Bush tried to, and failed because of acute charisma deficiency). But politicians are intrinsically well-equipped to do so, and her success is less illuminating of the mystery of celebrity than Nelson Mandela's, and his contrastive transformation from national politician to world emblem, a strong token of the hope of harmony.

II

Neither characters nor figureheads waver in their narratives. They are what they are; they do not choose to be, but, finding themselves in the right part, they can act directly, feelings and the will at perfect poise.

Celebrities of this kind are slightly fearful to us; they inhabit their own special category. "Persons" are different. Persons have their own will and stand by their personal responsibility. "Treat me as a person" is a plea for self-determination. Those celebrities—they are innumerable—to whom we assign personhood ("personality" being something different and unsound, flashy, a thing on show, detachable from a person) are largely those with whom we might like to be friends.

Kylie Minogue is one such person-celebrity. She was invented by the pop industry at sixteen, a bright, merry, sufficiently pretty confection to be packaged and sold. She might have gone the way of O'Hagan's Maria Tambini. Instead she made herself into herself, intensely likeable, inoffensively attractive, authoress of unmemorable but amiable songs, bursting with lovable old life and living it amenably, steady in her relationships, courteous and kindly in her interviews.

When she succumbed to breast cancer in 2006, the fanzines covered themselves with sugary foam, but Kylie Minogue took her treatment reclusively, reported on herself with dispassion, was glimpsed hairless and wearing a snood, returned restored, indomitable, plainspoken, unself-pitying. Thereby she did much for the good name of fame and made her kind of celebrity-person stiffen the fibres of the polity.

There are dozens such; reckoning up a few should refresh our sense of the health of the body politic. Things are not so bad if celebrity is assigned to women like Kylie Minogue, Dolly Parton, Sharma Chakrabarty, or (with a bit more effort) Jane Fonda. These are persons who might without parabola be personal friends, persons for whom fame is an attribute of their talents and also of their good fortune, persons whose success is pleasurable to them, for sure, whose personhood has expanded to fill without undue strain the social space assigned to them. If they are celebrated, one says to oneself, then the deep, life-shaking question, "what are we worth to ourselves?" may be soundly answered. We are worth a bit of their worthiness.

Persons and selves come close to one another. It makes sense to say "Dolly Parton is a nice person" (and niceness is a key value in all this), but you could not say "she has a nice self." Yet selfhood betokens something close to personhood. It differs in that the self is something inviolable that defines you as you. In that great classic, *The Presentation of Self in Everyday Life*, Erving Goffman[7] leaves the self itself as an elusive but vital mystery in front of which we arrange for its social presentation but which is, whatever it is, us, ours, established over time by the continuity and connectedness of our experience.

A celebrity embodying selfhood is therefore pretty consequential, as well as (surely?) matter-of-fact, tough, not to be paltered with. He or she is not a character; a self has no self-defining narrative to live out or through. John Wayne was a character, but (to go no further than Hollywood) Morgan Freeman has a self. So does President Obama. A self cannot be nice but may be good[8] (may be bad also). The celebrities we might think of as selves are so in virtue of their intractability, the finality with which they embody their own mysterious inviolability. Rarer as particular instances than persons, they still represent something we each feel ourselves to possess, or if deprived of self-possession as many people are, to crave for ourselves.

Something of what I mean is apparent in the demeanour of so splendid a television specialist as Sir David Attenborough. After all, he resigned office as a very senior BBC administrator thirty years ago in order to resume duties as the house naturalist, did so to retrieve what he rightly believed to be his natural calling and his essential self.

Since before that date, Attenborough has taught his large following, in the tiny details and broad patterns of natural life from its minutest insects to its cosmological panoramas, the terms of what it is not too much to call an emerging religion. The wonderful spaciousness of the sky and seas and the multitudinous variety of the life lived in them corroborate the Romantic metaphysics which is by now the nearest thing people outside formal churches have to a shared religion (and none the worse for that). Attenborough teaches, though he would never, I guess, put it like that, the theology, liturgy, mathematics, and grammar of such a world and other-worldly view. His listeners believe him because of who he is, the self that he is: serious, joyful, highly intelligent, unself-regarding, changeless from thirty to eighty, brave.

He is steady and hopeful. There is no tragedy in his vision of nature and its many selves, only the plotless epic of seeing and believing. When, therefore, he concluded that the climatologists were right and that he must bear witness in a new series to the terrifying menace of a globe turning against humankind and driven to destructiveness by rich humankind's own help-less greed, he spoke from his very self with chilling, reasonable finality.

Probably I could make this instance rather more rugged by taking as an example not an Attenborough, who is also so obviously attractive a person, but an intellectual dissident such as Norman Mailer. Mailer was a considerable artist, and unaccommodating selfhood has been one of the life-goals of the bohemian and avant-garde tradition much present in these historical pages.

So when Mailer, in his classic of journalism *The Armies of the Night*,[9] distinguishes between "history in a novel" and "the novel as history," he is announcing his intention to insert himself as the antihero of both forms, and to live out the self of the novelist and the recorder of his divided, violent nation's agon in his own pages. Pursuing that self to the heart of a crucial political action, one of the very few occasions in political history when a protest march altered the sum of things, he has no idea where it will lead—for himself (so to say) it leads to posh parties and drunken brawls and, in political protest, to jail and the courtroom. He is surprised at himself, his self insists on the role. The result, as he hoped but could not intend, is a great book, a declaration of his artistic independence as that kind of celebrity.

Mailer is a rougher diamond than Attenborough. In each case, they discover the self they and their fame require them to be. That is the good that fame can do, whether or not America saved itself in 1968 or the world saves itself in 2050. Perhaps Attenborough also comes closer to my last type of celebrity but one, which is what Rorty calls a "presence" but might better be thought of as a secular saint. This is the presence which a strange strain in Russian culture seems so regularly to feed and produces with frequency its special version in the mouth of Dostoyevsky, in the presences of Myshkin or Alyosha. Persons we like; selves we know because we have them ourselves; presences are frightening.

Cordelia is a presence. "So young and so untender," her father, King Lear, says coldly when she refuses to fawn to him. "So young, my Lord, and true," she replies. She is fixed upon the right and the good and will not, cannot be turned back. She is steely yet loving, neither a character one could sketch nor a person with whom one could dally. "One rarely knows their occupation, whatever it is, it doesn't form them."[10] Presences have no past nor future that we can usefully imagine for them; even their psychology is incidental to what they are.

A celebrity-presence may be world famous but will remain isolated. People will hardly flock to gape at one; they would be courteously ignored if they did. Often presences, like saints, are prisoners, steelily refusing to bow to the insistence of crude power. Andrei Sakharov was one such. Born in 1921, he lived the exigent, painful life of most Russians during Stalin's terrible rule and abortive five-year economic plans and was a patriotic warrior against the Nazi invasion in 1941. The same patriotism led him, one of the most original physicists in the world, first to work on the earliest versions of nuclear weaponry, then during the Cold War on the Russian hydrogen bomb.

This is a case of a "presence" where knowing the occupation of the man renders his saintliness understandable. Yet it seems likely that his holy innocence would have declared itself in any walk of life. For as his work drew him away from weaponry towards the great questions of cosmology to which his genius contributed his famous theories of the asymmetry of the universe, he came quite gradually but absolutely to the view that the development of powers of global destructiveness must be first contained and then stopped. At the same time (from about 1967) he formed and used his enormous reputation to profess an advocacy of human rights which proved an acute embarrassment to the then assured might of a communist USSR dominant across the whole of Eastern Europe and silently tussling with China for the East itself.

He was subjected to the usual horrible hoo-ha: vilification by government, coarse abuse in *Pravda*, house arrest, fired from his work, and finally exiled to the grim city of Gorky, once Nijni Novgorod, five hundred kilometres east of Moscow, where, unbending and unshaken, in 1975 he received the Nobel Peace Prize.

In appearance and demeanour he was the embodiment of the saint: gentle, fearless, courteous, unswervingly true not to his own being—that remains a mystery—but to the verities which required his conduct. Of course it matters that he was a scientist; scientific method and presuppositions fired and made unbreakable his will as well as themselves being coterminous with his absolutism. Thus the only natural right of humankind, which is the right to be free,[11] was for him a law of human nature as controlling as the laws of physics.

Fame of his kind is untouchable, hardly visitable. It establishes itself as a touchstone of necessity. It is moreover inviolable, a mode of identity beyond achievement. It is no accident, as I said, that other occupants of such a role are often Russian. I think that Anna Politkovskaya was one such. She was the journalist shot in Moscow in 2006 almost certainly on the orders of the FSB (successors to the KGB) and approved by President Putin. She had written unremittingly about Russian violation of human rights, especially in Chechnya, of all the hellish actuality of such violation by way of rape, mass killings, slaughter of children, torture, plundering, and blowing up the towns (by rebels and by the state soldiery alike).

She wrote five hundred articles for the last Russian independent paper, *Novaya Gaseta*, she visited Chechnya, the most savage and dangerous place in the country, some fifty times, she was beautiful, she was (her friends in the movie about her say) innocent in her saintly way. She had acted as heroic mediator when Chechnyan terrorists took hostages, first nine hundred of them in a Moscow theatre. Then the state gassed the theatre, killing 125 hostages and all the terrorists. She was in turn poisoned, recovered, jailed, released, murdered. She was mourned in the Russian way, by her millions of readers who knew their president was a hardnosed provincial killer.

There are also saintly presences in the milder cultural air of Britain, and it will be illustrative to name just one in order to emphasise the strangeness and importance of the category. Dorothy Hodgkin was the child of archaeologists and born in Egypt in 1910, came home to England, Cambridge, and then Oxford, to become one of the greatest of the nation's biochemists.[12] She first worked on X-ray crystallographic studies of penicillin, then (with the earliest computers) on the structure of vitamin B, lastly and most famously on the drug insulin, which so changed for the better the life of all diabetic sufferers, and in 1964 was awarded a Nobel Prize for her creative labours.

It is to the point that she was a scientist of such distinction and in her scientific innocence so like to Sakharov. She was strongly sympathetic to Quakerism and a lifelong socialist, and these dual attributes constituted the holiness of her presence. That is to say, she looked at the world with her sad eyes and lovely bloodhound features, and seemlily asked of it to do the impossible as if it were the easiest thing in the world.

Thus, as chancellor of the University of Bristol from 1970 to 1988 (she died in 1994), she spoke out, with her unfailing sweetness and graciousness, for nuclear disarmament. This was 1983 when Ronald Reagan was making the world a much more dangerous place by declaring propaganda war on "the evil empire" of the USSR and scattering new missiles, out of range for the United States, along the east coast of England. Dorothy Hodgkin's Bristol, which had appointed as chancellor the scientist in the country it most admired, had at the time a department of physics filled with cold warrior stalwarts protesting in print their support for the president's nuclear démarche. Dorothy Hodgkin, true to her presence, left her inferiors yammering helplessly as the press gathered around to hear her lend her matchless celebrity (without avail) to the cause of a rationally disarmed Europe.

Presences are exalted figures. You cannot imitate them. They give sanctity to the best of our deep desires. Sometimes such desires are fulfilled.

III

My last category in this roll call of the varieties of individuality is the individual itself. This is the master category in our attempts to find out both who and what we are. It is the goal of most conscientious parents to bring their beloved child up so that she will become a distinctive individual. Not an individual*ist*, for that would be to overdo things, but someone with her own views on the world, with strong feelings, gaiety as well as solidity of disposition, virtuous but also spontaneous ... as the list extends, the good parent's powers of self-mockery must come into play.

Yet we want these things with great urgency to be among the possessions of our self-possessed child, and the distinctive individuals there are about may serve not as emulable but as encouragement—encouragement to find not the particular distinctiveness of others, but a distinctiveness of one's own.

This is the moment for a testy little aside on the fatuity of what are so repellently called "role models." When some celebrity or other fails to come up to scratch because of some dire behaviour such as being drunk or slapping a slapper in a nightclub, those pious worthies have their say in their column or their chat show that somebody's role-model has let them down. The implication is that those who admire the victim-celebrity in question, almost certainly young and silly, were seeking to copy his or her success, clothes, appearance, or very self. Now they are let down because the wretch in question has so lapsed from good behaviour or proved lax in lifestyle or can be despised in whatever other meaningless clichés might be lit upon.

"Role model," if it can be made to mean anything, turns out not just to be a synonym for celebrity, but to designate somebody's achieved individuality *and* his or her assured place in public esteem. Such a person hardly occupies a "role"—celebrity is too loose and baggy a concept to tell us much about merit and esteem—and cannot really be said to be a "model" if that term, in turn, suggests emulability. No, a role model simply points to something in the person (the individual) so named which merits admiration, which at the same time bears witness to values beyond his or her individuality, or rather, which are embodied *in* the person's life but are more than merely personal. Such a value might be something as large and undifferentiated as goodness. Outside the sometimes preposterous strainings of philosophic discourse, people have no trouble with the idea of goodness in an individual life.[13] To say of Nelson Mandela, George Soros, or, come to that, Dolly Parton or the great opera singer Janet Baker, that they are good people makes, after due weighing up of their lives and works, perfectly good sense. No more do people have difficulty with saying of someone that he or she is a beautiful (or lovely) person, meaning more than the beauty of their appearance, important though that is. Someone might say, indeed, of Princess Diana that she was a lovely person, although when we think of her torments and occasional silliness, we might feel that will not quite do.

Individuality, however, is a tougher, more lived-in as well as more durable and elusive value. It started life (let us say) in Luther's ninety-nine precepts nailed to the cathedral door: "Hier stehe ich, ich kann nicht anders." His was a heretical covenant with a just God. It mutated by way of Immanuel Kant into the battle of the individual conscience with the moral law, and as theism receded, it thinned and expanded into conscientious consciousness, Henry James's heroines trying to be "those on whom nothing is lost," and because of seeing so much, becoming the most receptive of subjectivities, turning all action into the making of serious choices. That the choices cannot be morally grounded only makes action all the harder, the subject more irresolute, feeling even more fleeting and compounded. The achievement of stouthearted individuality, never known for sure, is modernist salvation for the soul.

The best celebrities have it, do they? If they do, then perhaps and at this limit, success is less a matter of money and more a work of art. (That would be the best preference for this author, at any rate.) You look over the celebrities who, all unconsciously, model themselves on the characters in *Tender Is the Night*—all those billionaires on yachts in the Mediterranean, with their ownership of press and television, their weapons procurement, their six mansions, the dreary sameness of their leisure pleasures, sun, sea, sand, skis, sex, spliffs—and who would not step instinctively into the reassuring ordinariness of the middle station?

Yet celebrity is not middling. There is a paradox here, and if we puzzle it out rightly, it is one sufficiently encouraging about the present condition of our local humanity—in the Anglophone world, and in Europe, to presume no further. For the last celebrity to be called, with acclamation, onto the stage and under the bright light, is a poet, greatest poet of the day I shall risk saying, Seamus Heaney: "Famous Seamus."

To pick a poet to embody individuality is to ratify Romantic aesthetics. "What is a poet? He is a man speaking to man," said Wordsworth. Put aside, a bit tiredly, old sexism, and that will do well enough. The poet speaks to a being as human as we are. But also (we require of him) he speaks in a way "more alive than other people, more alive in his own age ... as it were, at the most conscious point of the race in his time ... the point at which the growth of the mind shows itself."[14] Well! That is to ask for a lot. But perhaps not too much for our egalitarian declaration of independence from celebrity. Scientists may be intensely conscious, politicians may mark a point at which the growth of mind shows itself, but poets are men and women speaking to men and women, and if they are good poets, they are hearkened to as teachers of how to live and live well, how to feel and think, not how to be copied, emulated, or envied, but how to take their words and meanings, and have them move in our own lives.

Much of this drastic action is made by moral luck. Heaney was born, as is common knowledge, of Catholic parents in the divided substate of Northern Ireland, at the liminal of northwestern Europe where, as on all such edges, prosperity comes hard and antique rivalries and hatreds drift into residues and harden and endure. He was born onto a farm of the old, mixed kind—hens, pigs, cows, shire horses, flax, hay; therefore old and natural and strenuous rhythms moved into his body and speech from the start. Then the Troubles erupted again at his door, when he was a young schoolteacher with the stern Christian Brothers education and a degree in English literature behind him, and knowing himself by then to be a poet and a person of powerful feeling and a frame of thinking to match, he had to turn to face the incorrigible geography of the Six Counties.

In itself, that geography is pretty small. Battles just as grim are fought out on many European edges: Sicily, Brittany, Catalonia, Kosovo. Heaney made of them his capaciously statesmanlike, wholly poetic, keenly actual, and exemplarily individual life's work.

He was much assailed for just this quiet balancing of the phantoms of hatred and the coming emptiness (W. B. Yeats's terrible phrases). One properly famous of his poems is his unanswerable response:

> Northern reticence, the tight gag of place
> And times: yes, yes. Of the "wee six" I sing,
> Where to be saved you only must save face
> And whatever you say, you say nothing.[15]

He wrote his way out of the North and into a cottage at Wicklow in the South, and he wrote and wrote: wrote marriage into the heart of his writing, where marriage, like murder, was the gift of his history as well as the joy of his life.[16] His people's accent is gnarled and thick as well as lifted with unexpected intonations; Heaney, knowing it by heart, can play its tune and play it off against the plainer gloss of international educated speech.

To talk like this is to talk of a life's work—Heaney is seventy; he won the Nobel Prize in 1995, learning of having done so, in a delightful anecdote, well after the rest of the world and while on holiday in a remote corner of the Peloponnesians. Not that he was there by accident. From the middle period of his work onwards, Heaney speaks to and from a crowd of other poets, friends and masters, plenty of them Greek—Aeschylus from two and a half millennia ago, Cavafy from the day before yesterday—Greeks alongside Dante, Virgil friends with Hugh MacDiarmid.

> Be the wee
> Contrary stormcock you always were,
> The weather-eye of a poetry like the weather

and timely unpoetic friends, Claire O'Reilly, Mick Joyce in heaven, his beloved wife "tail up like a skunk" rooting for a nightie in the bottom drawer.

He talks and talks, talks to us in the poems, talks dutifully and well in all that "overinterviewing": in one such interview his long-standing friend, Dennis O"Driscoll, asks him, "What has poetry taught you?" and Heaney, always the good, the ideal teacher, answers: "That there's such a thing as truth and it can be told—slant; that subjectivity is not to be theorised away and is worth defending; that poetry itself has virtue, in the first sense of possessing a quality of moral excellence and in the sense also of possessing inherent strength of reason by its sheer madeupness, its *integratis, consonatia* and *claritas*."[17] As you live with and through the poems, the realisation dawns—slowly, as art, like life, mostly does—that they have dramatised and spoken a biography. They are vividly populated with friends (and enemies) and poet-friends; they have a prodigious geographical reach, from California and Harvard to Lake Avernus and the home cemeteries of Czeslaw Milosz and Zbigniew Herbert, and they always come home to Ireland, both parts, North and South.

Once upon a time, T. S. Eliot, while he was writing *Little Gidding* during the London blitz of 1941, mused to a friend how hard it was to feel that writing poetry was a justified activity amid "what is going on now." Heaney quotes him, and goes on,

> Here is the great paradox of poetry and of the imaginative arts in general. Faced with the brutality of the historical onslaught, they are practically useless. Yet they verify our singularity; they strike and stake out the ore of self which lies at the base of every individuated life. In one sense the efficacy of poetry is nil—no lyric has ever stopped a tank. In another sense, it is unlimited. It is like the writing in the sand in the face of which accusers and accused are left speechless and renewed.[18]

Anyone might feel like that about their work. Then, insofar as they are lucky, they find themselves to have "struck and staked out the ore of self," and if the ore turns to sand, why it's none the worse for that. We write our lives on the sand, the tide washes it away. But what we have written, we have written.

Enough now about celebrities. The poets and artists, and when we can understand them, the scientists and mathematicians also, are the most use to us. Celebrity may massively mislead us, but I do not see that we can do without it. It gives us certain bearings. But those bearings guide us only inasmuch as we have some idea where we are in the first place. Celebrity, that is, cannot lead by its unkindly light. Too many of those who wear its flashy attire are lost souls. But they are lit by the shimmering phosphorescence of success, and people first follow them, and then pelt them.

They only pelt, it should be added, the lost souls, plenty of whom deserve the pelting they get. What I mean is that there are *structures* in all this tumult, as there are in all human dealings. Certain classes of celebrity count as peltable; the international rich are not, and they, as I have so frequently said in these pages, are the worst menace looming over the human (and the natural) future, and the celebrities who make its headlines. So many of the rich not only as a direct consequence of their monomania but because of the way money is now made, removed from the agency of others and the manufacture of blessed *things*, are indifferent and insolent towards the normal duties and courtesies of social life. Their moneymaking drives them away from the lived exchanges of class and power and domesticity. I mentioned George Soros a page or two ago, and he as being a good man of stupendous wealth. He is the exception who ... etc. There are no doubt a few more. But although avarice and greed have long been in the canon of deadly sins, and any number of moralists have decried the filthy rich, no one can doubt that, for the past four decades or so, they have had things all their own way and been celebrated for so doing—just as they were in Haussmann's Paris and the Astors' New York.

As in all perorations, I am trying for even-handedness in spite of my malediction spoken over irresponsible wealth and the separated rationality and self-exculpation it invents. At the rousing end of his great book *The Power Elite*, which moves so strongly behind these pages, C. Wright Mills declares:

> The men of the higher circles are not representative men; their high position is not a result of moral virtue; their fabulous success is not firmly connected with meritorious ability. Those who sit in the seats of the high and the mighty are selected and formed by the means of power, the sources of wealth, the mechanics of celebrity, which prevail in their society. They are not men selected and formed by a civil service that is linked with the world of knowledge and sensibility. They are not men shaped by nationally responsible parties that de-

bate openly and clearly the issues this nation now so unintelligently confronts. They are not men held in responsible check by a plurality of voluntary associations which connect debating publics with the pinnacles of decision. Commanders of power unequalled in human history, they have succeeded within the American system of organised irresponsibility.[19]

There is at present little chance of any such open debates being held, nor such checks on power devised. All the same, the large and varied landscape of celebrity has its beauties, its open and uplifting places, its bright sunshine and homely clearings. We cannot remind ourselves too often that there are very numerous kinds of celebrity, that they are all products of our complicated history, nor that quite enough of them stand and live for an inhabitable future, one in which men and women may live honest lives, may make their peace with nature, may know and name for what they are the excellent and manifold expressions of hope and virtue: trust and equality, say, from which may even follow the love that lasts a lifetime, and perhaps some friendly, godless equivalent of the light of the divine countenance.

When I was a boy I was given a folio-sized volume with lovely thick pages entitled *The Boy's Book of Heroes*. I was affected through and through by it. It included Jack Hobbs and George Mallory, Cecil Rhodes, Michael Faraday, David Livingstone, and, bless my soul, Garibaldi. It even included some women—two nurses, Edith Cavell and Florence Nightingale. A British boy's book, of course, but not so bad for 1946.

If anyone were to compile such an anachronistic thing today, could it flare out with like colour, life, inspiration? There is every reason to look for these treasures in celebrated lives, and to disparage as weak and feckless, or harsh and cruel, those that are just that. So this is a book aiming to catch at visions, lives in brief, searching in those who won regard, applause, great prizes, for a kind of hymn or creed to which people, even a people, could give assent, and say to themselves, as long as we have such lives, then we shall come through. So I looked for meaning in the past, and this was the way it came.

Notes

Chapter 1: The Performance of Celebrity

1. Guy Debord, *Society of the Spectacle* (Detroit: Black and Red, revised edition, 1977), paras. 36, 37.

2. Clifford Geertz, "Centres, Kings, Charisma," in *Local Knowledge: Further Essays in Interpretive Anthropology* (New York: Basic Books, 1983), p. 125. See also D. M. Bergeron, *English Civic Pageantry 1558–1642* (London: 1970).

3. Quoted in Bergeron, *English Civic Pageantry*, p. 15.

4. Max Weber, *The Theory of Social and Economic Organization* (New York: Free Press, 1904), part 3.

Chapter 2: A Very Short History of the Feelings

1. I follow Alasdair MacIntyre here, in his "Practical Rationalities as Social Structures," in *The MacIntyre Reader*, ed. K. Knight (Cambridge: Polity Press, 1998), pp. 133–35.

2. Clifford Geertz, *Negara: The Theatre State in Nineteenth Century Bali* (Princeton: Princeton University Press, 1980), pp. 124–32. See also my *Clifford Geertz: Culture, Ethics, Custom* (Cambridge: Polity Press, 2000), chap. 7.

3. Geertz, *Negara* , p. 123.

4. In his splendid and indispensable *The Pleasures of the Imagination: English Culture in the 18th Century* (Chicago: University of Chicago Press, 1997).

5. "Dissertation on the Passions," elisions in MacIntyre *MacIntyre Reader*, p. 125, on whom I depend here.

6. Roy Porter, "The Social Order," in *English Society in the 18th Century* (Harmondsworth: Penguin, revised edition, 1990), pp. 65ff.

7. David Hume, "Of Superstition and Enthusiasm," in *Selected Essays*, ed. S. Copley and A. Edgar (Oxford: Oxford University Press, 1993), p. 41.

8. *MacIntyre Reader*, p. 126.

9. The rest, as E. P. Thompson shows us, had a much more rough-and-ready emotional calculus, although one still matched to Hume's sequence. See his "The

Moral Economy of the Crowd in Georgian Britain," in *Customs in Common* (London: Allen Lane, 1990).

10. Quoted and translated by Adam Smith, *Essays on Philosophical Subjects*, ed. W. Wightman and J. Bryce (Oxford: Clarendon Press, 1980), p. 253.

11. "On the Romantic Sensibility in the Movements of the Heart," in Madame de Staël, *De L'Allemagne, Collected Writings*, ed. Renan (Paris: Gallimard, 1953).

12. See T. J. Clark, *Farewell to an Idea: Episodes in the History of Modernism* (New Haven: Yale University Press, 1996).

13. *Preface* to *Lyrical Ballads*, 1800, ed. H. Littledale (Oxford: Oxford University Press, 1911), pp. 232, 237.

14. E.g., in the movie starring Richard Gere and Julia Roberts, *Pretty Woman* (1990).

15. Instances finely developed by Richard Sennett in *The Fall of Public Man* (Cambridge: Cambridge University Press, 1977).

16. F. R. Leavis, "Anna Karenina," in *Anna Karenina and Other Essays* (London: Chatto and Windus, 1967), p. 21.

17. *MacIntyre Reader*, p. 128.

18. In, classically, *The Ambassadors* (1903).

19. A tale well told by Anthony Giddens in *The Transformation of Intimacy* (Cambridge: Polity Press, 1992).

20. The different designations are important as to whether one claims status as an "individual," a "character," a "person," and so on. See the concluding essay by the editor in *Identities of Persons*, ed. Amelie Rorty, as discussed in my envoi.

21. Philip Larkin, "Love Songs in Age," *Collected Poems* (London: Faber, 1988), p. 113.

CHAPTER 3: THE LONDON–BRIGHTON ROAD

1. I draw here and subsequently with admiration on Peter Ackroyd, *London: The Biography* (London: Minerva, 1997).

2. Thompson, "The Moral Economy of the Crowd."

3. Details from Porter, *English Society in the 18th Century*, p. 101.

4. See E. P. Thompson, *Whigs and Hunters: The Origins of the Black Act* (London: Allen Lane, 1975).

5. Porter, *English Society in the 18th Century*, pp. 67ff.

6. Ibid., p. 70.

7. J. H. Plumb, N. McKendrick, and J. Brewer, *The Birth of a Consumer Society: The Commercialisation of 18th Century England* (London: Europa Press, 1982).

8. As witness J. H. Plumb, *The Growth of Political Stability in England* (London: Macmillan, 1972).

9. Quoted by Brewer, *Pleasures of the Imagination*, pp. 333–34.

10. As Linda Colley shows in *Britons: Forging the Nation 1707–1837* (London: Vintage, 1996).

11. Brewer, *Pleasures of the Imagination*, p. 419.

12. Sophie de la Roche, quoted in *German Visitor to London Theatres* (New York : Octagon Press, 1978), p. 114.

13. Alexander Pope, *The Dunciad* in *The Poems*, ed. John Butt (London: Methuen, 1965), book 1,ll.32 following.

14. Brewer, *Pleasures of the Imagination*, p. 63.

15. See Andor Gomme and David Walker, *Architecture of Glasgow* (London: Lund Humphries, 1968), chap. 3; also Andor Gomme et al., *Bristol: An Architectural History* (London: Lund Humphries, 1979).

16. Porter, *English Society in the 18th Century*, p. 233.

17. See Charles Ryskamp et al., *Art in the Frick Collection* (New York: Harry N. Adams, 1996), p. 89.

18. Norbert Elias, *The Civilising Process* (Oxford: Blackwell, 2000); Michel Foucault, *Discipline and Punish: The Birth of the Prison* (Harmondsworth: Penguin, 1979).

19. See R.G.S. Eyre's classic study, *The Novel in Women's Magazines, 1740–1780* (Oxford: Oxford University Press, 1967), a splendid source book for a history of the sentiments.

20. Quoted from Dr. Johnson by Mrs. Thrale, *The Anecdotes of Mrs. Piozzi in Their Original Form*, ed. R. Ingrams (London: John Murray, 1984), p. 45.

21. Quoted in Joseph Wood Krutch , *Samuel Johnson* (New York: Harcourt, Brace and World, 1963), p. 117.

22. See Jenny Uglow's excellent biography, *Hogarth* (London: Random House, 2001).

23. I follow Martin Postle here in his catalogue essay, "The Modern Apelles," in *Joshua Reynolds: The Creation of Celebrity*, ed. M. Postle (London: Tate Gallery 2005), pp. 17–34. See also Ellis Waterhouse, *Reynolds* (London: 1973).

24. Quoted by Postle, "The Modern Apelles," p. 19.

25. Quoted by ibid., p. 26.

26. Quoted by ibid., p. 30.

27. Colley, *Britons*, pp. 208ff, "Majesty."

28. Ibid., p. 241.

29. See "The Invention of the Seaside" in my *The Delicious History of the Holiday* (London: Routledge, 2000).

30. Ian Nairn and Nikolaus Pevsner, *The Buildings of England: Sussex* (Harmondsworth: Penguin, 1965), p. 439.

31. *Selected Letters of Byron*, ed. V. H. Collins (Oxford: Oxford University Press, 1928), April 6, 1819.

32. I owe these details about the everyday life of these monsters to T.A.J. Barnett, *The Rise and Fall of a Regency Dandy* (London: John Murray, 1947). This is the story of Scrope Berdmore Davies, playboy, beau, and close friend and travelling companion of Byron's.

33. Frederick Raphael, *Byron* (London: Sphere Books, 1989), p. 67. I depend extensively on Raphael's splendid and vivid biography.

34. I have in mind the excellent movie *Witness* (1985) made by Peter Weir, in which Harrison Ford, an outsider cop on the run, has an affair with Rachel Lapp (played by Kelly McGillis), an Amish widow.

35. *George Gordon, Lord Byron: Letters and Journals*, ed. Leslie Marchand (London: John Murray, 1912), vol. 8, p. 112.

36. *Theory of the Mortal Sentiments*, ed. D. Raphael and A. Macfie (Oxford: Clarendon Press, 1976). Smith revised the sixth edition just before he died in 1790.

37. See Emma Rothschild's brave work of rehabilitation, *Economic Sentiments: Adam Smith, Condorcet and the Enlightenment* (Cambridge: Harvard University Press, 2001), p. 27.

38. Quoted by ibid., p. 54.

39. Ibid., p. 149.

40. "On the Middle Station of Life," in *Selected Essays*, ed. Copley and Edgar, p. 10.

41. Ibid., p. 7.

42. Quoted by Rothschild, *Economic Sentiments*, p. 228.

43. Copley and Edgar, eds., *Selected Essays*, p. 7.

CHAPTER 4: PARIS: HAUTE COUTURE AND THE PAINTING OF MODERN LIFE

1. Charles Taylor, *Sources of the Self: The Making of Modern Identity* (Cambridge: Harvard University Press, 1989), p. 373.

2. First of all correlated by Edmund Burke in his *Philosophical Enquiry into the Origin of Our Ideas of the Sublime and the Beautiful*, 1757.

3. Taylor, *Sources of the Self*, pp. 410ff.

4. See Eric Hobsbawm and Georges Rudé, *Captain Swing* (London: Lawrence and Wishart, 1969).

5. I take much here from Eric Hobsbawm, *Nations and Nationalism* (Cambridge: Cambridge University Press, 1984).

6. I follow E. P. Thompson in calling it that. See "The Peculiarities of the English," in his *The Poverty of Theory* (London: Merlin Press, 1978).

7. Cf. Taylor, *Sources of the Self*, p. 424.

8. Simon Schama thinks it would all have happened anyway, but without the guillotine. See his *Citizens: A Chronicle of the French Revolution* (New York: Knopf, 1989).

9. These details of the fragmentariness of France are taken from Graham Robb, *The Discovery of France* (London: Bloomsbury, 2006).

10. This medley of historical generalisations is taken, successively, from Eric Hobsbawm, *Industry and Empire* (London: Weidenfeld and Nicolson, 1968); Thompson, "The Moral Economy of the Crowd"; Robert Hughes, *The Fatal Shore: The Transportation of Convicts to Australia 1787–1868* (London: Harvill Collins, 1987).

11. Charles Dickens, *Dombey and Son* (1848), ed. with an introduction by Raymond Williams (Harmondsworth: Penguin, 1983), pp. 103, and 473.

12. I take these examples from T. J. Clark's retelling of the tale in *The Absolute Bourgeois: Artists and Politics in France 1848–1851* (London: Thames and Hudson, 1973).

13. The story of the coup is best and most ironically told by Marx in "The Eighteenth Brumaire of Louis Napoleon," in Marx and Engels, *Selected Works* (London: Lawrence and Wishart, 1968), pp. 97–174.

14. Ibid., p. 138.

15. T. J. Clark, *The Painting of Modern Life: Paris in the Art of Manet and His Followers* (London: Thames and Hudson, 1985), "The View from Notre-Dame."

16. Quoted by ibid., p. 39.

17. Walter Benjamin, *The Arcades Project*, trans. by Howard Eiland and Kevin McLaughlin (Cambridge: Harvard University Press, 1991), p. 879.

18. Ibid., p. 3.

19. Ibid., p. 7.

20. As told by Bill Lancaster in *The Department Store: A Social History* (London: Leicester University Press, 1995).

21. Affectionately remembered by Asa Briggs in *Friends of the People: The Centenary History of Lewis's* (London: Batsford, 1956).

22. See M. B. Miller, *The Bon Marché: Bourgeois Culture and the Department Store, 1869–1920* (London: Allen and Unwin, 1981).

23. Figures in Lancaster, *Department Store*, p. 20.

24. Susan Porter Benson, *Counter Cultures: Saleswomen, Managers and Customers in American Department Stores, 1890–1940* (Urbana: University of Illinois Press, 1986).

25. Clark, *Painting of Modern Life*, pp. 41ff.

26. Ibid., p. 210.

27. Taken as his definition by F.W.J. Hemmings in *Baudelaire the Damned* (London: Hamish Hamilton, 1982).

28. I take much here from Christopher Prendergast, *Paris and the nineteenth Century* (Oxford: Blackwell, 1992), "The High View: Three Cityscapes."

29. Hemmings, *Baudelaire the Damned*, pp. 199–200.

30. Edmond and Jules Goncourt, *Pages from the Goncourt Journal*, ed. and trans. Robert Baldick (Harmondsworth: Penguin, 1984), p. 399.

31. I repeat with admiration much of Richard Sennett's pioneering argument in *The Fall of Public Man* (Cambridge: Cambridge University Press, 1976).

32. Ibid., pp. 187ff. See also James Laver's classic *A Concise History of Costume and Fashion* (New York: Abrams, 1950).

33. Immortalised of course by Henry James, *The Awkward Age*, first published in 1899.

34. Shown to me years ago by B. S. Raine, a descendant of the Victorian hunting memorialist Surtees.

35. Charles Dickens, *Little Dorrit* (1857) (Harmondsworth: Penguin, 1967), p. 503.

36. Sennett, *The Fall of the Public Man*, pp. 193–94.

37. I compress into a sentence the vast theorisation of these developments by Michel Foucault. See, for a start, *Souci de Soi* (Paris: Gallimard, 1984).

38. This famous concept was invented by David Riesman in his book of that title, which he applied to the 1950s United States. The idea applies just as happily to 1890.

39. Robert Graves, *Selected Poems* (Harmondsworth: Penguin, 1961), p. 161.

40. Most of these details come from Ruth Brandon's rather long but excellent biography, *Being Divine: A Biography of Sarah Bernhardt* (London: Secker and Warburg, 1991).

41. *My Double Life: The Memories of Sarah Bernhardt* (New York: SUNY Press, 1999).

42. Henry James, *Collected Travel Writings* (New York: Library of America, 1993), p. 732.

43. This short account rests entirely on James Morton, *Lola Montez: Her Life and Conquests* (London: Portrait, 2007).

CHAPTER 5: NEW YORK AND CHICAGO

1. Ambroise Vollard, *Recollections of a Picture Dealer* (New York: Dover, 2002).

2. Introduction to *Families of Fortune: Life in the Gilded Age*, by Alexis Gregory (New York: Vendome Press, 1993), p. 7.

3. Figures taken and recalculated from ibid., p. 10.

4. Another Trianon was built down the road at Rosecliff in 1898.

5. Theodor Adorno, *Minima Moralia* (London: New Left Books, 1974), p. 224.

6. Justin Kaplan, *When the Astors Owned New York* (New York: Plume Books, 2007), p. 29.

7. Gustavus Myers, *History of the Great American Fortunes* (New York: Monthly Press, 1937), p. 47.

8. These details and much else from C. Wright Mills's classic, *The Power Elite* (New York: Oxford University Press, 1956), chaps. 3 and 4.

9. Dixon Wecter, *The Saga of American Society* (New York: Scribner's, 1937), pp. 234–35. "Society" in the title means "High."

10. Mills, *The Power Elite*, p. 72.

11. As John dos Passos satirises him, in his great novel *The Big Money* (1937) (New York: Washington Square Press, 1961), pp. 525–34.

12. Gore Vidal, *Hollywood* (London: Abacus, 1994), p. 115.

13. Benson, *Counter Cultures*, chap. 1.

14. First published in 1885. Here referred to in the edition (New York: Bantam, 1960).

15. I take much in what follows from Charles Ponce de Leon, *Self-Exposure: Human Interest Journalism and the Emergence of Celebrity, 1890–1940* (Chapel Hill: University of North Carolina Press, 2002).

16. Don Seitz, *Joseph Pulitzer: His Life and Letters* (New York: Simon and Schuster, 1924), p. 622.

17. Ponce de Leon, *Self-Exposure*, p. 60.

18. Taylor, *Sources of the Self*, pp. 393ff.

19. Paul Gallico, *Liberty*, October 29, 1929, p. 54, quoted by Ponce de Leon.

20. Geertz, *Negara*, "Conclusion."

21. Thorstein Veblen, *The Theory of the Leisure Class* (1901), welcomed in a famous review by Howells here cited in the edition (New York: Scribner's, 1964).

22. *Life of Hawthorne* in Henry James, *Critical Essays* (New York: Scribner's, 1937), vol. 9, p. 49.

CHAPTER 6: THE GEOGRAPHY OF RECOGNITION

1. At various points in this chapter I am using the argument of my book, *The Delicious History of the Holiday*.

2. Hear her story as adventurer-anthropologist-explorer told by Mary Russell in *The Blessings of a Good Thick Skirt* (London: Flamingo, 1994).

3. Van Gogh, *Collected Letters*, ed. Mark Roskill (London: Flamingo, 1993), p. 268.

4. This short history of transport owes much to Mary Blume and her book *Côte d'Azur: Inventing the French Riviera* (New York: Thames and Hudson, 1992).

5. Ibid., p. 117.

6. F. Scott Fitzgerald, *Tender Is the Night* (1934) (Harmondsworth: Penguin, 1955), p. 101.

7. The phrase is R. G. Collingwood's in *The Principles of Art* (Oxford: Clarendon Press, 1937), pp. 57ff.

8. Fitzgerald, *Tender Is the Night*, p. 138.

9. Ibid., p. 122.

10. Ibid., p. 180.

11. Evelyn Waugh, *Vile Bodies* (1930 and in print ever since) (Harmondsworth: Penguin, 1996), pp. 96–97.

12. Ibid., p. 120.

13. Quoted from Lindbergh's journals in Philip Roth, "Postscript: A True Chronology of the Major Figures," in *The Plot Against America* (New York: Vintage Books, 2005), pp. 369–70.

14. Vidal, *Hollywood*, p. 112.

15. A.J.P. Taylor, *English History 1914–1945* (Oxford: Clarendon Press, 1965), pp. 312–13.

CHAPTER 7: THE GREAT DICTATORS

1. This is Richard Sennett's argument in a nutshell. See Sennett, *The Fall of Public Man*, pp. 290ff.

2. The title of Lionel Trilling's book acutely relevant to my argument in this chapter. See his *Sincerity and Authenticity* (New York: Oxford University Press, 1974).

3. Sennett, *The Fall of Public Man*, p. 221.

4. I take much in the foregoing from Ian Kershaw, *Hitler: Hubris 1889–1936* (New York: W. W. Norton, 1998).

5. Ibid., p. 519.

6. Paul Ginsborg, *Italy and Its Discontents* (Basingstoke, Palgrave, 2003), pp. 296–97.

7. I am relying on two biographies for these details: Denis Mack Smith's classic, *Mussolini* (London: Weidenfeld and Nicolson, 1981), unyielding in his contempt for his subject; and R.J.B. Bosworth, *Mussolini* (London: Arnold, 2002).

8. Mack Smith, *Mussolini*, p. 129.

9. Charlie Chaplin, dir., *The Great Dictator* (1940).

10. In Tim Parks, *Italian Neighbours* and *An Italian Education*. See also Ginsborg, *Italy and Its Discontents*, pp. 68–93.

11. Mack Smith, *Mussolini*, facing p. 147.

12. As Elias Canetti teaches us in *Crowds and Power* (Harmondsworth: Penguin, 1981).

13. Kershaw, *Hitler*, p. 403.

14. See, e.g., his famous malediction on popular art, "The Culture Industry," in the collection he shared with Max Horkheimer, *Dialectic of Enlightenment* (London: Verso, 1979). For a similar critique, from a very different viewpoint but written about the same time, see Collingwood, *The Principles of Art*.

15. George Orwell, *England, Your England* (London: Secker and Warburg, 1968), p. 34.

16. Canetti, *Crowds and Power*, p. 19.

17. Geertz, *Local Knowledge*, p. 122. See Philip Kieff's excellent critique of psychologism, *The Triumph of the Therapeutic* (New York: Random House, 1966).

18. I borrow here from a classic paper by Edward Shils, "Charisma, Order and Status," *American Sociological Review* (April 1965).

19. A point taken from David Runciman's excellent study, *Political Hypocrisy: The Mask of Power from Hobbes to Orwell and Beyond* (Cambridge: Polity Press, 2008).

20. As Scott Fitzgerald almost put it in *The Great Gatsby* (New York: Scribners, 1925), p. 76.

21. I take these qualities from a variety of sources, including Rexford Tugwell's *The Democratic Roosevelt* (New York: Penguin, 1969); the warhorse John Gunther's *Roosevelt in Retrospect* (New York: Harper, 1950); and Stephen Graubard, *The Presidents* (London: Penguin, 2004).

22. *FDR's Fireside Chats*, ed. R. D. Buhite and D. W. Levy (New York: Penguin, 1993), pp. 12–17. Given on March 12, 1933.

23. Ibid., p. 173.

24. Gore Vidal, *Palimpsest: A Memoir* (London: Abacus, 1996).

25. Arthur Schlesinger, *A Thousand Days* (London: André Deutsch, 1965), p. 191.

26. The article first appeared in *Esquire* and was reprinted in Norman Mailer, *Cannibals and Christians* (New York: Doubleday, 1964), p. 88.

27. Schlesinger, *A Thousand Days*, p. 105.

28. Policies variously proposed by him to the Party Congress in 1986 and at Reykjavik the same year. See my *The Cruel Peace: Everyday Life and the Cold War* (New York: Basic Books, 1991), pp. 355–62.

29. Vidal, *Palimpsest*, p. 312.

30. Ibid., p. 289.

31. Paul Krugman, *The Conscience of a Liberal* (New York: W. W. Norton, 2007), pp. 11–12.

32. No one can write of these matters without using Guy Debord's slightly mad and doctrinaire little book, *Society of the Spectacle*, brought to birth by the events of May 1968.

33. I am drawing here on Peter Stallybrass and Allon White, *The Politics and Poetics of Transgression* (Brighton: Harvester, 1986).

34. I depend here on many sources, including in particular Joe Klein, *The Natural* (New York: Doubleday, 2002); and John B. Thompson, *Political Scandal* (Cambridge: Polity Press, 2000).

35. Joan Didion, *Political Fictions* (New York: Vintage Books, 2002), pp. 215–16.

36. Walter Cronkite, *A Reporter's Life* (New York: Ballantine Books, 1997), p. 220.

Chapter 8: The Stars Look Down

1. Richard Dyer, *Heavenly Bodies: Film Stars and Society* (London: Routledge, rev. ed., 1986), p. 3.

2. I take much here from Nicholas Garnham, *Capitalism and Communication* (London: Sage, 1990), chap. 2.

3. E.g., A.J.P. Taylor, *English History, 1914–1945*, as quoted, pp. 314–15.

4. I take much of what follows from Garry Wills, *John Wayne's America: The Politics of Celebrity* (New York: Simon and Schuster, 1997), and even more from Michael Wood's review of the book, *New York Review*, April 24, 1997, and a long conversation with Wood in 2006.

5. Joan Didion, *Slouching towards Bethlehem* (New York: Washington Square Press, 1981), pp. 44–45.

6. Wills, *John Wayne's America*, p. 268.

7. D. H. Lawrence, *Selected Literary Criticism*, ed. Anthony Beal (London: Heinemann, 1955), p. 329.

8. Wills, *John Wayne's America*, p. 316.

9. Marc Eliot, *Jimmy Stewart: A Biography* (New York: Harmony, 2006).

10. Graham McCann, *Cary Grant: A Class Apart* (London: Fourth Estate, 1996), p. 3.

11. I follow much of what follows from Stanley Cavell's splendid *Pursuits of Happiness: The Hollywood Comedy of Remarriage* (Cambridge: Harvard University Press, 1981).

12. McCann, *Cary Grant*, p. 133.

13. Cavell, *Pursuits of Happiness*, p. 170.

14. Evelyn Waugh, *Brideshead Revisited* (London: Dent, Everyman ed., 1993), p. 246.

15. This is a suppressed quotation from John Berger, *About Looking* (London: Writers and Readers Cooperative, 1980), pp. 197–98.

16. Quoted by Graham McCann, *Marilyn Monroe* (Cambridge: Polity Press, 1988), p. 175.

17. I take this account from Norman Mailer's justly famous *Marilyn: A Biography* (which is also a photo album) (New York: Grosset and Dunlap, 1973), pp. 120–21.

18. McCann, *Cary Grant*, p. 160. I am also grateful for several conversations with Professor Ross Miller, Arthur Miller's nephew.

19. Mailer, *Marilyn*, p. 130.

20. Arthur Miller, *Timebends: A Life* (London: Methuen, 1987), p. 307.

21. Dyer, *Heavenly Bodies*, chap. 2.

22. Miller, *Timebends*, p. 359.

23. Simone de Beauvoir, *Brigitte Bardot and the Lolita Syndrome* (New York: Reynard Press, 1960).

24. Martha Gellhorn, *The Face of War* (New York: Atlantic Monthly Press, 1988), p. 180.

25. Ibid.

26. So famous it became the title of a film about one of his greatest moments, facing down Senator McCarthy: *Good Night and Good Luck*, dir. George Clooney, 2006.

Chapter 9: From Each According to His Ability

1. The sociology of his great victory is vividly explored by Timothy Garton Ash in his *We, the People* (Cambridge: Granta, 1990).

2. The phrase is the architectural historian Mark Girouard's in his *The Queen Anne Movement 1860–1900* (Oxford: Clarendon Press, 1977).

3. Walter Benjamin, "The Storyteller," in *Illuminations* (London: Jonathan Cape, 1970), p. 102.

4. Charles Dickens, *David Copperfield* (Harmondsworth: Penguin, 1974), p. 71.

5. In a conversation with me reported in my *The Name of the Game* (London: Heinemann, 1978).

6. As he says in his autobiography, *Golf Is My Game* (London: Chatto and Windus, 1959), p. 111.

7. Alistair Cooke, *Letter from America*, broadcast by the BBC, September 1972.

8. These details taken from Lawrence Loudino, *Tiger Woods: A Biography* (Albany NY: Greenwood Press, rev. ed., 2007), and the Wikipedia site on Woods.

9. A point made for me by Colin Crouch, *Coping with Post-Democracy* (London: Fabian Society 598, 2000).

10. As admirers of that astonishing book will recognise, I am influenced here by John Berger's *G* (London: Weidenfeld and Nicolson, 1972).

11. My guide through this evanescent history is Simon Firth, *The Sociology of Rock* (London: Picador, 1979).

12. I learned much about their music from Wilfred Mellers, *Twilight of the Gods: The Beatles in Retrospect* (London: Viking, 1974).

13. Robert Darnton, *Bohemians before Bohemianism* (Wassenaar: Netherlands Institute for Advanced Study, 2006).

14. Much of what follows is from *Eric Clapton: The Autobiography* (London: Random House, 2008), with extensive additions, naturally, from *New Musical Express* and press sources.

15. I owe much here to the scholar of Queen, Hilary Britland.

16. James Scott, *Weapons of the Weak* (New Haven: Yale University Press, 1985).

17. Stuart Hall and T. Jefferson, *Resistance through Rituals* (London: Hutchinson, 1976).

18. Bob Dylan, *Chronicles I* (London: Simon and Schuster, 2004), pp. 82–83.

19. Bob Spitz, *Dylan: A Biography* (London: Michael Joseph, 1989).

20. Quoted by Christopher Ricks in his *Dylan's Visions of Sin* (London: Viking Penguin, 2003), p. 1.

21. Ibid., p. 156.

22. See ibid., pp. 421–27.

CHAPTER 10: STORIES WE TELL OURSELVES ABOUT OURSELVES

1. Wittgenstein, *Philosophical Investigations* (Oxford: Basic Blackwell, 1953), part 2, p. xi.

2. Clifford Geertz, *The Interpretation of Culture* (London: Hutchinson, 1975), p. 448.

3. I borrow this phrase from Raymond Williams, *The English Novel from Dickens to Lawrence* (London: Chatto and Windus, 1970), where it is a controlling idea.

4. Details from Cronkite, *A Reporter's Life*.

5. Ibid., p. 261.

6. As is well argued by Raymond Geuss in his *Public Goods, Private Goods* (Princeton: Princeton University Press, 2001).

7. Figures from Tony Judt, *Postwar: A History of Europe since 1945* (London: Penguin, 2005), p. 188.

8. Details from John Cole, *As It Seemed to Me: Political Memoirs* (London: Orion Books, 1996).

9. Max Clifford interview about a client in *Heat*, November 1–7, 2008.

10. Christopher Lasch, *The Culture of Narcissism: American Life in an Age of Diminishing Expectation* (New York: W. W. Norton, 1979).

11. Philip Larkin, "The Building," in *Collected Poems* (London: Faber and Faber, 1988).

12. Bernard Malamud, *The Natural* (New York: Dell, 1971).

13. This is a suppressed but urgent quotation from F. R. Leavis in his essay "Thought, Language and Objectivity," in *The Living Principle: English as a Discipline of Thought* (London: Chatto and Windus, 1975), p. 58.

14. George Orwell, "Raffles and Miss Blandish," in *Collected Essays* (London: Heinemann Mercury, 1961), p. 237.

15. Quoted in Tara Brabazon's excellent *Thinking Popular Culture* (Farnham: Ashgate, 2008), p. 70.

16. *Great Interviews of the Twentieth Century no. 2: Diana, Princess of Wales* (London: Guardian News and Media, 2007), pp. 13ff.

17. Ibid., p. 10.

18. Hugh Young, *The Hugo Young Papers*, ed. Ion Trewin (London: Allen Lane, 2008), p. 267.

19. Quotations which follow are from Emily Nussbaum's article, *Observer Magazine*, October 26, 2008.

20. Jim Hunter, *The Flame* (London: Faber and Faber, 1966), here quoted in the Pantheon edition (New York, 1966).

21. Ibid., pp. 118–19.

22. Andrew O'Hagan, *Personality* (London: Faber and Faber, 2004).

23. Ibid., p. 44.

24. Ibid., p. 282.

ENVOI: CHERISHING CITIZENS

1. Geertz's (1981) words, already quoted from *Negara*, p. 135.

2. Amelie Oksenberg Rorty, "A Literary Postscript," in the collection she edited, *The Identities of Persons* (Berkeley: University of California Press, 1976), pp. 301–23.

3. Ibid., p. 317.

4. Here updated by Alisdair MacIntyre, in his *After Virtue: A Study in Moral Theory* (London: Duckworth, 1981).

5. E.g., Lord David Puttnam, *Observer*, September 28, 2008.

6. Claude Levi-Strauss, *Structural Anthropology* (London: Allen Lane, 1968), chap. 1.

7. (Harmondsworth: Penguin, 1971).

8. I have in mind Iris Murdoch's parable, *The Nice and the Good* (London: Chatto and Windus, 1969).

9. Norman Mailer, *The Armies of the Night* (London: Weidenfeld and Nicolson, 1968).

10. Rorty, "A Literary Postscript," p. 318.

11. I follow Herbert Hart in making this claim, in his paper "Are There Any Natural Rights?," *Philosophical Review* 64 (1955), pp. 175ff.

12. Details from an unpublished autobiography loaned me by her daughter.

13. Iris Murdoch stands up for a plain, blunt defence of the word in *The Sovereignty of Good* (London: Routledge and Kegan Paul, 1970).

14. Phrases quoted from F. R. Leavis, *New Bearings in English Poetry* (London: Chatto and Windus, rev. ed., 1959).

15. Seamus Heaney, *North* (London: Faber and Faber, 1978), p. 59.

16. As his lovely collection, *Field Work* (London: Faber and Faber, 1976), betokens.

17. Dennis O'Driscoll, *Stepping Stones: Interviews with Seamus Heaney* (London: Faber, 2008), p. 485.

18. Seamus Heaney, *Finders Keepers: Selected Prose 1971–2001* (New York: Farrar, Straus, Giroux, 2002), p. 207.

19. Mills, *The Power Elite*, p. 361.

Illustrations

1. *Mrs Siddons*, 1785, by Thomas Gainsborough   45
2. *The Mall in St. James's Park*, c. 1783, by Thomas Gainsborough   50
3. Brighton Pavilion   61
4. Portrait of George Gordon, 6th Baron Byron of Rochdale in Albanian Dress, 1813, by Thomas Phillips   65
5. *Music in the Tuileries Gardens*, 1862, by Edouard Manet   90
6. *A Bar at the Folies-Bergere*, 1881–1882, by Edouard Manet   91
7. Sarah Bernhardt, 1862   103
8. The Breakers, Newport, R.I.   112
9. Madeleine and John Jacob Astor IV with their dog, Kitty   114
10. Italian fascist dictator Benito Mussolini leading his officers in a spirited run in full military regalia   161
11. *Indiscreet* (1958), Ingrid Bergman and Cary Grant   199
12. GI Monroe in Korea   201
13. Bobby Jones, cover of *Time* magazine, c. 1930s   227
14. American film actor and director Paul Newman dressed in a sponsor logo-covered racing jacket at Moroso Motorsports Park, Jupiter, Florida, mid-1980s   273

Index

Adorno, T. W., 165–66
Aeschylus, 284
Ali, Muhammed, 255
Aristotle, 272
Arlott, J., 225
Armani, G., 246
Asquith, A., 209
Astaire, F., 49, 116
Astor family, and John Jacob, 109–10,
    113–14, 115, 270, 286
Attenborough, D., 276–67
Austen, J., 9, 26, 64, 76, 79

Bach, C.P.E., 72
Bach, J. C., 48
Baddeley, S., 46
Baez, J., 234, 240
Bagehot, W., 170
Baker, J., 282
Baker, S., 211
Baldwin, S., 171
Bardot, B., 143, 206, 264
Baudelaire, C., 75, 77, 88, 89, 90, 92,
    93–96, 98, 116, 139, 234, 236
Beardsley, A., 234
Beatles, the, 14, 233–34
Beauvoir, S. de, 206
Beaverbrook, Lord, 123
Beckett, S., 272
Beckham, D., 16, 225
Beethoven, L., 25, 75
Belfrage, C., 248
Bellamy, R., 196
Benjamin, W., 10, 85, 86, 108, 221–22
Bennett, A., 58

Bennett, J. G., 124
Bernhardt, S., 8, 102–6, 107, 236, 237
Best, G., 16
Black, W., 126
Blake, W., 75
Blanc, F., 141
Blanqui, 99
Blume, M., 142
Bonnard, P., 140
Boswell, J., 21, 52, 137, 138
Boucicant, A., 187, 189
Bow, C., 126
Boyd, P., 237
Brando, M., 264
Brandt, W., 15
Brewer, J., 21, 39, 48
Brueghel, P., 54
Brummel, Beau, 64
Burden, Senator, 110
Burgoyne, General J., 55
Burke, E., 43, 52, 55
Burke, K., 20
Burney, F., 55, 76
Bush, George W., 275
Byron, K., 209
Byron, Lord G. G., 26, 62–70, 74, 75, 82,
    99, 105, 116, 138, 236, 237, 270

Cagney, J., 188
Calder, A., 208
Cameron, D., 12
Campbell, D., 153
Capone, A., 131
Carnegie, A., 110, 125
Caroline of Brunswick, Queen, 60

Caron, L., 198
Cash, J., 240
Cavafy, A., 284
Cavell, E., 287
Cavell, S., 197
Cavour, 141
Cézanne, P., 140, 143
Chakrabarty, S., 276
Chanel, C., 12, 244
Chaplin, C., 162, 187
Charlton, B., 255
Chase, J. Hadley, 257
Chekhov, A., 99, 258
Chesterfield, Lord, 53
Chopin, F., 28, 75
Churchill family and Winston, 111, 156, 174–75
Cibber, C., 44, 46
Cicero, 138
Clancy Bros., 241
Clapton, E., 234, 235, 236–38
Clark, T. J., 84, 89
Claude (Lorraine), 137
Clifford, M., 254
Clinton, W. J., 15, 184–86, 230
Clive, K., 46
Cobb, T., 226
Cole, J., 251–52
Coleridge, S. T., 76
Condorcet, E. de, 19
Cook, J., 55
Cook, T., 135
Cooke, A., 226, 228
Cookson family, 39
Coolidge, C., 172–73
Cooper, A., 240
Coppola, F. F., 131–32
Courbet, G., 77, 98, 139, 234
Coward, N., 210
Cronkite, W., 14, 180, 185, 216, 248, 249–50, 251, 252

Culley, G., 39
Curtis, T., 128, 198, 203

Dante Alighieri, 284
Darnton, R., 235
Daubrun, M., 93
Davis, B., 157
Dawson, L., 268
Day, D., 255, 264
Debord, G., 5–6
Degas, E., 90, 100
Del Santo, L., 237
Dempsey, J., 129
Diana, Princess, 14, 16, 170, 261–63, 264, 282
Dickens, C., 75, 79–82, 94, 98, 119, 127, 131, 222
Dickinson, A., 178
Diderot, D., 43
Didion, J., 184–85, 190–91
Dillinger, J., 131
DiMaggio, J., 200, 204
Dimbleby, D., 250
Dimbleby, R., 14
Donne, J., 4
Dougherty, J., 202
Dreyfus, Capt., 105
Durkheim, E., 20
Duval, J., 93
Duveen, Lord J., 108
Dyck, Sir A. van, 44
Dyer, R., 188, 204
Dylan, B., 234, 236, 240–44

Edward VII, King, 135, 141
Edward VIII, King, 30, 170
Edwards, H., 250
Eiffel, G., 87, 88
Elias, N., 50
Eliot, G., 28
Eliot, T. S., 30, 94, 203, 241, 285

Elizabeth I, Queen, 5, 6, 7, 129
Elliott, D., 211
Estes, Sleepy J., 241

Fairbanks, D. Snr., 187, 226
Fantin-Latour, H., 90
Faraday, M., 287
Fayed, D., 264
Fellini, F., 177, 263
FHM, 254, 271
Fielding, H., 26
Fisher, K., 46, 55, 57
Fitzgerald, F. Scott, 12, 138, 142, 144–48, 149, 202, 282
Fitzherbert, Mrs., 60, 170
Flynn, E., 188
Fonda, J., 276
Ford, A., 250
Ford, H., 110
Ford, J., 193
Forster, E. M., 29, 139
Foucault, M., 51–52
Fourier, C., 86, 99
Fox, C. J., 38, 52, 55, 58
Freeman, M., 276
Freud, S., 51, 96
Frick, H. C., 108, 110, 113, 125
Fulton family, 110

Gainsborough, T., 9, 23, 49–50, 85
Galbraith, J. K., 109
Galella, R., 264
Gallico, P., 129
Gardner, A., 237
Garibaldi, G., 141, 287
Garland, J., 49, 116
Garrick, Sir D., 8, 21, 42–46, 52, 55, 56, 57, 59, 129, 270
Gaulle, C. de, 15, 177
Gautier, T., 90
Geertz, C., 6, 7, 20, 21, 130, 168, 247

Geldof, B., 234, 236, 240
Gellhorn, M., 20, 142, 148, 213–15
George III, King, 21, 58–59
George VI, King, 11, 156, 171–72
Gibbon, E., 52, 53
Gilbert, W. S., 139
Gillray, J., 60
Ginsberg, P., 160, 162
Gish, L., 188
Glamour, 4
Goering, H., 153
Goethe, J. W., 75
Goffman, E., 276
Goldman, M., 110
Goldsmith, D., 23, 52, 55, 79
Goncourt Bros., 85, 95
Gonzalez, P., 255
Gorbachev, M., 30, 180
GQ, 254, 271
Grant, C., 13, 157, 187, 188, 194–98, 199, 209
Graves, R., 102
Greeley-Smith, N., 126
Green, H., 268
Guccio, G., 246
Guggenheim, M., 110
Guiccioli, T., 69
Guthrie, W., 240, 241

Halifax, Lord, 163
Hamilton, Lady Emma, 46, 102
Handel, G. F., 47, 72
Hardcastle, W., 14
Harding, W., 172
Harlow, J., 188
Haussmann, Baron, 9, 84, 85, 88, 286
Havel, V., 219
Hawkins, J., 53, 209, 210
Haydn, J., 48
Hayek, F. von, 71
Heaney, S., 283–85

Heat, 254, 255
Hegel, J.W.G., 19, 51
Hello!, 4, 150, 254
Hemingway, E., 12, 70, 144, 213
Hendrix, J. P., 18, 234
Hepburn, K., 126
Herbert, Z., 285
Herder, J. G., 19, 75
Hine, L., 122
Hitchcock, A., 187
Hitler, A., 11, 20, 30, 100, 153, 156, 158,
    159–60, 163, 164–69, 174, 176, 178
Hobbs, J., 287
Hodgkin, D., 18, 280
Hogarth, W., 54, 75
Holland, H., 61
Howells, W. D., 124–25, 130
Hudson, T., 54
Hugo, V., 104
Hume, D., 19, 22, 24–25, 26, 27, 29, 32,
    62, 67, 71–73, 74, 132, 217
Hunt, R. M., 111
Hunter, J., 265–67

Ibsen, H., 99
Irving, H., 8

Jagger, M., 234, 240
James, H., 28, 29, 30, 104–5, 106, 124,
    125, 130, 148, 272, 282
Jennings, P., 250
Johnson, C., 209
Johnson, Dr. J., 8, 39, 43, 53, 55, 57, 191
Johnson, L. B., 250
Jones, B., 16, 129, 226–28, 229, 230
Jonson, B., 150
Joyce, M., 284
Jura, V., 219

Kant, I., 19, 282
Kean, E., 8, 64, 99
Keats, J., 26

Kelly, G., 197
Kelly, Y., 237
Kennedy, Jack, 176, 204, 263
Kennedy, Joe, 176
Kennedy, J. F., 15, 168, 176–79, 180, 181,
    182, 183, 216
Kingsley, M., 139
Kinnaird, D., 69
Kolakowski, L., 219
Korda, A., 187
Krugman, P., 181
Kyi, Aung San Suu, 18

Lamartine, A. de, 75, 89
Lamb, Lady C., 64, 66, 68, 70
Lancaster, B., 128
Lane, F., 255
Lang, F., 187
Larkin, P., 33, 87, 255
Lasch, C., 254
Lawrence, D. H., 12, 192
Lawrence, Sir T., 44
Lean, D., 209
Leavis, F. R., 28
Leigh, J., 194
Lemmon, J., 198
Lenglen, S., 129
Lévi-Strauss, C., 274
Liddell family, 39
Life (magazine), 13
Lindbergh, C., 153–55
Liszt, F., 28, 100
Livingstone, D., 287
Lloyd George, D., 11
Loren, S., 244
Loy, M., 188
Ludwig, King, 106
Luther, M., 282

MacDiarmid, H., 284
MacIntyre, A., 25, 29
Macklin, C., 46

Macmillan, H., 177
Mailer, N., 70, 178, 203, 277–78
Malevich, K., 26
Mallory, G., 287
Malone, E., 53
Mandela, N., 15, 274, 275, 282
Manet, E., 10, 90, 91, 92, 96
Mann, T., 28
Marvell, A., 209
Marvin, L., 193
Marx, K., 5, 27, 51, 209
Matisse, H., 140, 143
Matthews, S., 16, 223–25, 228
May, B., 239
McAllister, W., 115, 116
McCartney, P., 17, 236
McEnery, M., 238
McKendrick, N., 39
McKenna, V., 210
McLean, G., 193
Mellon, A., 110
Mercury, F., 18, 234, 235, 238–39
Millbanke, A., 66
Miller, A., 202, 203–4, 205
Mills, C. Wright, 116, 117, 145, 286–87
Mills, J., 209, 211
Mills and Boon, 67
Milosz, C., 285
Minogue, K., 275–76
Monet, C., 90, 108
Monroe, M., 14, 176, 178, 188, 190,
    200–205, 206, 209
Montez, L., 106–7
Moore, T., 63
Morgan, J. P., 108, 110, 125
Morisot, B., 90
Morny, Duc de, 104
Morris, W., 209
Morrison, J., 18
Morton, Jelly Roll, 241
Moses, R., 84
Mountbatten, Lord L., 210

Mozart, W. A., 48, 66, 67, 72
Murphys, the, 12
Murray, J., 63
Murrow, E., 14, 215–16, 248, 249, 252
Mussolini, B., 11, 20, 30, 100, 156, 158,
    160–63, 164, 168–69
Myers, G., 115

Napoleon, B., 99
Nash, J., 61
National Enquirer, 4, 254
Nelson, H., 99, 102
Newman, P., 17, 272–74
Nietzsche, F., 51, 80, 132
Nightingale, F., 287
Niven, D., 209
Nixon, R., 181, 183, 230
Nordegren, E., 229
North, Lord, 58
Northcliffe, Lord, 123, 212
Novak, K., 194

Obama, B., 276
O'Driscoll, D., 284
O'Hagan, A., 267–69, 275
OK!, 254, 255
Oldfield, A., 46
Ollivier, E., 141
Omai, Prince, 55, 56
Onassis, A., 263
O'Reilly, C., 284
Orme, R., 55
Orwell, G., 166, 257
Oxford, Lady, 66

Pacino, A., 132
Paganini, N., 237
Paris Match, 13
Parker, D., 172–73
Parks, T., 162
Parton, D., 276, 282
Pavlow, M., 209

Peck, G., 194
Perugino, P., 44
Petacci, C., 162
Philip, Prince, 261
Picasso, P., 12, 140
Pickford, M., 117, 129, 157, 187
Picture Post, 13
Pissarro, C., 90, 91
Pitt, W., the younger, 58
Plumb, J. H., 39
Politkovskaya, A., 279–80
Pope, A., 44, 63
Porden, W., 61
Porter, R., 23–24
Poussin, N., 137
Powell, J. E., 238, 266
Powell, M., 209, 210
Pressburger, E., 209
Prince Regent (George IV), 9, 20, 52, 58, 59–62, 63, 75, 99, 170, 172, 184, 270
Pringle, H., 127
Private Eye, 4
Proust, M., 28
Puccini, G., 235
Pulitzer, H., 10, 118, 123, 124, 125, 150, 212
Putin, V., 279

Raleigh, W., 209
Rather, D., 250
Reagan, R., 15, 179–82, 183, 192, 219, 280
Redgrave, M., 209
Renoir, A., 10, 90
Reynolds, Sir J., 8, 19, 39, 52, 53, 54–58, 68, 245
Rhodes, C., 287
Richthofen, M. von, 12
Ricks, C., 243–44
Riefenstahl, L., 166–69
Robinho, S., 233
Rockefeller, J. D., 110, 122, 125

Rockwell, N., 127
Rolling Stones, the, 234
Roosevelt, F. D., 154, 156, 172–75, 176, 180, 182–83, 184
Roosevelt, T., 121, 173
Rorty, A., 271, 274
Rossini, G., 75
Rousseau, J-J., 25, 62, 75
Ruskin, J., 75
Russell, R., 196, 197
Rutherford, Mrs. W., 184
Ryan, R., 132, 194

Sabatier, A., 93
Sachs, J., 110
Saint, Eve M., 198
Sakharov, A., 18, 278–79
Sand, G., 28
Santee, W., 255
Schiller, F., 75, 76
Schwarzenegger, A., 219
Seeger, P., 241
Segovia, 12
Sennett, R., 99, 158
Seurat, G., 90
Shakespeare, W., 42, 43, 46, 105
Shelley, P. B., 26, 70, 76
Sheridan, D., 209
Sheridan, R. B., 8, 23, 25, 52, 55, 56, 68, 79
Siddons, Dame S., 8, 19, 44–45, 55, 56, 57, 129
Simpson, W., Mrs., 170
Sinden, D., 210
Sisley, A., 90
Smith, A., 19, 21, 24, 52, 53, 67, 71–73, 74
Soros, G., 282, 286
Spitz, B., 242
Springer, J., 18, 258–59
St. Johns, A., 126, 127
Staël, Mme. de, 26, 75, 76

Stalin, J., 11, 30, 156, 163, 164, 166–67, 168–69, 174
Stanford family, 110
Steen, J.,54
Steffens, L., 122, 126, 128
Sterne, L., 55
Stevens, W., 113
Stewart, J., 14, 191, 193–94, 200, 272
Stravinsky, I., 237
Streep, M., 244
Sullivan, Sir A., 139
Sunday Sport, 4, 254

Tarbell, I., 122, 126, 128
Taylor, C., 75, 76
Taylor, Lord, 90
Temple, S., 267–68
Terry, E., 8
Thatcher, M., 15, 168, 177–78, 274–75
Thrale, H., 55
Tintoretto, 138
Tocqueville, A. de, 19
Tolstoy, L., 28
Toulouse-Lautrec, H.M.R. de, 10
Turner, J.M.W., 25, 75
Tyers, J., 49

Ukah, S., 55

Vadim, R., 143
Van Gogh, V., 140
Vanderbilt family, 109, 110, 111, 116
Veblen, T., 117, 130
Verdi, G., 27–28, 75, 217
Versace, G., 246
Vidal, G., 119, 155, 177, 181
Virgil, 284
Vollard, A., 108
Vuillard, E., 90

Walpole, Sir R., 21, 38, 40
Walters, B., 249, 250

Warhol, A., 256
Warren, E., 55–57
Watteau, J.-A., 44
Waugh, E., 149–52, 197–98
Wayne, J., 188, 190–93, 195, 201, 211, 272, 276
Weber, M., 7, 142, 171
Welles, O., 118, 119
Wellington, Duke of, 99
Wells, H. G., 88
Wharton, E., 130
Whitbread family, 39
Wilde, O., 234
Wilkes, J., 8, 38
Willard, J., 122
Wills, G., 191, 192
Wilson, R., 23
Wilson, Woodrow, 11, 119
Winchell, W., 127–28
Winckelmann, J. J., 137
Windsor, Duke and Duchess of, also Edward VIII, King, 12, 142, 170–71
Winfrey, O., 18, 260–61
Wittgenstein, L. L., 247
Wodehouse, P. G., 107, 149
Woffington, P., 46
Wolsey, Cardinal, 4
Woods, T., 16, 228–30
Woodward, J., 274
Woolf, V., 28, 29, 30, 148
Wordsworth, W., 19, 25, 26, 66, 75, 76, 255, 283
Wortley Montague, Lady M., 8, 137
Wren, C., 37, 112

Yeats, W. B., 253, 284
Young, H., 263

Zavaroni, L., 268, 269
Zoffany, T., 44, 46
Zola, E., 89, 105
Zukor, E., 187